25 Aug. 2018

To Abby,
 It has been [n...] '19
with you this summ[er...] Thank you so
much for all your hard work, your
awesome friendly, helpful personality!
Enjoy your time in the kitchen.
  With Love Lori

Cooking with Spirits for the Spirit

P.S.
I hope you come
back next Spring!! :)

Cooking with Spirits for the Spirit

A Meditative Approach to Cooking

JANET HALL SVISDAHL

iUniverse, Inc.
Bloomington

Cooking with Spirits for the Spirit
A Meditative Approach to Cooking

Copyright © 2012 Janet Hall Svisdahl

All rights reserved. No part of this book may be used or reproduced by any means, graphic, electronic, or mechanical, including photocopying, recording, taping or by any information storage retrieval system without the written permission of the publisher except in the case of brief quotations embodied in critical articles and reviews.

iUniverse books may be ordered through booksellers or by contacting:

iUniverse
1663 Liberty Drive
Bloomington, IN 47403
www.iuniverse.com
1-800-Authors (1-800-288-4677)

Because of the dynamic nature of the Internet, any Web addresses or links contained in this book may have changed since publication and may no longer be valid. The views expressed in this work are solely those of the author and do not necessarily reflect the views of the publisher, and the publisher hereby disclaims any responsibility for them.

Any people depicted in stock imagery provided by Thinkstock are models, and such images are being used for illustrative purposes only.

Certain stock imagery © Thinkstock.

ISBN: 978-1-4759-6051-8 (sc)
ISBN: 978-1-4759-6131-7 (e)

Printed in the United States of America

iUniverse rev. date: 12/10/2012

This book
is dedicated to
my husband, Randy,
and to our children and grandchildren.
May they be kept healthy and whole in body, mind, and spirit!

Contents

Foreword 1
Preface 3
Acknowledgments 5
Author's Note 7
The Art of Meditation 9
Wine and Beer Guide 13
Appetizers 21
Cocktails 53
Breads/Grains 67
Breakfasts 85
Lunch — Supper — Some Sides 103
Soups & Stews 141
Dressings 155
Salads 163
Seafood & Fish 181
Meats & Marinades 213
Poultry 239
Sauces 251
Pasta 257
Rice Dishes 273
Desserts 285
A Selection of Four Complete Holiday Dinners 305
   Holiday Dinner 1 307
   Holiday Dinner 2 325
   Holiday Dinner 3 335
   Holiday Dinner 4 343
Conclusion 355

Foreword

By Jenny Roberts

Janet Hall Svisdahl began her cooking career at age eleven, experimenting with creative flair on her five siblings, mother, and father, and sometimes, when things got rough and takeout pizza was the order of the day, our three cats. Rachel, our eldest sister, was Janet's biggest critic when it came to food, but without Rachel, this recipe book would not have been written. She is the inspiration for all things excellent.

At twenty-two, having refined her talent, Janet took over as manager and cook for Robin's Nest Restaurant (Bella Coola). As her twin sister, I went with her, serving as hostess, waitress, and part-time cook. Together we took Bella Coola by storm. It was not unusual to have cars in the parking lot outside Robin's Nest Restaurant waiting for an empty table on any night of the week.

Janet also cooked at Big John's Restaurant, The Waterfront Restaurant (Bella Coola), and Saint John's Fishing Lodge (somewhere on the waters of British Columbia).

Today Janet continues to feed old friends and new at her homes in Holberg and Bella Coola. She is always ready to set out an extra plate for her sisters or for whoever happens to drop by.

"Taste and taste again!" is truly Janet's motto. *Cooking with Spirits for the Spirit* is her first cookbook.

Preface

Cooking with Spirits for the Spirit is dedicated to the spirit of living simply, pleasurably, and prayerfully.

Along with its recipes—many gleaned internationally from family and friends—*Cooking with Spirits for the Spirit* contains spiritual quotes, poems, and sayings for meditative exercise. These contributions have been carefully gathered from laypeople, poets, religious leaders, presidents, and even kings, like apples of gold in settings of silver.

This book is intended as a holistic approach to health regarding one's entire well-being and is intended to feed body, mind, and spirit.

Feasting builds community, promotes harmony, and fosters goodwill, especially when imbibed of the fruit found in love, joy, and peace.

Careful planning takes stress out of cooking. It's wise to purchase and prepare ingredients ahead of time. For convenience I've included a beer and wine guide, a cocktail section, and a complete holiday meal selection from appetizers to desserts to take the stress out of your holiday.

In this hectic world, thought is needed to carve a slice of restful enjoyment for yourself. With this in mind, I've also included a brief section on how to meditate.

When you come into your kitchen, be as salt. Enliven your surroundings! Pepper everything you can with kindness. When all is prepared, set an extra plate at your table. You never know—a knock at your door may find you entertaining an angel unawares.

Acknowledgments

A special thanks to my brother Bill Hall, who suggested the title of this cookbook.

A special thanks as well to Olivia Haysey (thirteen), a promising first-time illustrator with a spirited future ahead of her in the world of art! Olivia sketched many of the designs for *Cooking with Spirits for the Spirit*.

And thank you to Dreamstime for the use of your graphics. I couldn't have done it without you.

Author's Note

Though this book is titled *Cooking with Spirits for the Spirit*, many of the recipes do not have spirits, such as beer, wine, or other liquors, included in their ingredients. However, it is my sincerest desire that when you enter your kitchen, whether you cook with spirits or not, you always cook with spirit!

The Art of Meditation

Achieving inner stillness and peace is something most people in our hectic world desire. Stillness can be obtained. Peace can be gotten, but like most things, there is a cost. The cost is time, and will is key. Choosing to let go a busy schedule for a few precious moments of your time every day, you can learn how to achieve inner peace and serenity.

Seek a solitary place where you can be alone. Soothing music calms your mind, and it is a good idea to select a peaceful assortment ahead of time. You may want to use other props as well. Ceremony is very powerful and anticipatory. Use whatever is meaningful for you. It may be a special article you wish to place either in front of you or on your person. Head coverings, shawls, prayer beads, candles, a chalice, or incense all can be meaningful. Use your imagination. Perhaps you'd rather not use any props at all. That is fine as well.

When you feel you are prepared, sit relaxed with your spine straight and loose and the palms of your hands open and slack. Close your eyes. Take a deep breath and then another, allowing all the tension to leave your body. Keep breathing deep and rhythmically. Quietly refuse to let wandering thoughts master you. Let them pass by, like a silent, gliding swan on a still pond. Let everything go. You can pick up those wandering thoughts later. This is the time to relax and visualize whatever is beautiful to you.

You may want to pray. The simpler the prayer the better. Restful repose is what you seek. Do not allow anything that is not worthy to settle in your mind.

When you are ready to leave the place of meditation, be conscious of your breathing. It should still be deep and slow. Be conscious too of movement. The simple, deliberate act of moving in a slow, peaceful manner aids greatly in generating the feeling and experience of peace.

A Meditative Poem
Anonymous

If I can throw a single ray of light,
Across the darkened pathway of another;
If I can aid some soul to clearer sight
Of life and duty and thus bless my brother;
If I can wipe from any human cheek a tear
I shall not have, then, lived in vain while here.
If I can guide some erring one to truth, inspire
within his heart a sense of duty; if I can plant
within my soul of rosy youth a sense of right,
a love of truth and beauty; if I can teach
one man that God and Heaven are near; I shall
not have, then, lived in vain while here.
If from my mind I can banish doubt and fear and
keep my life attuned to truth, love and kindness;
if I can scatter light and hope and cheer and
help remove the curse of mental blindness; if
I can make more joy, more hope, less pain I
shall not have lived and loved in vain.
If by life's road side I can plant a tree beneath
whose shade some wearied head may rest though
I may never share its shade or see its beauty I
shall yet be truly blessed though no one knows
my name, nor drops a flower upon my grave, I
shall not have lived in vain while here.

Wine and Beer Guide

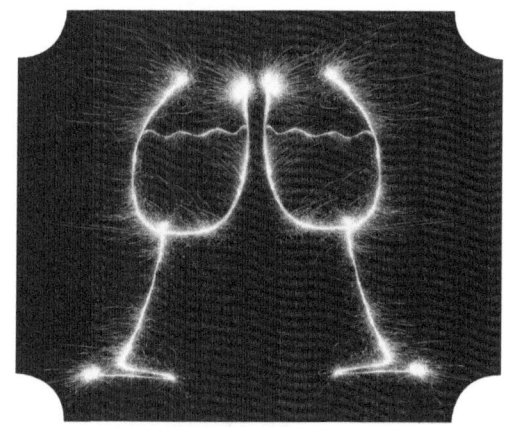

Sipping Wine
Italian Pinot Grigio
Australian Traminer Riesling
Sauvignon Blanc
Piesporter Style
Chamblaise

Appetizers
Pinot Gris
Sonoma Valley Pinot Noir
Cabernet Sauvignon
Chilean Sauvignon Blanc
Sparkling wine
Blush

Beef
Cabernet Sauvignon
Chilean Merlot
French Merlot
South African Pinotage
Shiraz/Zinfandel
Italian Barolo
Italian Amarone
Merlot
California Trinity Red

Pork
Dry Riesling
California Pinot Noir
California Shiraz/Zinfandel
Australian Chardonnay
Johannisberg Dry Riesling

Veal
Italian Montepulciano
Italian Sangiovese

Fish & Seafood
Sauvignon Blanc
Chilean Chardonnay
Pinot Gris
Johannisberg Dry Riesling
New Zealand Pinot Noir
Sauvignon Blanc
Gewürztraminer
South African Chenin Blanc
Liebfraumilch

Lamb
Cabernet Sauvignon
Chilean Pinot Noir
Italian Barolo
Spanish Tempranillo

Vegetable Stews
French Merlot
Sauvignon Blanc
Gewurztraminer
Pinot Gris

Beef Stews
Spanish Rioja
Shiraz
Argentine Malbec
Australian Shiraz
Spanish Rioja

Salads
Australian Chardonnay
Piesporter Style
Sauvignon Blanc
White Zinfandel
Blush

Poultry
Australian Chardonnay
German Muller-Thurga
South African Chenin Blanc
Sauvignon Blanc
Riesling
Gewurztraminer
Chardonnay Semillon
Luna Bianca

Pasta
Chardonnay
Merlot
Montepulciano
Valpolicella
Barolo
Chardonnay
Chilean Merlot
White Merlot
Sauvignon Blanc
Bergamais

Pizza
Bergamais
Valpolicella
Chilean Carmenere
Spanish Tempranillo
Pinor Noir

Fruit/Cheese
Sangiovese
Pinot Gris
Sauvignon
Port
Sparkling Wine

Desserts
Cream Sherry
Ice wine
Riesling
Port

Beer

*Ale, Brew, Bock, Suds, Draft, Lager, Stout, Weiss,
Porter, Pilsner, Pilsener, Brewski, Cerveza*

Whatever you name it, beer is called the poor man's champagne, though universally it is every man's beverage, no matter what snack bracket one is in.

Delightful to drink alone or with almost any meal, beer reigns supreme as a most versatile libation. Below is a brief description of various beers, their taste, and suggested uses.

Pilsner
Light/Crisp Bready/Slightly Bitter
Creamy soups
Vegetables
Bread
Pizza

Pale Ale
Rich/Dry Bittersweet
Cheese fondues
Fish
Meat and poultry

Porter
Smoky/Crisp Nutty/Liquorice undertones
Barbecue
Beef/Pork
Stew/Chili
Baked beans

Stout
Roasted with chocolate/coffee notes
-Darkest of beers-
Chocolate
Desserts
Cakes
Brownies
Chili

Amber Ale
Slightly Sweet
Woody/Caramel
Meats
Chicken

Amber
Caramel
Shellfish
Gravies

India Pale Ale
Lots of flavor with a lingering bitterness
Mexican food

Fruit Beer
Fruity/Sour
Salads
Desserts
Fruit pies

Belgium White Ale
Light/Citrusy
Seafood
Bread Batter
Broths
Soups

Appetizers

Oriental Chicken Bites 23

Spring Rolls 24

Soy Dipping Sauce 24

Barbecued Lemon Shrimp 25

Lisa's Spinach Dip 26

Hot Artichoke Dip 26

Mini Balls of Fire 27

Sherry in the Cheese 28

Stuffed Jalapeños 29

Debbie's Baked Garlic Delight 30

Baked Brie 31

Roasted Pepper and Goat Cheese Tarts 32

Bacon-Wrapped Dates 32

Hummus 33

Glenda's Fried Pita 33

Mushrooms. 34

Deluxe Nachos 35

Crispy Potato Skins. 36

Spicy Chicken Wings. 37

Tequila Lime Wings 38

Guacamole 40

De-Deviled Salmon Eggs 40

Rum Riblets 41

Sherried Hot Crab Dip. .42

Trio of Olive and Lemon Tapenade. 43

Stuffed Mushrooms. 44

Smoked Salmon Spread. 45

Jerk Chicken 46

Jerk Fritters. 47

Shrimp Spring Rolls 48

Sushi 50

Antipasto 51

Prawn Coconut Fritters. 52

Oriental Chicken Bites

1 lb. ground chicken (448 g)
1/4 cup cilantro, chopped (50 ml)
2–3 green onions, chopped
2 cloves of garlic, minced
1 tbsp. grated lemon zest (15 ml)
2 tsp. cornstarch (10 ml)
1 tsp. minced gingerroot (5 ml)
3 tbsp. soy sauce (45 ml)
Dark brown sugar
Commercial sweet Asian chili sauce

Preheat your oven to 400°F (200°C). Line a large baking sheet with tinfoil. Spray it with cooking oil. In a large bowl, combine chicken, green onions, garlic, lemon zest, cornstarch, gingerroot, and soy sauce. Form the mixture into one-inch balls (2.5 cm). Roll the balls lightly in the brown sugar. Place on the prepared baking sheet. Bake for fifteen minutes, turning once. Transfer to a serving dish. Serve with sweet Asian chili sauce. Serves six to eight.

Spring Rolls

1/2 cup cold cooked rice (125 ml)
2 tsp. minced garlic (10 ml)
2 tsp. fresh ginger, grated (10 ml)
1 tbsp. sesame oil (15 ml)
4 shitake mushrooms
1 large carrot, shredded
3 green onions, sliced
1/2 bunch cilantro sprigs
3/4 cup medium shrimp, cooked and chilled (175 ml)
3/4 cup cellophane noodles, cooked and chilled (175 ml)
12 rice paper rounds

Stir the garlic, ginger, and sesame oil into the rice. Put mushrooms in a cup of warm water for 5 minutes to rehydrate. Remove and slice thin. Dip rice paper rounds in bowl of cold water until pliable. Distribute the rice mixture in the center of each softened rice paper round. Sprinkle with the shrimp. Place the green onion on top. Add the shredded carrot. Roll the rounds into tube shapes, tucking in the sides, adding a sprig of cilantro into each. Serve with soy dipping sauce. Serves twelve.

```
"There must be illumination before
revelation can get to a person's soul."
-A.W. Tozer
```

Soy Dipping Sauce

2 tbsp. soy sauce (30 ml)
2 tbsp. sugar (30 ml)
2 tbsp. water (30 ml)
1 tbsp. lime juice (15 ml)
1 minced garlic clove

Combine all the ingredients in small bowl and stir well. Taste the mixture and adjust the seasonings according to your preference.

Barbecued Lemon Shrimp
(With Vodka Sauce)

3 tbsp. sugar (45 ml)
1 tbsp. lemon zest (15 ml)
1/3 cup lemon juice (75 ml)
1/3 cup vodka (75 ml)
1/3 cup olive oil (74 ml)
1 1/2 tsp. minced gingerroot (7 ml)
1 large garlic clove, chopped
1/4 tsp. salt (1 ml)
1/4 tsp. pepper (1 ml)
1 lb. (448 g) of large peeled shrimp
1/2 tsp. cornstarch (2 ml)

Soak wooden skewers for the shrimp for half an hour in cold water. Preheat the barbeque grill to medium-high. Spray the barbecue grates with oil.

Prepare Vodka Sauce
In a medium saucepan on low heat, combine sugar, zest, and lemon juice. Heat until the sugar dissolves. Let cool. Stir in vodka, oil, ginger, garlic, salt, and pepper. Taste and adjust seasonings as desired.

Put the shrimp in medium bowl and stir in a few spoons of the lemon sauce. Thread the shrimp on the presoaked skewers. Place on grill. Grill for five minutes or until the shrimp is opaque, turning once. Remove to a platter. Whisk cornstarch into the remaining sauce and bring to a boil. Reduce heat and then simmer until thickened. Serve with shrimp. Serves eight.

"An honest man is always a child."
—Socrates

Lisa's Spinach Dip

I got this recipe from my daughter Lisa when she was living in her South Carolina–inspired home in the wilderness of Canada. Never at a rush, Lisa prepares her meals in her well-appointed kitchen, calmly and peacefully, an attitude that taught me that food is a sacred gift and should be honored in its approach. This dip recipe is so good; be careful not to eat too much or you might spoil your appetite for dinner.

1 ten-ounce package frozen chopped spinach, thawed and squeezed dry (300 ml)
1 cup sour cream (250 ml)
1 cup mayonnaise (250 ml)
1/2 cup green onion, chopped (125 ml)
1 tbsp. parsley flakes (15 ml)
1 tsp. lemon juice (5 ml)
1/2 tsp. seasoned salt (2 ml)
2 1/2 tbsp. dry soup mix (37 ml)
1/2 cup water chestnuts, drained and chopped (125 ml)
1 round sourdough bread loaf, hollowed out

Preheat oven to 325°F (160°C). Save the bread that was hollowed out of the loaf and cut it into cubes. Set aside. Mix the spinach, sour cream, mayonnaise, green onion, parsley, lemon juice, seasoned salt, dry soup mix, and water chestnuts in a medium bowl. Fill the bread hollow with mixture. Wrap the bread in tinfoil and place in the oven. Bake for 1 1/4 hours or until piping hot all through. Place bread on serving platter. Arrange the bread cubes around the platter and use for dipping. Serves twelve.

Hot Artichoke Dip

1 jar artichoke hearts (450 ml)
1/2 cup Parmesan cheese (125 ml)
1 cup mayonnaise (250 ml)
1/2 tsp. garlic salt (2 ml)
1/2 tsp. lemon juice (2 ml)

Mash the artichoke hearts, Parmesan cheese, mayonnaise, garlic salt, and lemon in a medium bowl. Turn into a round, lightly greased casserole dish. Bake in 350°F (180°C) oven for ten minutes. Serve with crackers. Makes two cups or 6 servings.

> "Learning without thought is labor lost.
> Thought without learning is perilous."
> —Confucius

Mini Balls of Fire

1 egg, beaten
1/4 cup dried breadcrumbs (50 ml)
1/4 cup milk (50 ml)
2 tbsp. cilantro or mint (30 ml)
2 tsp. hot pepper, diced (10 ml)
1/2 tsp. salt (2 ml)
1/2 tsp. cinnamon (2 ml)
1/2 tsp. ginger (2 ml)
1/2 tsp. nutmeg (2 ml)
1/2 tsp. black pepper (2 ml)
A dash of ground cloves
1 lb. ground burger or lamb (448 g)
Commercial chutney

In a large bowl, combine egg, breadcrumbs, milk, herbs, and spices with ground burger or lamb. Shape into small balls. Place on an ungreased baking sheet. Bake at 350°F (180°C) twenty to twenty-five minutes. Serve with chutney on the side. Serves six.

Sherry in the Cheese

4 tbsp. sherry (60 ml)
3 tbsp. butter, softened (45 ml)
1 1/4 tsp. Dijon mustard (6 ml)
1/2 tsp. salt (2 ml)
A dash of cayenne
1 1/2 cups sharp cheddar cheese, grated
(375 ml)

In a medium bowl, mix sherry, butter, Dijon mustard, salt, cayenne, and cheese until well blended. Taste and then adjust seasonings as desired. Serve with whole grain crackers. Serves four to six.

"But maybe, by raising my voice, I can help the greatest of all causes. Goodwill among men. And peace on earth."
—Albert Einstein

Stuffed Jalapeños

12 fresh jalapeño peppers, sliced lengthwise and de-seeded
1 cup shredded cheddar blend cheese (250 ml)
1 package cream cheese (200 g)
1/2 tsp. Italian seasoning (2 ml)
1/4 tsp. habanero salt (1 ml) (optional)
2 eggs, beaten
2 tbsp. cream (30 ml)
2/3 cup finely crushed breadcrumbs (150 ml)
Cajun spice
Sour cream (optional)

Mix the cheddar cheese, cream cheese, Italian seasoning, and habanero salt together in medium bowl. Set aside. Beat the eggs with the cream on a large plate, and pour the breadcrumbs on a second plate.

Fill the jalapeño peppers generously with cheese mixture. Dip the peppers in the eggs and cream mixture. Roll in the crushed breadcrumbs, coating well. Arrange on a large, ungreased cookie sheet, cheese side up. Sprinkle with Cajun spice. Bake at 350°F (180°C) for twenty to twenty-five minutes or until hot all through. If desired, serve with sour cream. Serves twelve.

"Boldness be my friend!"
—William Shakespeare

Debbie's Baked Garlic Delight

10 whole heads of garlic
2 tsp. butter (10 ml)
1/2 cup olive oil (125 ml)
2 cups good-quality chicken stock (500 ml)
3 tbsp. fresh thyme or marjoram, coarsely chopped (45 ml)
1 cup goat cheese, crumbled (250 ml)
1 cup sundried tomatoes (250 ml)

Chop the tips from garlic heads and put the garlic heads in an oven-proof baking dish. Dab butter on each head. Sprinkle with olive oil. Add chicken stock until it measures halfway up the garlic. Sprinkle with the thyme or marjoram. Bake in a preheated oven at 350°F (180°C) for one and a half hours, basting frequently with the stock. Add the goat cheese and sprinkle with the sundried tomatoes. Return to oven. Bake another five to ten minutes or until the cheese melts. Serve with baguette slices. Serves ten.

"The shell must break before the bird can fly."
–Tennyson

Baked Brie
(with Brandy Caramel)

1/2 cup sugar (125 ml)
2 tbsp. water (30 ml)
2 tbsp. liquid whipping cream (30 ml)
2 tbsp. brandy (30 ml)
2 tbsp. butter (30 ml)
1/4 tsp. salt (1 ml)
1/4 tsp. fresh rosemary, chopped finely (1 ml)
1/3 cup walnut pieces (75 ml)
2 tbsp. dried cranberries (30 ml)
1 six-ounce wheel of Brie
Apple or pear wedges

Preheat oven to 375°F (190°C). Lightly butter a pie pan. Set aside. In a saucepan over medium-high heat, stir in the sugar and water. Bring to a boil. Boil for five minutes or until deep gold in color, brushing the sides of the pot with water to prevent crystallizing.

Remove from heat. Stir in whipping cream, brandy, and butter. Return to heat and liquefy, and then remove from heat. Add the salt and rosemary. In a small bowl, stir the walnuts with the cranberries.

Place the Brie in the center of the pie pan. Top with walnuts and cranberries. Bake until soft to the touch, about ten minutes. Remove from oven. Drizzle with the rosemary caramel sauce. Let it cool slightly before transferring to a serving dish. Serve with crusty bread, apple wedges, or pear wedges. Serves two to four.

Roasted Pepper and Goat Cheese Tarts

18 frozen mini tart shells
3/4 cup roasted red peppers (175 ml)
3/4 cup soft goat cheese (175 ml)
3 eggs
1 cup liquid whipping cream (250 ml)
1/4 tsp. each salt and pepper (1 ml)

Preheat oven to 375°F (190°C). Place the mini tart shells on a large baking sheet. Combine the roasted peppers with the goat cheese. Divide among the mini tart shells. Beat the eggs lightly with the whipping cream, salt, and pepper. Pour into mini tart shells, filling just to the rim. Bake for twenty to twenty-five minutes. Serves nine to eighteen.

```
"Humble love, and not proud science,
    keeps open the door of heaven."
            -E. Young
```

Bacon-Wrapped Dates

This recipe comes from my niece Laura, a soft- spoken woman who is an inspiration to the flustered, the busy, and the frazzled. Laura is never at a rush while juggling her children, husband, cats, and dogs in her hectic schedule. She moves in a space emitting peace and certitude. These bacon-wrapped dates are just about as sweet as she is.

12 slices maple-smoked bacon, halved
24 dates, fresh, pits removed
2/3 cup pure maple syrup (150 ml)
1/3 cup brown sugar (75 ml)
Pinch each of chili powder, cayenne, and black pepper.

Sprinkle bacon with chili powder, cayenne and pepper. Wrap each date with bacon. Put in a buttered eight-by-eight-inch (20x20 cm) baking dish. Drizzle with maple syrup. Sprinkle with brown sugar. Bake at 375°F (190°C) for thirty minutes. Serves twelve to twenty-four.

Hummus

1 nineteen-ounce can garbanzo beans (540 ml)
3 cloves of garlic, crushed
1 tbsp. lemon juice (15 ml)
1/4 tsp. salt (1 ml)
1/4 tsp. pepper (1 ml)
1/2 tsp. cumin (2 ml)
1/4 cup Tahini paste (50 ml)
1/4 cup boiling water (50 ml)

Put garbanzo beans, crushed garlic, lemon juice, salt, pepper, and cumin in blender. With blades running slow, add tahini paste and boiling water. Blend until smooth. Serve with pita rounds. Serves six.

Glenda's Fried Pita

1 package fresh pita rounds (about six)
1 tbsp. olive oil (15 ml)
1 tbsp. butter (15 ml)
seasoning salt

Melt olive oil and butter in medium-hot frying pan. Place pita rounds in a pan and fry each side, holding down with a dinner plate, until gently golden. Sprinkle both sides with seasoning salt. Place in warm oven, wrapped in tinfoil, until ready to serve. Serves four to six.

```
"The cautious seldom err."
        —Confucius
```

Mushrooms
(with Wine Sauce)

1/2 cup good-quality olive oil (125 ml)
6 cloves of garlic, minced
Red chili flakes to taste
2 1/2 lbs. fresh whole white mushrooms (1 kg)
1 tbsp. white flour
Salt and pepper to taste
1 loaf crusty French bread, sliced thick

Preheat oven to 375°F (190°C). Wrap the French bread in tinfoil and seal well. Place in a hot oven for ten minutes or until heated through. Meanwhile, heat the oil in a heavy saucepot and then add the garlic. Fry for two to three minutes. Sprinkle with chili flakes. Add whole the mushrooms and stir gently until the liquid draws out of mushrooms. Add salt and pepper to taste. Simmer for ten minutes or until all the liquid has evaporated. Sprinkle flour over the mixture and stir. Remove the pan from heat. Prepare the wine sauce. Makes four to six servings.

Wine Sauce

2 garlic cloves, minced
1 bunch Italian parsley, finely chopped
2/3 cup white wine (150 ml)
Salt and pepper to taste.

Put the garlic, parsley, wine, salt, and pepper in a small sauce pot. Bring it to a boil. Reduce heat and then slowly add the wine sauce to the mushrooms. Return to heat. Bring to a boil, stirring constantly. Reduce heat and then simmer for five minutes or until sauce thickens. Serve warm with French bread.

"The spectacular beauty of creation in all
its simplicity and in all its complexity,
reveals a spectacular God simply present
with an infinitely complex character."
Anonymous

Deluxe Nachos

1 lb. ground beef (448 g)
1 onion, chopped
2 cloves of garlic, minced
1 fourteen-ounce can refried beans (398 ml)
1/2 cup canned green chili peppers (125 ml)
1/2 tsp. cumin (2 ml)
1 tsp. chili powder (5 ml)
Dash of cayenne pepper
1 package nacho seasoning mix
1 2/3 cups shredded cheddar cheese (400 ml)
2/3 cup sliced black olives (150 ml)
1 large package tortilla chips
Garnish: guacamole, sour cream, and salsa (optional)

Brown the beef and onion in medium-hot skillet until beef is no longer pink inside. Add garlic, refried beans, green chili peppers, cumin, chili powder, and cayenne. Add nacho seasoning mix. Cook the mixture, adding water as needed as sauce thickens. Put half the bag of tortilla chips on a large pizza pan. Add half the meat mixture. Sprinkle with half the black olives. Add the remaining tortilla chips. Sprinkle top with cheese and remaining olives. Bake at 350°F (180°C) until cheese melts. Serve with your choice of guacamole, sour cream, and salsa. Serves six to eight.

Crispy Potato Skins

12 large russet potatoes
1/2 cup butter, melted (125 ml)
1/2 lb. bacon, cooked and crumbled (227 g)
2 1/2 cups shredded cheese (625 ml)
2/3 cup diced green onion (150 ml)
Seasoning salt to taste
1 cup prepared salsa (250 ml)
1 cup sour cream (250 ml)

Bake potatoes at 400°F (200°C) until a fork easily pierces through, about forty-five to sixty minutes. Let cool. Slice the potatoes in half lengthwise. Scoop out the insides to the edge of the shell. Discard the insides, or save for another dish. Brush the skins with melted butter. Put the skins, cut side up, on a baking sheet. Bake at 425°F (220°C) for ten minutes or until crispy. Sprinkle with shredded cheese and crumbled bacon. Salt to taste. Bake two to three minutes more or until cheese melts. Before serving, sprinkle with chopped green onions. Serve with salsa and sour cream on the side. Serves twelve.

"Go to your bosom: Knock there, and ask
your heart what it doth know."
—William Shakespeare

Spicy Chicken Wings

2 lbs. chicken wings (908 g)
1 cup ketchup (250 ml)
Dash of whiskey
1/3 cup onions, diced (75 ml)
3 tbsp. honey (45 ml)
3 tbsp. vinegar (45 ml)
2 garlic cloves, minced
1 tsp. chili powder (5 ml)
Dash of cayenne pepper
Dash of black pepper

Cut each chicken wing at the joint to make two sections. Place on a baking sheet. Bake in preheated oven at 375°F (190°C) for twenty to twenty-five minutes. Take out of the oven. Drain the fat from sheet and put sheet on heat-protective surface.

In a medium bowl, combine ketchup, whiskey, onions, honey, vinegar, garlic, chili powder, cayenne, and black pepper and mix well. Taste and then adjust seasoning to taste. Slather mixture over the wings, using a basting brush, and then return to oven. Bake for ten minutes, turning wings once. Brush with more sauce. Bake another ten minutes or until cooked through and crispy. Serves four.

Tequila Lime Wings
(Marinated with Tequila Lime Dipping Sauce)

3 lbs. chicken wings, split at joint and wing tips removed
(1 1/2 kg)
Salt and pepper

Preheat oven to 350°F (180°C). Line a baking sheet with tinfoil or parchment paper. Put wings on baking sheet and sprinkle lavishly with salt and pepper. Bake for forty-five minutes, turning halfway through. While baking, prepare tequila lime marinade. Serves four.

"Do not journey into yourself; journey
through yourself into God."
Anonymous

Tequila Lime Marinade

1 tbsp. lime zest (15 ml)
1/2 cup lime juice (125 ml)
1/3 cup tequila (75 ml)
3 cloves of garlic, minced
1 tbsp. honey (15 ml)
2 tbsp. smoky hot sauce (30 ml)
1–2 chipotle peppers in adobo sauce
1 tsp. cumin (5 ml)
Salt and pepper to taste

In a blender, put zest, lime juice, tequila, garlic, honey, hot sauce, chipotle peppers, cumin, salt, and pepper. Blend until smooth. Place baked wings in a large bowl and toss with 3/4 cup marinade (175 ml), reserving the rest. Marinate the wings for thirty minutes. While marinating, prepare the dipping sauce.

Tequila Lime Dipping Sauce

Reserved tequila lime marinade from previous recipe (50 ml)
1/2 cup cilantro, chopped (125 ml)
1/4 cup mayonnaise (50 ml)
1/4 cup sour cream (50 ml)
1 tbsp. honey (15 ml)
Oil

In a small bowl, mix the reserved marinade, cilantro, mayonnaise, sour cream, and honey. Stir well and then set aside. Preheat barbeque to medium-hot. Brush barbeque grill with oil. Remove the wings from marinade and place on grill. Turn the wings frequently with tongs until heated through. Remove to warm platter. Serve the wings hot, with tequila lime dipping sauce on the side.

```
"I may not draw aside the unseen veil that hides
  the unknown future from my sight, nor know if
 for me waits the dark or light. But I can trust.
 I have no power to look across the tide to see
 while here the land beyond the river, but this I
   know-I will be God's forever. So I can trust."
                    Anonymous"
```

Guacamole

2 large avocados, mashed
1/2 onion, diced
Several dashes green Tabasco sauce
2 tbsp. fresh cilantro, chopped (30 ml)
2 tbsp. lime juice (30 ml)
2 cloves of garlic, minced
1/4 tsp. salt (1 ml)
Dash of cumin

Mash the avocados, onion, Tabasco sauce, cilantro, lime juice, garlic, salt, and cumin with fork until smooth. Chill for at least one hour. Serve with tortilla chips or deluxe nachos. Serves four.

De-Deviled Salmon Eggs

1 dozen hard-boiled eggs, chilled
1/2 cup mayonnaise (125 ml)
1 cup canned salmon (250 ml)
1 tsp. lemon juice (5 ml)
1 1/4 tsp. Dijon mustard (6 ml)
1 1/4 tsp. Worcestershire sauce (6 ml)
1/2 tsp. salt (2 ml)
Dash of pepper
Dash of smoky paprika

Slice eggs in half lengthwise. Scoop the yolks into a medium bowl and add mayonnaise, salmon, lemon juice, mustard, Worcestershire, salt, and pepper. Mash well with a fork. Scoop the mixture into the egg white halves. Arrange on a serving platter. Sprinkle with paprika. Serves twelve.

"Twenty years from now you will be more disappointed by the things you didn't do than by the ones you did do. So throw off the bowlines. Sail away from the safe harbor. Catch the trade winds in your sails. Explore. Dream. Discover."
—Mark Twain

Rum Riblets

4 lbs. pork ribs, cut into bite-size pieces (1800 g)
1 cup dark brown sugar (250 g)
1/3 cup hot chili sauce (75 ml)
1/3 cup ketchup (75 ml)
1/3 cup dark rum (75 ml)
1/3 cup dark soy sauce (75 ml)
1 tbsp. Worcestershire sauce (15 ml)
1 tsp. dry mustard (5 ml)
3 garlic cloves, crushed
1/4 tsp. black pepper (1 ml)

Wrap ribs in tinfoil. Bake in preheated oven at 325°F (165°C) for 1 1/2 hours. Unwrap foil. Pour off juices. In a medium bowl, combine brown sugar, chili sauce, ketchup, rum, soy sauce, Worcestershire sauce, dry mustard, garlic, and pepper. Pour half the mixture over the ribs. Bake ribs for another 1 1/2 hours, uncovered. Place under broiler and broil six inches (15 cm) from heat, basting with the remaining sauce until crispy. Serves eight.

Sherried Hot Crab Dip

1 eight-ounce package cream cheese (250 g)
2 tbsp. mayonnaise (30 ml)
2 tbsp. dry sherry (30 ml)
1 1/2 tsp. lemon juice (7 ml)
Dash of Tabasco sauce
1 cup crabmeat, drained (250 g)
Salt and pepper to taste
1/3 cup almonds, slivered (75 ml)

Heat oven to 350°F (180°C). Mix cream cheese, mayonnaise, sherry, lemon juice, and Tabasco sauce. Stir in crabmeat. Sprinkle with salt and pepper to taste. Spoon the crab mixture into a small, shallow baking dish. Top with the slivered almonds. Bake until hot and bubbly, approximately fifteen to twenty minutes. Serve warm with crackers. Serves six.

"If chosen men had never been alone, in deepest silence, open-doored to God, no greatness would ever have been dreamed, or done."
Anonymous

Trio of Olive and Lemon Tapenade

1 large garlic clove, chopped
2 tbsp. brined capers, drained (30 ml)
1 cup black olives, pitted (250 ml)
1 cup green olives, pitted (250 ml)
1 cup Kalamata olives, pitted (250 ml)
1/3 cup roasted red peppers, chopped (75 ml)
1/4 cup fresh basil, chopped (50 ml)
2 anchovies, coarsely chopped
zest of half a lemon
2 tsp. balsamic vinegar (10 ml)
1/3 cup parsley, chopped (75 ml)
1/3 cup olive oil (75 ml)
Dash of pepper
Toasted baguette, crostinis, or crackers.

Put garlic, capers, olives, red peppers, basil, and anchovies in blender. Blend until coarsely chopped. Add lemon zest, vinegar, parsley, olive oil, and dash of pepper. Transfer to bowl and then cover with wrap. Let it rest one hour before serving with crackers. Serves eight to ten.

Stuffed Mushrooms

16 whole mushrooms
1/3 cup onion, minced (75 ml)
1 tbsp. butter (15 ml)
1/2 cup crushed breadcrumbs (125 g)
1/3 cup pecans, finely chopped (75 ml)
2 tbsp. parsley (30 ml)
1 five-ounce package garlic and herb soft cheese, crumbled (142 g)
Salt and pepper to taste
4 tbsp. melted butter (60 ml)

Preheat oven to 375°F (190°C). Remove stems from the mushrooms and set caps in a baking dish. Finely chop the stems. In a hot skillet, fry the mushroom stems and onions in butter until soft, about four to five minutes. Stir in breadcrumbs, pecans, and parsley. Transfer to a bowl and blend in cheese. Season with salt and pepper to taste. Spoon the mixture into the mushroom caps. Melt the butter and pour it over mushrooms in a baking dish. Bake for twenty minutes or until hot. Serves four to six.

"To clasp the hands in prayer is the beginning of
an uprising against the disorder of the world."
–Karl Bath

Smoked Salmon Spread

1 eight-ounce package of cream cheese, softened (250 g)
5 ounces of smoked salmon, chopped finely (150 g)
1/4 cup chives, chopped (50 ml)
2 tbsp. lemon juice (30 ml)
3 tbsp. liquid whipping cream (45 ml)
2 tsp. prepared horseradish (10 ml)
Dash of Tabasco sauce
Salt and pepper to taste
Jalapeño jelly

Blend the cream cheese, salmon, chives, lemon juice, whipping cream, and horseradish in a blender and then pour into a serving bowl. Season to taste with Tabasco, salt, and pepper. Cover and put in the fridge. Let it stand for one hour or up to two to three days to allow the flavor to develop. Serve with crackers dabbed with jalapeño jelly. Serves six.

Jerk Chicken
(with Fritters and Sauce)

4 lbs. chicken drumsticks (1800 g)
1/3 cup jerk marinade sauce (75 ml)

Jerk Marinade Sauce
Combine thoroughly in blender:
2 large onions, chopped
2 scallions, chopped
2 sprigs thyme
3 cloves of garlic, chopped
1/4 cup vegetable oil (50 ml)
1/4 cup soy sauce (50 ml)
1/2 cup beer (125 ml)
1/4 cup vinegar (50 ml)
6 whole scotch bonnet peppers
Salt to taste
1 small piece of ginger, grated
1/2 cup tomato paste (125 ml)
1 cup pineapple juice (250 ml)

Put the chicken drumsticks and a third of the jerk sauce in a plastic bag, making sure the chicken is well coated, adding more sauce if needed. Put in the fridge and marinade for six hours or overnight. Preheat oven to 400°F (200°C). Remove the drumsticks from the marinade and arrange on a foil-lined baking sheet. Bake for thirty-five minutes or until crisp. Serve drumsticks with fritters and sauce. Serves eight.

"The only ones among you who will be really happy are those who will have sought and found how to serve."
—Albert Schweitzer

Jerk Fritters

1 cup black beans, drained (250 ml)
2 cups banana, mashed and separated(500 ml)
1 cup cornmeal (250 ml)
1 large organic egg
2 green onions, chopped
3 tbsp. lime juice (45 ml)
2 tsp. cumin (10 ml) separated
Salt to taste
2 tbsp. olive oil (30 ml)
1 sixteen-ounce jar of roasted red pepper, drained (500 ml)
Lime wedges for garnish

Mash beans in a large bowl with half of the mashed banana. Add cornmeal, egg, green onions, and lime juice. Add one teaspoon of the cumin and a pinch of salt to taste. Heat oil in large skillet over medium-high heat. Drop generous spoons of fritter batter into a hot skillet. Flatten slightly with the back of a spoon to form patties. Cook, turning as needed, until golden brown on both sides, about four minutes. Drain on a paper towel. Keep warm. Serve with fritter sauce. Serves four to six.

Fritter Sauce

In a small bowl, combine roasted red pepper with remaining banana and cumin. Blend well until smooth. Spoon into small saucepan and heat until warm. Spoon onto a warmed platter. Top with fritters and jerk chicken (see previous recipe). Garnish with lime wedges.

"The time is upon us for right living. As you ask God to guide your understanding of what remains for you to become a stronger person of worth, to live tightly before Him, remember that time is of the essence. God needs your example today."
Anonymous

Shrimp Spring Rolls
(with Dipping Sauce)

1 lb. frozen shrimp, thawed and chopped (454 g)
1 can water chestnuts, drained and chopped (227 ml)
1 green onion, chopped finely
1/3 cup fresh cilantro, chopped (75 ml)
1/2 tsp. fresh grated ginger (2 ml)
Dash of pepper
1 tbsp. dark soy sauce (15 ml)
1/4 tsp. Chinese five spice (1 ml)
16 spring roll wrappers (purchase wrappers in Asian section of your grocery store)
1 large organic egg, beaten
Oil for frying

In a medium bowl, lightly stir shrimp, water chestnuts, green onion, cilantro, ginger, salt, pepper, soy sauce, and Chinese five spice. Set aside.
Lay one spring wrapper on work surface point up. Place two tablespoons of the shrimp mixture across the bottom and roll up tightly, folding in the sides as you go. Lightly brush the wrapper with egg to seal. Repeat with remaining wrappers and filling.

In a heavy skillet, heat half an inch of oil (1 cm) over high heat until sizzling. Reduce heat to medium. Drop spring rolls in the hot oil in batches. If the oil is not at a sizzle as you fry, increase heat. Fry until golden brown on all sides, approximately three to four minutes. Remove and drain rolls on paper towels. Serve with dipping sauce. Makes eight servings.

Dipping Sauce

3 tbsp. rice wine vinegar (45 ml)
2 tbsp. water (30 ml)
3 tsp. fresh grated ginger (30 ml)
2 tsp. sugar (10 ml)
1/2 tsp. hot pepper sauce (2 ml)
Dash of soy sauce

In a medium bowl, whisk together vinegar, water, ginger, sugar, hot sauce, soy sauce, and salt. Taste and then adjust seasonings as desired.

> "If you can roll with the punches when trouble comes your way, keeping an uncomplaining tongue, spring will bloom in your heart."
> —J. S.

Sushi

Sushi is so versatile that almost anything goes for a filling. For inspiration go for lunch at your nearest Japanese restaurant and take note of what the menu offers. You will find open sushi (traditionally raw fish atop rice wrapped with nori) or closed sushi (cooked or steamed fish or seafood rolled with various fillings inside rice-wrapped nori). While making sushi, feel free to experiment with fillings like Shitake mushrooms, shredded carrots, tofu, egg, salmon, or tuna. This is a popular recipe, and using canned or imitation crab, it is very easy to put together. The inspiration for this dish comes from my Japanese friend Keiko, whose husband, Joel, was a martial arts student of my father, Graham.

1 lb. sushi rice or short-grain rice (450 g)
10 sheets nori (dried seaweed)
1/2 cup rice vinegar (125 ml)
1 1/2 ounces of sugar (42 g)
1/2 tsp. salt (2 ml)
1 can of crabmeat, drained and minced (213 g)
or 1 package imitation crabmeat, chopped
2 ripe avocados, chopped finely
1 cucumber, peeled, diced finely
1 scallion, minced
Vinegar for sealing
Garnish: Pickled ginger, wasabi (Japanese horseradish),
Asian dipping sauce, or soy sauce

Wash rice until the water runs clear and cook according to package directions. Cool completely. Transfer to a large dish, and add vinegar, sugar, and salt. Toss lightly. Place a bamboo sushi mat on your work surface. Lay one sheet of nori shiny side down on top of the mat. Cover evenly with a layer of cool rice, using water-dampened fingers to make it spread easier. In a medium bowl, mix very lightly crab, avocado, cucumber, and scallion. Spoon a portion of the mixture evenly over the rice. Roll the sushi tightly into a cylinder shape, using vinegar to seal the seams. Cut with a very sharp knife into eight pieces. Continue this process with each new sheet of nori until all sheets are used. Place the sushi in the fridge to chill thoroughly. Serve with pickled ginger, wasabi, and your dipping sauce of choice.

"Trust. But verify."
—Ronald Regan

Antipasto
(for a Crowd)

1 cup olive oil (250 ml)
1 head of cauliflower, chopped
5 cloves of garlic, smashed
4 cups ketchup (1 L)
2 cups hot ketchup (500 g)
1 cup red wine (250 ml)
1 1/3 cups tomato paste (325 ml)
1 tbsp. oregano (15 ml)
2 large green peppers, chopped
2 cans drained and chopped black olives (200 ml) each
1 cup green olives, chopped (250 ml)
1 jar sweet pickles, chopped (650 ml)
1 cup pimientos, chopped (250 ml)
1 jar pearl onions, chopped (125 ml)
3 cups canned artichokes, chopped (675 g)
2 ten-ounce cans mushroom pieces, drained (284 ml)
2 large carrots, diced
Salt and pepper to taste
3 cans solid tuna (213 g)
2 cans anchovies, chopped

Heat a large pot with olive oil. Add cauliflower and garlic. Sauté for two minutes. Mix in ketchup, wine, tomato paste, and oregano. Add the chopped vegetables and salt and pepper to taste. Simmer for ten minutes. Add anchovies and tuna. Bring to a boil, stirring constantly. Remove from heat. Chill and serve for immediate use, or place in containers for freezing. Can keep in fridge two weeks. Serve with crackers.

Prawn Coconut Fritters

1 cup canned corn kernels (250 ml)
1/4 cup coconut cream (50 ml)
1 egg, lightly beaten
1/3 cup unbleached white flour (75 ml)
1/2 tsp. salt (2 ml)
1/2 tsp. sugar (2 ml)
1 tsp. cumin (5 ml)
1/2 cup coarsely chopped prawns (125 g)
1/4 cup olive oil (50 ml)
1 lemon, sliced
6 sprigs cilantro

In a large mixing bowl, mix corn, coconut cream, egg, flour, salt, sugar, cumin, and prawns together lightly. Heat olive oil in skillet over medium-high heat. Place golf ball–size fritters in hot oil, frying in batches, for three minutes per side or until golden. Drain on a paper towel. Season with additional salt if desired. Keep warm until serving. Garnish with lemon slices and cilantro sprigs. Serves eight.

Cocktails

"Your vision will become clear only when you can look into your own heart. Who looks outside, dreams; who looks inside, awakes."
—Carl Jung

Wine Punch	55
Sangria	55
Graham's Margaritas	56
Wine Spritzer	56
Daiquiri	57
Bloody Mary	57
Desert Locusts	58
Hot Buttered Rum	58
Peach Bellini	59
Chi Chi	59
Mai Tai	60
Holiday Punch	60
Soda Pop Punch	61
American Flyer	61
Christmas Jed Nog	62
Classic Martini	63
Maiden's Prayer	63
Foghorn	63
Bella Coola	64
Acapulco	64
Tiger's Milk	65
Long Island Iced Tea	65
Gin Sling	66
Side Car	66
Manhattan	66

Wine Punch

2/3 cup water (150 ml)
1/4 cup sugar (50 ml)
1 cinnamon stick
1/2 tsp. whole cloves (2 ml)
4 cups apple juice (1 L)
1 1/2 cups apricot or papaya nectar (365 ml)
1/4 cup lemon juice (50 ml)
2 bottles chilled white wine

In a saucepan combine water, sugar, cinnamon, and cloves. Simmer for ten minutes. Chill and strain. Combine apple juice with apricot or papaya nectar and lemon juice. Add chilled wine. Mix well. Taste and adjust seasonings if desired. Serves twelve.

"The conscious water saw its God, and blushed."
—Richard Crashaw

Sangria

"Laughter is wine, healing the heart."
Anonymous

In a large punch bowl combine:

4 cups rosé wine (.95 L)
2 cups unsweetened grapefruit juice (500 ml)
1/2 cup cognac (125 ml)
4 tbsp. sugar (60 ml)
3 lemons, sliced
1 orange, sliced
4 cups club soda (.95 liter)

Stir well. Chill until serving. Serves ten.

Let no one ever come to you without
leaving better and happier.
Be the expression of God's kindness:
kindness in your face,
Kindness in your eyes, kindness in your smile."
–Mother Theresa

Graham's Margaritas

1 cup crushed ice (250 ml)
4 oz. frozen lime concentrate (125 ml)
2 oz. fresh lime juice (60 ml)
2 oz. water (60 ml)
6 oz. tequila (185 ml)
2 oz. triple sec (60 ml)

Dip the rims of four margarita glasses in water and then in salt. Put glasses in freezer to chill. In a blender, mix lime concentrate, lime juice, water, tequila, and triple sec with crushed ice. Pour into frozen glasses. Serves six.

"Drinking spirits cannot cause spiritual damage."
–José Bergamin

Wine Spritzer

1 cup dry white or rosé wine (250 ml)
1/4 cup club soda (50 ml)

Combine wine and soda in cocktail shaker and
shake well. Pour over ice. Serves two.

"The fountains from which love flows are found in God."
Anonymous

Daiquiri

1 six-ounce can frozen lemon or lime concentrate (180 g)
1 cup light or golden rum (250 ml)
2 trays of ice cubes
1 cup frozen raspberries
sugar to taste (optional)

Blend ingredients in blender until very slushy. If desired, add sugar to taste. Serves six.

"Love is the key to Heaven."
Anonymous

Bloody Mary

4 cups tomato juice (1 L)
1 cup vodka (250 ml)
2 tsp. Worcestershire sauce (10 ml)
1/4 tsp. celery salt (1 ml)
Dash of Tabasco sauce
Ice cubes
6–8 celery stalks for garnish

Blend tomato juice, vodka, Worcestershire sauce, celery salt, and Tabasco sauce in a large pitcher. Taste and adjust seasonings as desired. Serve over ice. Garnish with celery stalks. Serves eight.

Desert Locusts

1 pint vanilla ice cream (500 ml)
1/3 cup crème de cacao (75 ml)
1/4 cup green crème de menthe (50 ml)

Blend in blender till smooth. Serve immediately. Serves four to six.

> "The first glass, for myself, the second, for my friends, the third, for good humor, the fourth, for my enemies."
> —Sir William Temple

Hot Buttered Rum

3/4 cup brown sugar (175 ml)
1/3 cup butter (75 ml)
1/4 tsp. lemon peel (1 ml)
1/4 tsp. cinnamon (1 ml)
Dash of allspice
Dark rum
Boiling water

Mix the first five ingredients together with a wooden spoon. Put in the fridge until ready to use. (Mix keeps up to four weeks.) For one serving, place one heaping tablespoon of mix into a large mug. Add one to two ounces of rum (30–60 g). Fill with boiling water. Stir well and serve.

Peach Bellini

1/2 cup peach schnapps (125 ml)
2/3 cup sparkling wine (150 ml)
1 tsp. lemon juice (5 ml)
1 tsp. sugar (5 ml)
Mint sprigs for garnish

Into two champagne flutes, layer peach schnapps, wine, lemon, and sugar. Top with mint sprigs.

> "As fermenting in a vessel works up to the top whatever it has in the bottom, so wine in those who have drunk beyond measure, vents the most inward secrets."
> –Michel E. Montaigne

Chi Chi

3 oz. vodka (90 ml)
4 tbsp. coconut cream or thick coconut milk
1 cup pineapple juice (250 ml)
1 1/2 cups crushed ice (375 ml)

Combine ingredients in blender and blend until smooth. Pour into two tall glasses.

> "Action may not always bring happiness, but there is no happiness without action."
> –Gandhi

Mai Tai

1 oz. dark rum (30 ml)
1 oz. light rum (30 ml)
1 oz. orange curacao (30 ml)
2 oz. orange juice (60 ml)
1/2 oz. lime juice (15 ml)
Dash of simple syrup
1 pineapple slice
1 cocktail cherry

Combine ingredients except for pineapple slice and cherry in a tall glass. Stir gently. Top with pineapple and cherry.

Holiday Punch

2 forty-ounce bottles Ocean Spray cranberry cocktail (1.89 L each)
1 can frozen orange juice, thawed
1 can frozen grapefruit juice, thawed
1 can frozen lemonade, thawed
2 cans soda water
2 cans ginger ale
Vodka (optional)

Combine ingredients in large punch bowl. If adding vodka, add according to desired amount Chill. Serves twenty.

> "John the Baptist came neither eating nor drinking, and they said, he has a demon. The son of man came eating and drinking, and they said, here is a glutton and a drunkard. But wisdom is proved right by her actions."
> —Jesus

Soda Pop Punch

1 six-ounce can frozen fruit juice (lemon, lime, orange, or pineapple) (200 ml)
3 cups carbonated water (750 ml)

Mix together well in blender. Add ice if desired. Serves four.

American Flyer

1 1/2 oz. light rum (45 ml)
1 tbsp. lime concentrate (15 ml)
1 1/2 tsp. sugar syrup (7.5 ml)
Champagne

To make simple syrup, mix one part sugar to two parts water. Boil for five minutes. Remove from heat and let stand.

Shake rum, lime, and sugar syrup together in a cocktail shaker. Pour into a champagne flute. Fill with champagne.

Christmas Jed Nog

I have never known anyone who loves Christmas as much as my friend Jed, who adorns the season with blazing glory. Jed generously supplied this amazing recipe, but you won't want to make it only at Christmas. This is good for any celebration that involves a crowd.

2 cups white sugar (500 ml)
1 1/2 cups bourbon (375 ml)
1 1/2 cups brandy (375 ml)
1 cup rum (250 ml)
9 eggs
1 quart vanilla ice cream (1 L)
1 quart whole milk (1 L)
Fresh-grated nutmeg for garnish

Mix sugar, bourbon, brandy, and rum together. Let stand for two hours. Beat eggs for half an hour in a blender or food processor. Add ice cream and milk. Add sugar, bourbon, brandy, and rum. Pour into a large punch bowl. Garnish with a sprinkling of nutmeg.

```
"The heart of Christmas is a sacred beauty fulfilled."
                    Anonymous
```

Classic Martini

Icy coldness is a must. Store gin with glasses in the freezer.

2 oz. dry gin (60 ml)
1/2 oz. dry vermouth (15 ml)
1 lemon twist
1 green olive

Stir gin and vermouth with ice, cracked or cubed but not crushed. Strain into a chilled cocktail glass. Run lemon peel around rim of glass and twist over rim. Drop in olive. Serves one. Note: if you do not care for gin, use vodka.

Maiden's Prayer

1 oz. gin (30 ml)
1 oz. Cointreau (30 ml)
1/2 oz. lemon juice (15 ml)
1/2 oz. orange juice (15 ml)
1 orange peel twist

Shake ingredients—except for peel—vigorously with ice in a cold cocktail shaker. Strain into chilled cocktail glass. Twist orange peel over and then drop in. Serves one.

Foghorn

2 oz. gin (60 ml)
1/2 oz. lime juice (15 ml)
3 oz. ginger ale (45 ml)
Lime wedge

Pour gin and lime into ice-filled glasses. Top with ginger ale. Stir gently. Add more ginger ale if desired. Squeeze lime wedge over drink and drop in. Serves one to two.

"Religion is an important force whether you are
a Christian, Muslim, Buddhist, a Jew, or a Hindu.
Religion is a great force and has command over
one's own morality, behavior, and attitude."
—Nelson Mandela

Bella Coola

1 1/2 oz. gin (45 ml)
1/2 oz. Campari (15 ml)
1/2 oz. Limon cello (15 ml)
1/2 oz. orange liqueur (15 ml)
1 oz. orange juice (30 ml)
Ice
Lime peel spiral

Shake liquid ingredients vigorously with ice. Strain into chilled cocktail glasses. Garnish with lime peel spiral. Serves two.

Acapulco

1 oz. gold tequila (30 ml)
1 oz. gold rum (30 ml)
2 oz. grapefruit juice (60 ml)
3 oz. pineapple juice (90 ml)

Shake ingredients vigorously with ice. Strain into large chilled cocktail glasses. Serves one to two.

"The only true 'happy hour' in a person's life
is the one God creates deep in the heart."
Anonymous

Tiger's Milk

1 oz. dark rum (30 ml)
1 oz. brandy (30 ml)
4 oz. half and half (125 ml)
2 tsp. sugar (10 ml)
Dash of ground nutmeg

Shake ingredients vigorously with ice. Strain into chilled cocktail glasses. Sprinkle with nutmeg. Serves one to two.

```
"What we choose changes us. Who we love transforms
us. How we create reshapes us. What we do remakes us."
             -Dr. Eugene Callender
```

Long Island Iced Tea

1 oz. white rum (30 ml)
1 oz. gin (30 ml)
1 oz. vodka (30 ml)
1 oz. tequila (30 ml)
1 oz. Cointreau or triple sec (30 ml)
1 oz. lime juice (30 ml)
1 oz. orange juice (30 ml)
3 oz. chilled cola (90 ml)
2 lemon wedges

Pour all liquid ingredients except for cola into two ice-filled glasses. Top with cola. Stir gently. Squeeze lemon wedge over drink. Serves two.

Gin Sling

1 tsp. sugar syrup (5 ml)
2 tsp. lemon juice (10 ml)
3 oz. gin (90 ml)
Soda water

Shake sugar syrup, lemon juice, and gin in a cocktail shaker. Pour in a tall glass. Fill with soda water.

Side Car

1 part Cointreau
2 parts lemon juice
8 parts brandy

Shake over ice in a cocktail shaker. Strain into a tall glass.

Manhattan

1 part vermouth
5 parts bourbon or rye whiskey
1 dash angostura bitters

Pour over ice. Stir gently—don't shake. Strain into glass.

```
"You give little when you give of your possessions.
It is when you give of yourself that you truly give."
                    -Khalil Gibran
```

Breads/Grains

Well "Bread" Children

"Take one large, grassy field, half a dozen children, two or three small dogs, and a pinch of brook and some pebbles. Mix the children and the dogs together and put them in the field, stirring constantly. Pour the brook over the pebbles and sprinkle the field with flowers. Spread over all a deep blue sky and bake in the sun. When brown, set to cool in a bathtub."
—Mrs. Robert Murphy

Quick Beer Bread. 69
Whole Wheat Bread 70
Irish Soda Bread 71
Whole Wheat Cheese Loaf 71
Southern Cornbread 72
Garlic Cheese Bread 73
Cinnamon Bread 74
Monkey Bread 75
Angela's Ninety-Minute Bread 76
Russian Black Bread 78
Easy Caramel Sticky Buns 79
Donna's Easy Louisiana Biscuits 80
Sweet Potato Biscuits .80
Indian Bannock 81
Scones 82
Scottish Oatcakes 83

```
"I am the bread of life,
who so ever feeds on me
will never go hungry."
     -Jesus Christ
```

Quick Beer Bread

When making no-yeast quick breads, it is important to sift your flour. If you do not, the bread may tend to be heavy. If you do not purchase flour presifted and do not have a sifter, spoon the required amount of flour into a measuring container spoon by spoon to keep the flour from becoming compressed.

>3 cups presifted white flour (750 ml)
>3 level tsp. baking powder (15 ml)
>1 level tsp. salt (5 ml)
>1/4 cup sugar (50 ml)
>1 twelve-ounce can of beer of choice (350 ml)
>(must be regular beer, not nonalcoholic, to make batter lighter)
>1/3 cup melted butter (75 ml)

Preheat oven to 375°F (190°C). In a large bowl, mix presifted flour, baking powder, salt, and sugar. Make well in the center. Pour in beer and then mix lightly. Spoon batter into greased nine-by-five-inch loaf pan (23 x 13 cm). Pour melted butter over the top. Bake for hour. Cool bread for fifteen minutes on a wire rack before cutting.

Note: Do not put warm bread in plastic to store until thoroughly cool or else you'll have soggy bread.

Whole Wheat Bread

3 level cups whole wheat flour (750 ml) sifted
1 level tbsp. baking powder
1 tbsp. sugar
4 tbsp. flax seeds
2 cups club soda

Preheat oven to 400°F (200°C). Grease a nine-by-five-inch loaf pan (23x13 cm). In a large bowl, measure dry ingredients. Mix well. Add club soda. Stir with a wooden spoon until just combined. Do not over mix. Pour batter into the pan. Bake forty-five to fifty minutes or until top of bread is golden and a toothpick inserted in center comes out clean. Cool bread for several minutes on wire rack before taking out of pan.

```
"Got any rivers they say are un-crossable?
Got any mountains they say, 'Can't tunnel
through?' We specialize in the wholly impossible,
    doing the things they say you can't do."
-Faith song of the Panama Canal builders
```

Irish Soda Bread

3 cups unbleached white flour, sifted (750 ml)
1 tbsp. baking powder (15 ml)
1/3 cup brown sugar (75 ml)
1 tsp. salt (5 ml)
1 tsp. baking soda (5 ml)
1 large organic egg, lightly beaten
2 cups buttermilk or sour milk (500 ml)
To make sour milk, add 2 tbsp. lemon juice (30 ml) to enough milk to make 2 cups
1/4 cup butter, melted (50 ml)

Preheat oven to 325°F (165°C). Liberally grease a nine-by-five-inch loaf pan (23x12°C). In a medium bowl, combine flour, baking powder, sugar, salt, and baking soda. In a separate bowl, blend egg, buttermilk, or sour milk Add all at once to the flour mixture. Mix just until blended. Stir in the melted butter. Pour batter into a loaf pan. Bake sixty-five to seventy minutes or until a toothpick inserted in the center comes out clean. Cool on a wire rack. When completely cool, wrap bread in saran wrap or tinfoil and store for several hours or overnight for the best flavor.

Whole Wheat Cheese Loaf

2 cups whole wheat flour (500 ml)
2 cups unbleached white flour (500 ml)
2 tsp. baking powder (10 ml)
1 tsp. baking soda (5 ml)
1 tsp. salt (5 ml)
2 cups cheddar cheese, grated (500 ml)
2 tbsp. maple syrup (30 ml)
1 3/4 cups buttermilk or sour milk (375 ml)

In a large bowl, mix flour, baking powder, soda, and salt together. In a separate bowl, combine cheese, syrup, and buttermilk. Mix into the dry ingredients. Stir lightly just until mixed. Pour batter into greased loaf pans. Bake in 375°F (190°C) oven for forty-five minutes or until toothpick inserted in center comes out clean.

"I would rather live my life as if there is a God and die to find out there isn't, than live my life as if there isn't and die to find out there is."
—Albert Camus

Southern Cornbread

1 1/2 cups cornmeal (375 ml)
1 1/2 cups white flour (375 ml)
3 tsp. baking powder (15 ml)
1/2 tsp. baking soda (2 ml)
1 tsp. salt (5 ml)
4 tbsp. sugar (60 ml)
1/4 cup fresh jalapeño or green pepper, chopped (50 ml)
1 cup corn kernels, drained (250 ml)
1 cup shredded cheddar cheese (250 ml)
1 1/2 cups buttermilk or sour milk (375 ml)
2 eggs
6 tbsp. melted butter (90 ml)

In a large bowl combine corn flour, white flour, baking powder, baking soda, salt, and sugar. Stir in jalapeño or green pepper, corn, and cheese. In a separate bowl, combine buttermilk or sour milk, eggs, and butter.

Using a wooden spoon, stir wet ingredients into dry ingredients, mixing lightly. Pour batter into a nine-by-thirteen-inch cake pan (22x33cm). Bake in a preheated oven at 400°F (200°C) for thirty minutes or until a toothpick inserted in center comes out clean.

Garlic Cheese Bread

8–10 thick day-old bread slices
1 cup whole milk (250 ml)
1/4 lb. salted butter (52 g)
1/2 tsp. paprika (2 ml)
1/4 cup Parmesan cheese (50 ml)
Garlic powder to taste

Heat milk, butter, paprika, and garlic in small saucepan until just boiling. Turn off heat. Dip each bread slice into the pan, coating both sides with mixture. Sprinkle Parmesan cheese on a dinner plate. Press each bread slice into cheese, adding more cheese to the plate if necessary to coat all the pieces. Arrange on a baking sheet. Bake in an oven at 400°F (200°C) for five minutes. Serves eight to ten.

"Though it's worth every exertion, those who determine to simplify their lives, quickly discover it is a rigorous solo voyage against the wind."
Anonymous

Cinnamon Bread

1 1/2 cups flour (375 ml)
1/2 tsp. salt (2 ml)
2 tsp. baking powder (10 ml)
1 tsp. cinnamon (5 ml)
1 cup sugar (250 ml)
1/2 cup shortening (125 ml)
1 tsp. vanilla (5 ml)
1/2 cup milk (125 ml)
1 egg

Topping:
3 tbsp. powdered sugar (45 ml)
1/2 tsp. cinnamon (2 ml)

In a large bowl, mix flour, salt, baking powder, cinnamon, and sugar. In a separate bowl, mix shortening, vanilla, milk, and egg. Pour wet ingredients into dry ingredients and mix just until blended. Spoon batter into a greased and floured nine-by-five-inch loaf pan (23x12cm).
Sprinkle with topping. Bake at 350°F (180°C) for fifty minutes.

```
"All the beauty and joy we meet on earth represent
    only the scent of a flower we have not found,
    the echo of a tune we have not heard, news
    from a country we have never yet visited."
                    —Philip Yancey
```

Monkey Bread
A fun family favorite

2 loaves frozen bread dough, thawed
1 cup melted butter

Break off pieces of each loaf of dough to the size of a child's fist. Roll all the pieces in melted butter. Arrange in even layers in an ungreased angel food cake pan. When all pieces are added, cover the angel food cake pan with a clean, dry tea towel. Let dough rise in a warm place free of draft until double in size or dough rises to the top of pan. Bake in preheated oven at 350°F (180°C) for twenty-five to thirty minutes or until bread makes a hollow sound when rapped. Invert on platter. Let guests break off pieces. Serve with extra butter on the side if desired.

"One of the most relieving, enriching things in the wide world is that sense of liberation when the conscience goes free. When through forgiveness, God gives freedom to the laboring conscience, the heart suddenly knows itself clean, and the burden lifts. Even the mind is set free."
—A. W. Tozer

Angela's Ninety-Minute Bread

My mother gave me this recipe when I moved from the city to the simplicity of country living. Once a week for a year (before I moved back to the city) I would make this bread, feeling very homey and rustic. I like this recipe of Mom's because it is easy to make and very versatile. You can use any flour combination you like as long as the ratio of white flour is predominant (in order not to make the bread too heavy). You can also use a bit of vegetable or fruit juice in place of some of the water the recipe calls for. This bread is a yeast bread, so you have to knead each loaf well. Kneading is simply pushing the heels of your hands firmly into the dough on a well-floured surface, turning the dough around and around, over and over, for several minutes to make dough elastic and to get the air bubbles out. Makes four loaves.

4 tbsp. yeast (60 ml)
1 tbsp. white sugar (15 ml)
1 cup warm water (250 ml)
4 tbsp. oil (60 ml)
8 tbsp. sugar (120 ml)
2 eggs
4 tsp. salt (20 ml)
3 cups water (750 ml)
8 cups flour (960 g)
(You can use a combination of different flours such as white, whole wheat, or rye. Just make sure to begin and end with white.)
2 tbsp. whole bran (30 ml) (optional)
2 tbsp. wheat germ (30 ml) (optional)
2 tbsp. flax seeds (30 ml) (optional)

In a small bowl, combine yeast with sugar and warm water. Let sit for five minutes. In a separate large bowl, mix oil, sugar, eggs, salt, and water. Add your flours of choice to mixture, stirring vigorously with a wooden spoon. Mix in bran, wheat germ., and flax if desired. Add the yeast mixture, stirring well, adding additional flour if dough seems too sticky to handle. Cover the bowl with a clean tea towel and let rest fifteen minutes. After fifteen minutes, place the dough on a floured surface. Separate into four even loaves. Knead each loaf for several minutes to make it elastic and to get the air bubbles out. Put each loaf into a greased nine-by-five-inch loaf pan (23x12cm). Cover pans with clean tea towel, and let rise away from draft until doubled in size. Bake in a preheated 400°F (200°C) oven for thirty-five to forty-five minutes or until bread makes a hollow sound when rapped or a toothpick inserted in center comes out clean. Timing varies when using different flours. If desired, brush tops with beaten egg white to make the top crusty or brush with melted butter to make tops soft. Cool thoroughly on wire racks.

> "Bread is the staff of life."
> Anonymous

Russian Black Bread

2 cups beer (500 ml)
1/2 cup water (125 ml)
2 envelopes dry yeast
1/4 cup vinegar (50 ml)
1/4 cup molasses (50 ml)
1/4 cup unsweetened cocoa powder (50 ml)
1/4 cup melted butter (50 ml)
1 tbsp. sugar (15 ml)
1 tbsp. salt (15 ml)
2 tsp. caraway seed (10 ml)
1 tbsp. onion powder (15 ml)
1/4 tsp. garlic powder (1 ml)
1/2 tsp. fennel (2 ml)
1 tbsp. instant coffee (15 ml)
1 cup bran (250 ml)
2 cups white flour (500 g)
4 cups rye flour (946 ml)
2 cups wheat flour (473 ml)

In a medium sauce pot, warm beer until tepid, neither hot nor cold. Remove from heat. Pour into a large bowl. Add yeast. Stir to combine.
Add vinegar, molasses, cocoa, melted butter, sugar, salt, caraway, onion powder, garlic powder, fennel, and coffee. Add bran and mix well. Add flour.

Knead for ten to fifteen minutes, adding additional flour as needed. (Dough will be a bit sticky.) Place in a greased bowl. Cover bowl with a clean tea towel and let rise until doubled in size. When doubled, punch down dough with your fists. Cut dough in half. Shape into rounds. Put on round greased cake pans. Cover and let rise until doubled in size. Bake in a preheated 375°F oven (190°C) for fifty to sixty minutes. Let cool on wire racks.

"Grace is available for each of us every day—our spiritual daily bread—but we've got to remember to ask for it with a grateful heart and not worry about whether there will be enough for tomorrow."
—Sarah Ban Breathnach

Easy Caramel Sticky Buns

2 loaves frozen bread dough, thawed
1 cup butter, divided (250 ml)
1 1/2 cups brown sugar, divided (375 ml)
2 cups toasted walnuts, chopped and divided (500 ml)
1/2 cup raisins (125 ml)
1 tbsp. cinnamon (15 ml)
2 tsp. orange zest (10 ml)

In a saucepan, melt 3/4 cup of the butter (175 ml) with 3/4 cup of the brown sugar (175 ml). Cook for two minutes or until bubbly. Pour into greased nine-by-thirteen-inch pan (22x33 cm.) Sprinkle with half the walnuts. Set aside. Stir together the rest of the butter, sugar, and walnuts. Stir in cinnamon and zest. Mix well. Set aside.

Roll the dough into square shapes. Sprinkle with the walnut mixture. Roll up. Cut into one-inch pieces (2.54 cm). Place pieces in the baking dish, seam side down. Cover with a tea towel and let rise until double in size. Bake in a preheated 350°F (180°C) oven for twenty-five minutes. Put on wire rack. Let stand for five minutes. Invert on a platter.

Glaze

2 tbsp. cream (30 ml)
1/4 tsp. vanilla (1 ml)
Dash of lemon juice.
1 cup confectioner's sugar (250 ml)

Mix well. Drizzle over buns.

Donna's Easy Louisiana Biscuits

4 cups Bisquick brand biscuit mix (500 g)
2/3 cup club soda (150 ml)
1 cup sour cream (250 ml)
1/4 cup melted butter (50 ml)

In a medium bowl, lightly mix Bisquick mix with club soda and sour cream. Roll dough out onto a lightly floured board. Roll one inch thick (2.54 cm). Cut with a cookie cutter. Place biscuits on a greased baking sheet. Brush with melted butter. Bake in a preheated 400°F oven (200°C) for about ten minutes or until tops are golden and bottoms are crisp yellow. Serve warm. Makes fourteen to sixteen.

> "I have read Plato and Cicero, sayings very wise and beautiful; but I have never read in either of them: 'Come to me, all ye that labor and are heavy burdened, and I will give you rest.'"
> —Augustine

Sweet Potato Biscuits

4 cups flour (1 L)
1/2 cup sugar (125 ml)
2 level tbsp. baking powder (30 ml)
2 tsp. salt (10 ml)
1 tsp. baking soda (5 ml)
2 large sweet potatoes, cooked and mashed, equaling 2 cups (500 ml)
1 cup butter, melted (250 ml)
1 1/3 cups buttermilk (325 ml) or sour milk.

Combine flour, sugar, baking powder, salt, and baking soda. In a separate bowl, combine sweet potatoes, melted butter, buttermilk, or sour milk. Make a well in dry ingredients and add in wet ingredients. Stir lightly to mix. Roll dough out onto floured surface to one inch thick (2.54 cm). Cut with biscuit cutter. Place biscuits on ungreased baking sheet. Bake at 350°F (180°C) for about twenty-five minutes or until golden and bottoms of biscuits are very light brown. Makes fourteen to eighteen.

Indian Bannock

2 1/4 cups white flour (550 ml)
1/3 cup wheat germ (75 ml)
1 tsp. baking powder (5 ml)
1/2 tsp. baking soda (2 ml)
2 tbsp. brown sugar (30 ml)
1/2 tsp. salt (2 ml)
1/4 cup butter, softened (50 ml)
1/2 cup warm, mashed potatoes (125 ml)
1 cup milk (250 ml)

In a large bowl, blend flour, wheat germ, baking powder, soda, sugar, and salt. Cut in butter with a pastry blender or two forks until the mixture is the consistency of cornmeal. Make well in the center. Add warm potatoes and milk. Stir gently. Turn out onto lightly floured board. Knead for thirty seconds. Pat dough to one inch (2.54 cm) thick. Place bannock on lightly greased baking sheet. Bake in 425°F oven (220°C) for twenty-five minutes. Cut into wedges. Serve warm. Makes eight servings.

"Requests give direction to love, but demands stop the flow of love."
Anonymous

Scones

2 cups flour (500 ml)
4 tsp. baking powder (20 ml)
2 tsp. sugar (10 ml)
1/2 tsp. salt (2 ml)
1/4 cup butter (50 ml)
2 eggs
1/2 cup cream (125 ml)
1 egg white
1 tsp. water (5 ml)
Sugar for sprinkling (optional)

In a medium bowl, blend flour, baking powder, sugar, and salt together. Add butter. Work the butter in with a pastry blender until the dough resembles coarse crumbs. Add eggs. Add cream. If needed, use a bit more cream to make the dough firm enough to handle. Turn dough out onto a lightly floured board. Knead for half a minute. Pat and roll one inch thick (2.54 cm). Cut into diamond shapes with a sharp knife, cutting across dough diagonally. Using a pastry brush, brush scones with egg white mixed with water. Sprinkle scones with sugar if desired. Bake in hot oven at 450°F (230°C) for fifteen minutes or until browned. Makes eight to twelve.

Scottish Oatcakes

2 cups steel-milled oatmeal (500 ml)
1 cup unbleached white flour (250 ml)
1/2 cup dark brown sugar (125 ml)
1 tsp. baking soda (5 ml)
1/2 tsp. sea salt (2 ml)
1/2 cup butter (125 ml)
Cold water

In a large bowl, mix together oats, flour, sugar, soda, and salt. Cut in butter. Add enough cold water to hold the dough together. Roll to a quarter inch thick (6.35mm). Cut in squares. Bake in preheated 375°F oven (190C) for ten to fifteen minutes.

"God will prepare everything for our perfect happiness in Heaven, and if it takes my dog being there, I believe he will be there."
-Billy Graham

Breakfasts

"Begin the day with God.
He is your Sun and Day
His is the radiance of your dawn
To Him address your day."
Anonymous

Welsh Rarebit 87
Cornmeal Griddle Cakes 88
Eggs in Purgatory. 89
Bourbon French Toast 90
French Omelet 91
Omelet 92
Baked Omelet 92
Greek Yogurt Parfait 93
Banana Pancakes 93
Jalapeño Breakfast Pie 94
Eggs Benediction 95
Crepe Suzette. 96
Avocado Toasts 97
Lori's Mile-High Granola. .98
Low-Carb Granola 99
Cointreau Grapefruit. 99
Strawberry Smoothie 100
New Orleans Black Muffins 101
Banana Bran Muffins. 102

"Break your fast of the night with a grateful heart, with pleasant speech, with good food!"
Anonymous

Welsh Rarebit

2 English muffins, split and lightly toasted
8 slices bacon, crisply cooked
4 vine-ripened tomato slices, set aside
1 1/2 cups shredded cheddar cheese (375 ml)
3/4 cup beer (175 ml)
1 tsp. dry mustard powder (5 ml)
1/2 tsp. Worcestershire sauce (2 ml)
Dash of cayenne
1 large beaten egg, set aside

Place toasted muffins on two plates. Top with bacon. Place in warm oven. For cheese sauce, in small saucepan on medium heat, combine cheddar cheese, beer, mustard powder, Worcestershire sauce, and cayenne. Stir gently until cheese melts. Stir half of the cheese sauce into the beaten egg, and pour back into the saucepan. Cook gently until sauce thickens. Remove English muffins from oven. Top with cheese sauce. Top with tomato slices. Serve immediately. (Note: You can substitute the beer with milk if desired.)

Cornmeal Griddle Cakes

2 cups white cornmeal (500 ml)
2 tbsp. sugar (30 ml)
2 tsp. salt (10 ml)
2 cups boiling water (500 ml)
2 eggs
1 cup milk (250 ml)
4 tbsp. melted butter (60 ml)
1 cup flour (250 ml)
4 tsp. baking powder (20 ml)
Fresh raspberries
Warm maple syrup

Combine cornmeal, sugar, and salt in large bowl. Add boiling water. Stir vigorously until lump free. Cover and let sit for twenty minutes. In a separate bowl, beat eggs. Add milk and melted butter. Add to cornmeal mixture. Beat until smooth. Mix flour and baking powder. Stir lightly into the cornmeal mixture. Spoon batter onto hot, greased griddle. Cook griddle cakes until golden on both sides, about one to two minutes. Remove and place on warm platter. Garnish with raspberries. Serve with butter and warm maple syrup Serves four.

"An attitude of worship puts one's mind and spirit in line with wordless things and into the flow of power."
Anonymous

Eggs in Purgatory

2 slices crusty Italian bread
Olive oil
2 large organic eggs
1/4 cup hot and spicy spaghetti sauce, warmed (50 ml)
Fresh-grated Romano or Parmesan cheese
Pinch of crushed chili peppers

Create a hole in center of each slice of bread. Place slices in a medium-hot skillet drizzled with a bit of olive oil. Crack an egg into the hole of each slice of bread in the skillet. Cook for two minutes and then gently flip. Cook one more minute. Remove eggs and bread from skillet. Put on two warm plates. Spoon spaghetti sauce, cheese, and crushed chili peppers atop each slice. Serve immediately.

"A man's true wealth in the here-after is the good he does in this world to his fellow man."
—Muhammad

Bourbon French Toast

This is for a crowd, but you can easily half the recipe.

1 1/2 tsp. cinnamon (7 ml)
1/4 cup bourbon (50 ml)
1 cup liquid whipping cream (250 ml)
1/4 cup liquid honey (50 ml)
1 tsp. vanilla (5 ml)
1/4 tsp. nutmeg (1 ml)
1/2 tsp. salt (2 ml)
1 loaf day-old French bread
Plain yogurt
Fresh fruit

Mix cinnamon, bourbon, whipping cream, honey, vanilla, nutmeg, and salt together. Heat griddle to medium heat. Dip bread slices in batter. Put in griddle. Brown each side until it is a gentle golden brown. Remove from heat. Serve immediately with plain yogurt and fresh fruit on the side.

"A good laugh is sunshine in a house."
—William Makepease Thackeray

French Omelet

Decide which filling you want and prepare before making omelet.

Asparagus Tarragon Filling
2 tbsp. butter (30 ml)
1 tsp. lemon juice (5 ml)
Dash of tarragon.
Salt and pepper
8 oz. cooked asparagus (250 ml)

In a saucepan on medium-high heat, melt and brown butter. Add lemon juice, tarragon, and salt and pepper to taste. Add cooked asparagus. Cook just till heated through. Fill omelet.

Fruit and Cheese Filling
1/2 cup orange juice (125 ml)
2 tsp. lemon juice (10 ml)
2 tsp. cornstarch (10 ml)
Dash of nutmeg
1/2 cup Sliced fruit of choice (125 ml)
1/2 cup Gouda cheese, grated (125 ml)

Pour orange and lemon juice into a small saucepan on medium heat. Whisk in cornstarch, and stir well. Add nutmeg. Stir until hot and thickened. Spoon a bit of sauce inside the omelet. Fold omelet. Spoon remaining sauce atop. Sprinkle with Gouda cheese and fruit.

Mushroom and Onion Filling
1 tbsp. butter (15 ml)
1/3 cup diced onions (75 ml)
8 oz. fresh mushrooms, sliced (250 ml)
Salt and pepper

Melt butter in hot skillet. Add onion and mushrooms, and fry until tender. Fill center of omelet with mixture. Add a sprinkling of grated cheese if desired. Fold one side of omelet 1/3 over center. Fold other side 1/3 over center. Slide onto warm plate.

Omelet

4 eggs
2 tbsp. water (30 ml)
Dash salt and pepper
2 tbsp. melted butter (30 ml)

In a medium bowl, combine eggs, water, salt, and pepper. In a large skillet, heat butter on medium heat until it sizzles. Pour in egg mix. As eggs begin to set, run a rubber spatula around edges, lifting the eggs to allow uncooked parts to flow underneath. When set but still shiny, remove eggs from heat. Spread desired filling across center, lifting 1/3 omelet over center. Repeat with remaining 1/3 on other side to overlap omelet. Tilt skillet onto plate. Divide in two.

Baked Omelet

4 large eggs, yolks and whites separated
1/2 tsp. lemon zest (2 ml)
1 tbsp. butter (15 ml)
cheese, salsa, or fried onions for garnish

Preheat oven to 375°F (190°C). In a medium bowl, beat egg whites until stiff peaks form. In a separate bowl, beat egg yolks until thickened. Stir in lemon zest. Fold in egg whites. Heat an eight-inch (20 cm) ovenproof pan over medium heat. Add butter. Pour in eggs and let heat for one minute. Then place mixture in oven. Bake for ten minutes or until egg is puffed and golden. Slide omelet onto warm serving plate, and cut into wedges. Garnish with cheese, salsa, or fried onions. Serves two.

Greek Yogurt Parfait

2 cups plain Greek yogurt (500 ml)
1 ripe, fresh peach, cored
1/4 cup blueberries (50 ml)
1/4 cup almonds (50 ml)
1/4 cup liquid honey (50 ml)
Granola

Divide yogurt into two tall glasses. Top with peaches, blueberries, and almonds. Drizzle with honey. Top with granola.

Banana Pancakes

2 cups white flour (500 ml)
2 cups plain yogurt (500)
1/8 cup milk (30 ml)
1/2 tsp. vanilla (2 ml)
3 eggs
3 tbsp. vegetable oil (45 ml)
2 tbsp. white sugar (30 ml)
2 rounded tsp. baking powder (10 ml)
1 rounded tsp. baking soda (5 ml)
1/2 tsp. salt (2 ml)
1 banana, sliced

Put flour, yogurt, milk, vanilla, eggs, oil, sugar, baking powder, soda, and salt in blender and blend until smooth. If batter seems a bit thick, add a little more milk until it is desired consistency. Pour in 1/4 cup
(50 ml) measurements onto lightly greased hot griddle. Cook until light and golden underneath, about one minute. Add banana slices to top before flipping. Cook other side one minute, or until light and golden on bottom. Makes four to six servings.

"We can never see the sunrise by
looking towards the west."
—Japanese proverb

Jalapeño Breakfast Pie

6 large organic eggs
2 cups sharp cheddar cheese, grated (500 ml)
1/2 cup fresh jalapeño peppers, chopped (125 ml)
1/2 cup black olives, sliced (125 ml)

In a medium bowl, beat the eggs until thick. Set aside. Sprinkle jalapeños on bottom of greased eight-by-eight-inch baking pan (20 x 20 cm). Sprinkle with grated cheese. Pour eggs over. Sprinkle with olives. Bake for half an hour in a preheated oven at 350°F (180°C). Serves four.

Eggs Benediction

4 slices country-style bacon or two slices country-style ham
4 large organic eggs
2 English muffins
Hollandaise sauce
Orange slices
Parsley sprigs

To make hollandaise sauce, in blender put:
3 egg yolks
2 tbsp. lemon juice (30 ml)
1/4 tsp. salt (1 ml)

Slowly add:
1/2 cup melted butter (125 ml)
Dash of cayenne pepper

Blend until thickened. Set aside.

Cook bacon until crisp. Drain on a paper towel and set in warm oven. Or fry ham slices in skillet until heated all through and put in warm oven.

To Poach Eggs:

Gently slide eggs into a skillet of simmering water. Simmer, uncovered, for three to five minutes, smoothing edges with a spoon to round. As eggs cook, toast English muffins. Remove eggs with a slotted spoon and put atop toasted muffins. Add bacon strips or ham. Top with hollandaise sauce. Place orange slices on side. Garnish with parsley. Serves two.

"If we would love, we must first learn to listen.
It is in listening that love matures."
Anonymous

Crepe Suzette

1 cup flour (250 ml)
1 1/2 cups milk (375 ml)
2 eggs
2 tbsp. sugar (30 ml)
1 tbsp. melted butter (15 ml)
1/4 tsp. salt (1 ml)

Place flour, milk, eggs, sugar, melted butter, and salt in medium bowl and beat until smooth. Heat a lightly greased skillet to medium heat. Spoon in two to four tablespoons of the batter, tilting the skillet to spread the batter thinly. Cook both sides of crepes until gently brown, loosening the edges with a small spatula. Invert the pan over a platter and slide the crepes onto it. Fold the crepes into quarters. Place in the oven to keep warm while cooking the remaining batter. Make sauce.

Sauce

1/4 cup butter (50 ml)
1/4 cup orange liqueur (50 ml)
1/4 cup orange juice (50 ml)
2 tbsp. sugar (30 ml)
2 tbsp. brandy (30 ml)

Melt butter in a chafing dish on medium heat. Add liqueur, orange juice, and sugar. Cook and stir until mixture is warm and bubbly. Remove crepes from oven and arrange folded crepes in the sauce. Simmer until sauce thickens slightly, spooning sauce over crepes as they heat. Pour brandy over crepes. Ignite carefully. When flame subsides, slide onto plates. Serve immediately. Makes six servings.

Avocado Toasts

4 tbsp. olive oil (60 ml)
1 1/2 tsp. cumin seeds (7 ml)
1/4 tsp. turmeric (1 ml)
1/8 tsp. cardamom (0.6 ml)
1 whole-grain baguette, sliced
2–3 avocados, peeled and chopped
1 lime
Salt and pepper to taste

Preheat oven to 450°F (230°C). In a small saucepan, heat olive oil until hot. Add cumin, turmeric, and cardamom. Turn off the heat and let the spices sit for ten minutes. Brush both sides of baguette slices with the oil, cumin, turmeric, and cardamom mixture. Place on an ungreased baking sheet and place in the preheated oven. Bake until the baguette is nicely toasted, about three to four minutes. Remove from the oven. Top slices with avocado. Arrange on a large serving platter. Before serving, squeeze generously with lime. Sprinkle with salt and pepper. Makes sixteen to eighteen pieces.

Lori's Mile-High Granola

This scrumptious recipe comes from my dear friend Lori, a health fanatic who went door to door to test this recipe on the good folk of her town. Lori's positive, upbeat attitude, coupled with ingenious creative industry, makes me understand that in order to have a great spirit, one must perform one's duty in the right spirit.

> 5 cups rolled oats (900 g)
> 2 1/2 cups soya flakes (375 g)
> 1 cup sunflower seeds (250 g)
> 6 oz. wheat germ (170 g)
> 1 cup coconut flakes (230 g)
> 1 cup almonds, slivered (230 g)
> 1 cup cashews, diced (230 g)
> 1 cup pecan pieces (230 g)
> 3/4 cup grape-seed oil (175 ml)
> 3/4 cup water (175 ml)
> 1 1/2 tsp. vanilla (7 ml)
> 1 cup brown sugar (250 ml)
> 1/2 cup flax seeds (125 ml) (optional)
> 1 cup dried cranberries (250 ml)(optional)

In a large bowl, combine oats, soya flakes, wheat germ, coconut flakes, and nuts. In a separate bowl, mix grape-seed oil, water, vanilla, and brown sugar. Pour over ingredients in the first bowl. Stir gently to combine. Place on a large, ungreased baking sheet and bake at 275°F (140°C) for sixty to ninety minutes, stirring every twenty minutes. Remove from oven and let cool. If desired, add cranberries and flax. Mix lightly. Store in airtight containers. Makes fifteen servings.

> "A friend is one who walks in the
> door when others walk out."
> Anonymous

Low-Carb Granola

1 cup raw sunflower seeds (250 ml)
1/2 cup flax seeds (125 ml)
1 cup unsweetened coconut (250 ml)
1 cup pecans, chopped (250 ml)
1 cup walnuts, chopped (250 ml)
1 cup almonds, chopped (250 ml)
1 stick butter, melted (85 g)
2 tsp. cinnamon (7 ml)
3 packages Splenda or other sugar substitute to taste

Mix sunflower and flax seeds with coconut. Add nuts. Drizzle with melted butter. Stir in cinnamon and sugar substitute. Place on baking sheet. Bake at 350°F (180°C) for thirty minutes. Let cool before storing. Makes about six servings.

Cointreau Grapefruit

2 large grapefruits
4 tbsp. Cointreau liqueur (60 ml)
2 tbsp. brown sugar (30 ml)
Dash of nutmeg

Cut grapefruits in half, and slice off the very bottom to make them stand up. Sprinkle with Cointreau. Mix sugar with dash of nutmeg. Sprinkle over fruit. Place on baking sheet and bake for five minutes at 350°F (180°C) until golden and bubbly. Serves four.

"The mouth—not just for eating, but for praying."
Anonymous

Strawberry Smoothie

2 cups fresh or frozen strawberries (500 ml)
1/2 cup soft, plain tofu (125 ml)
3 cups plain soymilk (750 ml)
1 tsp. liquid honey (5 ml)
2 scoops vanilla whey isolate powder
1 tbsp. hemp hearts (15 ml)
1 tbsp. flax seeds (15 ml)

Put all ingredients in a blender and blend well until smooth and serve immediately. Note: If using fresh strawberries, add a few ice cubes to make the smoothie very cold. Serves two.

"Listening has become a lost art. Lack of true listening is at the root of the poor communication between employees and employers, teachers and students, parents and children, husband and wife. Everyone has their own opinions, but few seem willing to really hear what the other is trying so hard to say. People are used to being talked at, but so few used to being talked with."
Anonymous

New Orleans Black Muffins
(These muffins are dense and chewy.)

1/2 cup molasses (125 ml)
3/4 cup hot water (175 ml)
1/4 cup full-fat milk (50 ml)
1 cup roasted pecans (250 ml)
1 cup unbleached white flour (250 ml)
2 cups whole wheat flour (500 ml)
3/4 cup sugar (175 ml)
3 tbsp. baking powder (45 ml)
1 tsp. baking soda (5 ml)
1 tsp. salt (5 ml)
!/2 cup roasted sunflower seeds
1/2 cup liquid honey

In a large bowl, combine molasses with hot water and stir well. Add milk. Stir and set aside. In a separate bowl, combine flour, sugar, baking powder, baking soda, and salt. Mix well. Add roasted pecans. Make a well in center and add molasses mixture. Stir until just combined. Spoon batter generously into well-greased muffin tins. Swirl tops with honey. Sprinkle with sunflower seeds. Bake in preheated oven at 300°F (150°C) for forty-five to fifty minutes or until set. Makes twelve. Note: To roast seeds and nuts, put in hot, dry skillet and stir constantly until browned and fragrant, about one minute.

Banana Bran Muffins

1 cup bran (250 ml)
1 cup buttermilk (250 ml)
4 tbsp. butter (60 ml)
1/3 cup brown sugar (75 ml)
2 eggs
1/2 cup molasses (125 ml)
2 tsp. orange zest (10 ml)
1 tsp. vanilla (5 ml)
1 1/2 cups white flour (375 ml)
1 tsp. baking powder (5 ml)
1/4 tsp. baking soda (1 ml)
1/2 tsp. salt (2 ml)
1 cup raisins, soaked (250 ml)
1 cup bananas, chopped (250 ml)
1/2 cup walnut pieces (125 ml)

Mix bran into buttermilk and set aside. Cream butter with sugar. Add eggs, beating well. Add molasses, orange zest, and vanilla. Add bran milk mixture. In a separate bowl, mix flour, baking powder, baking soda, and salt. Add bran mixture. Stir just till combined. Fold in chopped bananas, raisins, and walnuts. Generously fill greased muffin tin. Bake in preheated oven at 350°F (180°C) for twenty to twenty-five minutes or until a toothpick inserted in center of muffin comes out clean. Makes twelve large muffins.

Lunch
—
Supper
—
Some Sides

Megan's Sloppy Joes 106
Vegetarian Burgers 107
Spicy Hamburgers 108
Hamburgers with Mushroom Wine Sauce 109
Frankfurters 110
Easy Brown Beans 110
Hughie's Coleslaw 111
Ale-Braised Cabbage 112
German Cabbage 113
Sweet Potato Wedges 113
Dave's Spicy Potato Salad 114
Beer Potato Salad 115
Caliente Chili 116
Avocado Crab Louis 117
Fennel and Cheese Pasta 118
Spinach and Feta Quiche 119
Sauerkraut with Pork 120
Fiery Bean Burritos 121
Mediterranean Gyros 122
Falafel with Peanut Sauce 123
Chili Quitos 124
Easy Moussaka 125
American Meatloaf 126
Ratatouille 127
Spaghetti Squash 128
Lamb Patties 129
Curried Sweet Pepper Strips 130
Cajun Stuffed Potatoes 131
Twice-Baked Potatoes 132
Mediterranean Asparagus 132

Scalloped Corn 133
Antipasto Pizza 134
Asparagus Fritters 135
Citrus Crepes 136
Heavenly Hash Browns 137
Corned Beef Hash 137
Beef Stroganoff 138
Tostadas 139
Picnic Chicken 140

Megan's Sloppy Joes

2 lbs. lean ground lean beef (900 g)
1 large onion, chopped
1/4 cup water (50 ml)
3 tbsp. Worcestershire sauce (45 ml)
1/2 tsp. salt (2 ml)
1/2 tsp. pepper (2 ml)
1/2 tsp. garlic powder (2 ml)
1/2 tsp. onion powder (2 ml)
1 tsp. chili powder (5 ml)
1 tsp. red pepper sauce (5 ml)
1 twelve-ounce bottle chili sauce (375 ml)
2 cups sharp cheddar cheese, grated and set aside (500 ml)
10–12 whole wheat burger buns, split

In a large skillet, cook beef and onion over medium heat until beef is no longer pink, around eight to ten minutes. Add chopped onions, water, Worcestershire sauce, salt, pepper, garlic powder, onion powder, and chili powder. Stir in red pepper and chili sauce. Taste and adjust seasonings as desired. Simmer for thirty minutes. To serve, place buns on a large platter and top with sloppy Joe mix. Sprinkle with cheese. Serves ten to twelve.

Vegetarian Burgers

1 sixteen-ounce can kidney beans, drained (500 ml)
2 cups cooked chilled rice (500 ml)
2 tbsp. hot and spicy ketchup (30 ml)
1/2 tsp. garlic powder (2 ml)
1 tsp. oregano (5 ml)
Pinch of thyme
1/4 tsp. sage (1 ml)
Cajun salt to taste
1/4 cup onion, chopped (50 ml)
6 whole wheat buns

Combine beans, rice, ketchup, garlic powder, oregano, thyme, sage, and Cajun salt. Mash well. Add chopped onion. Form into six patties. Grill in hot skillet until browned on both sides. Serve on fresh buns.

"Clouds come floating into my life, no longer to carry rain or usher storm, but to add color to my sunset sky."
—R. Tagore

Spicy Hamburgers

1 lb. lean ground beef (448 g)
4 tbsp. chopped onion (60 ml)
2 garlic cloves, chopped
2 tbsp. parsley (30 ml)
1/2 tsp. crushed dried chilies (2 ml)
1 large organic egg
Dash of Tabasco sauce
Salt and pepper to taste
1 cup vine-ripened tomato, diced (250 ml)
4 whole wheat sesame seed buns

In a large bowl, combine beef, onion, garlic, parsley, chilies, egg, Tabasco, and salt and pepper. Gently mix in chopped tomatoes. form into four large patties. Grill on barbeque or in skillet on medium heat until meat is cooked through. Serve on warm sesame seed buns.

Hamburgers with Mushroom Wine Sauce

1 lb. ground beef (448 g)
4 tbsp. sour cream (60 ml)
4 tbsp. chives, chopped (60 ml)
1/2 tsp. curry powder (2 ml)
Salt and pepper to taste
4 Kaiser buns

Combine beef, sour cream, chives, curry powder, and salt and pepper to taste. Form into four patties. Place on medium-hot grill and grill for four to five minutes or until desired doneness. While burgers are grilling, prepare mushroom wine sauce.

Mushroom Wine Sauce

2 cups fresh mushrooms, chopped (500 ml)
1 cup onion, sliced (250 ml)
3 tsp. butter (15 ml)
1/2 cup red wine (125 ml)
Salt and pepper to taste

Sauté onions and mushrooms in butter on medium heat for four to five minutes. Add wine. Lower heat and simmer for five minutes. Season to taste with salt and pepper. Pour over grilled burgers. Serve with warmed Kaiser buns

"Every time you refuse to overlook a weakness or a flaw in another, real or perceived, your heart grows cold."
Anonymous

Frankfurters
with Roquefort

8 large frankfurters or smokies
4 large pita rounds or 8 large hotdog buns
Stoneground Dijon mustard
1 cup freshly grated Roquefort cheese (250 ml)
1 cup coarsely chopped onion (250 ml)

Grill frankfurters on medium-hot barbecue until crisp. Cut pita rounds or hotdog buns in half and warm briefly on grill or in oven. Spread with Dijon mustard and top with frankfurters or smokies. Sprinkle with cheese and chopped onion. If desired, serve with easy brown beans. Serves eight.

Easy Brown Beans

2 cans brown beans (398 ml each)
1/4 cup ketchup (50 ml)
4 dashes Worcestershire sauce
Dash of hot mustard powder
1 1/2 tsp. brown sugar (7 ml)
Dash of liquid smoke

Heat beans, ketchup, Worcestershire sauce, mustard powder, sugar, and liquid smoke in small saucepan until bubbly. Remove from heat. Taste and adjust seasonings according to preference. Serves four to six.

"The person of faith does not dare rest on human reason alone. He does not reject the place of human reason, but he knows there are things that human reason cannot do. The person of faith who puts their confidence in God has an access to knowledge that the person who merely thinks and reasons cannot have."
—A.W. Tozer

Hughie's Coleslaw

1 large green cabbage, chopped coarsely
1/2 package thick sliced bacon, cooked crisp and diced
1 large onion, diced

In a large bowl, toss cabbage, bacon, and onion together. Add enough dressing to desired creaminess, stirring well. Serves six to eight.

Dressing

1 cup mayonnaise (250 ml)
2–4 tbsp. white vinegar (30-60 ml)
1 tbsp. sugar (15 ml)
1/4 cup heavy cream (50 ml)
1/2 tsp. prepared horseradish (2 ml)
Salt and pepper to taste

In a medium bowl, whisk mayonnaise, vinegar, sugar, cream, and horseradish together. Taste and adjust seasonings as desired.

Ale-Braised Cabbage

1 large red cabbage, cored and finely diced
1 tbsp. olive oil (15 ml)
2–3 garlic cloves, minced
1 tsp. mustard seed (5 ml)
1/2 tsp. salt (2 ml)
2 bay leaves
1/4 cup water (50 ml)
1 1/2 cups beer (350 ml)
1 tbsp. lemon juice (15 ml)
1 tbsp. balsamic vinegar (15 ml)
1/2 cup dried cranberries (125 ml)

Heat oil in saucepan over medium heat. Add garlic and mustard seed to oil and stir for one minute. Add diced cabbage, salt, bay leaves, and water. Reduce heat to medium-low and cover. Cook for twenty minutes, adding a bit more water if necessary to keep from burning. Stir in beer. Bring to a boil and then reduce heat. Simmer for another twenty minutes. Stir in lemon, vinegar, and cranberries. Remove bay leaves before serving. Serves six to eight.

```
Buddha said, "I am a teacher in search of
   truth." Jesus said, "I am the truth."
Anonymous
```

German Cabbage

4 cups red cabbage, shredded (900 g)
1 onion, thinly sliced
1/2 apple, thinly sliced
1/3 cup chicken broth (75 ml)
1/3 cup white wine (75 ml)
2 whole allspice berries
1/2 tsp. caraway seeds (2 ml)

Combine broth, wine, allspice, and caraway in a large saucepan. In a large bowl, toss cabbage, onion, and apple together and add to saucepan. Bring to a boil. Turn heat to simmer. Cover and simmer for 1 1/2 hours. Serves six.

Sweet Potato Wedges

3 large sweet potatoes, scrubbed, and cut into quarter-inch wedges
(6.35 cm)
2 tbsp. olive oil (30 ml)
1 tsp. brown sugar (5 ml)
1 tsp. chili powder (5 ml)
1 tsp. salt (5 ml)
3 tbsp. maple syrup (45 ml)
1 1/2 tsp. apple cider vinegar (7 ml)

In a large bowl, toss sweet potato wedges with oil, sugar, chili powder, and salt. Spread on lightly greased cookie sheet. Roast at 475°F (240°C) for twenty minutes, shaking sheet once. Mix maple syrup with cider vinegar. Drizzle over wedges. Serves four to six.

"Conscience is that capacity within me that appends itself to the tallest belief I know, and then steadily prompts me of what that belief orders I do. Conscience is the eye of my soul."
Anonymous

Dave's Spicy Potato Salad

10 potatoes, quartered, cooked, and chilled
6 eggs hardboiled, cooled, and diced
Pinch each of dry mustard, sugar, salt,
cayenne pepper, smoky paprika,
sweet basil, marjoram, and oregano
1 lemon, freshly squeezed
2 large cloves of garlic, minced
4–6 fresh jalapeño peppers, diced
1 onion, chopped
1 red pepper, chopped
1 green pepper, chopped
2–3 celery stalks, chopped
12 slices bacon, cooked and crumbled

Dressing
1 1/3 cups mayonnaise (295 ml)
1 tsp. anchovy paste (5 ml)
9–10 dashes wine vinegar
Mix well.

Put potatoes with egg in a large bowl and set aside. In a small bowl, mix the spices together well and squeeze lemon over them. Set aside. In a medium-hot skillet, fry garlic, jalapeño peppers, onion, red pepper, green pepper, celery, and bacon until softened. Add the spice lemon mixture. Cook for another two to three minutes. Turn off the heat and set aside to cool. When thoroughly cool, tilt the skillet over the potatoes and eggs. Mix gently. Add dressing, adding more mayonnaise if needed. Chill. at least one hour. Serves ten to twelve.

"The genuine child of God is someone who cannot be explained by human reasoning."
Anonymous

Beer Potato Salad

3 lbs. cooked potatoes, cooled and cubed (1350 g)
2 cups celery, diced (500 ml)
1 green pepper, diced
1 onion, diced
1 1/4 cups mayonnaise (300 ml)
1 tsp. vinegar (5 ml)
1 tbsp. mustard (15 ml)
1/2 tsp. mustard powder (2 ml)
1 tsp. salt (5 ml)
1/2 tsp. pepper (2 ml)
Pinch of paprika
1 tsp. hot pepper sauce
1/2 cup beer (125 ml)

In a large bowl, combine potatoes, celery, green pepper, and onion. Toss lightly and set aside. In a separate bowl, combine mayonnaise, vinegar, mustard powder, salt, pepper, paprika, beer, and hot pepper sauce. Taste and adjust seasonings if desired. Pour over potato mixture. Toss lightly. Chill in fridge until cold at least one hour. Before serving, sprinkle with additional paprika. Serves six to eight.

Caliente Chili

1 lb. cubed beef chuck (448 g)
1 tbsp. cooking oil (15 ml)
1 jalapeño pepper, chopped
2 onions, chopped
1 green pepper, chopped
4 cloves of garlic, minced
1 canned adobo chipotle pepper, chopped
1 tbsp. chili powder (15 ml)
1 1/2 tsp. cumin (7 ml)
1 tsp. sugar (5 ml)
1 tsp. salt (5 ml)
1 tsp. black pepper (5 ml)
1 twenty-eight-ounce can diced tomatoes with juice (796 ml)
1 nineteen-ounce can kidney beans (540 ml)
1 can beer
1 unsweetened square of chocolate, melted
1 cup cheddar cheese, grated (250 ml)
1 cup fresh cilantro, chopped (250 ml)

Fry beef until well browned on all sides in medium-hot skillet. Remove from heat and set aside. In a separate skillet, fry jalapeño pepper, onion, green pepper, and garlic in oil until soft, adding additional oil if needed. Add chipotle pepper, chili powder, cumin, sugar, salt, and black pepper. Add canned tomatoes, kidney beans, beer, and melted chocolate. Simmer for ten minutes. Taste and adjust seasonings as desired. Add browned beef. Simmer for sixty minutes. Stir in grated cheese. Sprinkle with cilantro. Serves six to eight.

Avocado Crab Louis

1 egg yolk
2 tsp. Dijon mustard (10 ml)
1/2 tsp. Worcestershire sauce (2 ml)
2 tsp. red wine vinegar (10 ml)
Salt and pepper to taste
1/2 cup vegetable oil (125 ml)
1 tbsp. chili sauce (15 ml)
1/4 cup green onion, chopped (50 ml)
1/4 cup green olives, chopped (50 ml)
1 lb. lump crab meat (448 g)
4 avocados
Lettuce leaves
2 hard-boiled eggs, sliced

In a medium mixing bowl, whisk yolk, mustard, Worcestershire sauce, vinegar, salt, and pepper. Slowly add oil, beating rapidly until thickened. Add chili sauce, onions, and olives. Put crab in a separate mixing bowl and add half the sauce, blending gently so as not to break up lumps. Split avocados lengthwise and discard pits. Pile equal portions of crab mixture into each avocado. Spoon remaining sauce atop. Serve on lettuce leaves. Garnish with egg slices. Makes eight servings.

Fennel and Cheese Pasta

1/2 lb. whole grain pasta of choice (225 g)
4 tbsp. olive oil (60 ml)
1 onion, chopped
2 cloves of garlic, minced
5 anchovy filets, chopped
1/2 tsp. red chili flakes (2 ml)
1 fennel bulb chopped, fronds reserved
2 cups small red tomatoes, cut in half (500 ml)
2 tsp. marjoram (10 ml)
1 tbsp. fresh chopped basil (15 ml)
6 cups fresh baby spinach (1.5 L)
Fresh cracked pepper to taste
1/3 cup goat cheese, crumbled (75 ml)
4 tbsp. pine nuts, toasted (60 ml)

Cook pasta according to package directions. Drain and keep warm, reserving one cup of pasta water (250 ml). Heat olive oil in a medium-hot skillet. Add onion, garlic, anchovies, pepper flakes, and chopped fennel. Cook for five minutes and then lower heat to simmer. Add tomatoes, marjoram, and basil. Cook an additional two to three minutes or until tomatoes soften. Stir in spinach. Stir in pasta and enough pasta water until spinach wilts and noodles warm through. Sprinkle with fresh cracked pepper. Garnish with goat cheese, pine nuts, and fennel fronds. Serves two.

Spinach and Feta Quiche

1 commercially prepared piecrust
1 ten-ounce package frozen chopped spinach (283 g)
1 tsp. olive oil (5 ml)
1/2 cup onions, diced (125 ml)
1 clove of garlic, minced
1 tbsp. lemon juice (15 ml)
3 large eggs
1 cup milk (250 ml)
pinch nutmeg
pinch salt & pepper
1/2 cup feta cheese, crumbled (125 ml)
10 pitted black olives, sliced in half

Preheat oven to 450°F (230°C). Thaw spinach, squeezing out excess water. In a hot skillet, fry onions in olive oil for four to five minutes. Add garlic and then sauté for one minute. Add spinach and lemon and cook for another two minutes. Set aside. In a large bowl, whisk eggs and milk with salt, pepper, and nutmeg. Add to skillet mixture. Stir gently. Pour into prepared pie crust. Sprinkle with olives. Set in oven and bake for fifteen minutes. Lower heat to 350°F (180°C). Bake for another ten minutes or until crust is golden and toothpick inserted in center comes out clean. Serves four to six.

Sauerkraut with Pork

2 thick slices bacon, cooked, crumbled, and set aside (save bacon fat)
1 large onion, chopped finely
1 tsp. garlic, chopped
2 lbs. sauerkraut, drained (1 kg)
1 large bay leaf
1/2 tsp. caraway seeds (2 ml)
6 whole black peppercorns
1/2 cup white wine (125 ml)
1/2 cup chicken broth (125 ml)
1 thick ham steak, cut in four pieces
2 lbs. polish sausage (1 kg)
Mustard
8 small potatoes

In bacon fat in a medium-hot skillet, add onion and garlic. Sauté for three to four minutes. Add drained sauerkraut and stir gently. Add crumbled bacon and then lower heat. Tie the bay leaf, caraway, and peppercorns in a piece of cheesecloth. Add to skillet. Pour in wine and chicken broth. Add ham and sausage, pricking sausage with fork to let steam escape. Cover skillet tightly. Reduce heat. Simmer for sixty minutes. Meanwhile, steam potatoes until cooked through fifteen to twenty minutes. Discard cheesecloth from sauerkraut. Add salt to taste if desired. Arrange sauerkraut and meat on a platter. Pass the potatoes. Serve with mustard. Makes four servings.

Fiery Bean Burritos

At times when one would rather cry, brother Bill makes everything better by a good laugh, proving a good laugh is good medicine. Bill is a vegetarian, so I thought I'd do well to include a few meatless dishes in this book. This fiery bean burrito recipe is for anyone who loves spice. Using fewer jalapeños than the recipe calls for is wise if you are sensitive to heat.

1/4 cup olive oil (50 ml)
1 large onion, chopped
4 cloves of garlic, sliced thin
1–2 fresh jalapeño peppers, deseeded and sliced thin
1 tbsp. chili powder (15 ml)
1 sixteen-ounce can black beans, drained and mashed (400 ml)
1 fourteen-ounce can plum tomatoes, drained and chopped ((284 ml)
1 cup water (250 ml)
Dash of liquid smoke
Salt and pepper to taste
8 large flour tortillas, warmed
1 cup grated cheddar cheese (250 ml)
Salsa
Sour cream
Cilantro sprigs

Add oil to a large skillet and heat to medium-hot. Add chopped onions, garlic, and jalapeños. Sauté for four to five minutes. Add chili powder, beans, tomatoes, water, liquid smoke, salt, and pepper. Stir thoroughly, heating through. Taste and adjust seasonings as desired. To arrange, put a spoon of bean mixture on bottom center of each tortilla. Top with grated cheese and then roll up. For garnish, pass salsa, sour cream, or chopped cilantro as desired. Serves eight.

"You might as well try to hear without ears or breathe without lungs, as to try to live a Christian life without the Spirit of God in your heart."
—D. L. Moody

Mediterranean Gyros

1 lb. ground lamb or beef (448 g)
1/4 red onion, chopped
2 cloves of garlic, minced
2 tsp. salt (10 ml)
1 tsp. black pepper (5 ml)
1 tsp. cumin (5 ml)
1/4 tsp. nutmeg (1 ml)
Dash of cayenne pepper
1 tsp. oregano (5 ml)
2 tsp. lemon juice (10 ml)
4 pita rounds or flatbread
Chopped fresh lettuce
Chopped fresh tomatoes
Tzatsiki

Combine lamb or beef, onion, garlic, salt, pepper, cumin, nutmeg, cayenne, oregano, and lemon juice. Shape into thin, oblong patties. Put patties in refrigerator for one hour to firm. Grill patties for four to six minutes per side in medium-hot skillet. Remove from heat. Sprinkle center of pita or flatbread with fresh chopped tomato. Add meat patty. Sprinkle with lettuce. Drizzle generously with tzatsiki. Serves four.

Tzatsiki

1 large cucumber, chopped fine
1 cup thick plain Greek yogurt (250 ml)
4 small cloves of garlic, crushed
Salt to taste

Drain and push chopped cucumber through a sieve. Put cucumber in a small bowl and stir in yogurt. Add garlic. Add salt to taste. Mix well.

"Trying to do the Lord's work in your own strength is the most confusing, exhausting, and tedious of all work. But when you are filled with the Holy Spirit, then the ministry of Jesus just flows out of you."
—Corrie ten Boom

Falafel with Peanut Sauce

1 nineteen-ounce can of chickpeas (540 ml)
1/3 cup dry breadcrumbs (75 ml)
1/3 cup flour (75 ml)
3 tbsp. minced onion (45 ml)
1/4 cup parsley (50 ml)
3 cloves of garlic, minced
1 tsp. cumin (5 ml)
1/2 tsp. turmeric (2 ml)
1/2 tsp. coriander (2 ml)
1 tsp. chili powder (5 ml)
1/2 tsp. salt (2 ml)
1/4 tsp. cayenne (1 ml)
1 tbsp. lemon juice (15 ml)
1 package pita rounds
1 cup lettuce, chopped (250 ml)
1 cup fresh tomatoes, chopped (250 ml)

In a blender, puree un-drained chickpeas, breadcrumbs, flour, spices, and lemon juice until smooth. Remove falafel mix from blender and shape into oblong balls. Fry in hot oil for two to three minutes. Drain on paper towels. Cut top off of pita rounds. Add chopped lettuce and tomatoes. Fill with fried falafel. Top with peanut sauce. Serves four to six.

Peanut Sauce

In a small bowl blend well:

1/3 cup peanut butter (75 ml)
3 tbsp. water (45 ml)
1 tbsp. lemon juice (15 ml)
1 tbsp. oil (15 ml)
1 large crushed garlic clove
1/4 tsp. cumin

"Strive to have an impact for good. We cannot sit by and watch humanity destroy itself and offer no opportunity to spread the light. We are called by duty, responsibility, and love, to reach out to those around us."
Anonymous

Chili Quitos

1 lb. ground beef (448 g)
1 large onion, chopped
2 cloves of garlic, minced
4 tbsp. chili powder (60 ml)
Pinch of cumin
Pinch of black pepper
1 package nacho seasoning mix
1 cup pitted black olives with juice (250 ml)
1 fourteen-ounce can of tomato sauce (284 ml)
1 large bag tortilla chips
1 1/2 cups grated cheddar cheese (375 ml)

Brown ground beef in medium-hot skillet until no longer pink inside. Stir in onions, garlic, and seasonings. Add olives with juice. Add tomato sauce. Lower heat. Simmer, covered, for twenty-five minutes. Sprinkle with grated cheese and stir lightly. Just before serving, add tortilla chips. Serves six.

"Be kinder to people than necessary because everyone you meet is fighting some kind of unseen battle."
Anonymous

Easy Moussaka

3 tbsp. olive oil (45 ml)
1 small onion, chopped
4 cloves of garlic, minced
1 1/2 lb. ground lamb (675 g)
2/3 cup red wine (150 ml)
1 cup tomato sauce (250 ml)
1/2 tsp. each salt and pepper (2 ml)
1/4 tsp. each cinnamon and cloves (1 ml)
1 eggplant, peeled and sliced quarter-inch thick (6.35 mm)
1 package plain cream cheese
1/3 cup heavy cream (75 ml)
1/4 tsp. nutmeg (1 ml)
1/3 cup feta cheese (75 ml)

Heat olive oil in a heavy pan. Add onion and cook till tender, about four to five minutes. Add garlic and lamb. Cook and stir until lamb is no longer pink. Pour in wine. Add tomato sauce, salt, pepper, cinnamon, and cloves. Bring to boil. Reduce heat. Simmer for ten minutes. Brush eggplant slices with oil and arrange in a single layer on baking sheet. Bake for ten to twelve minutes in hot oven at 400°F (200°C) and then remove. Meanwhile, in a small pot, cook cream cheese with heavy cream and nutmeg until cheese melts. Set aside. Reduce oven to 350°F (180°C). Spread a thin layer of lamb sauce on bottom of lightly oiled baking dish. Add half the eggplant slices. Cover with remaining lamb sauce. Top with remaining eggplant. Pour cream sauce on top. Crumble feta cheese and sprinkle on top. Bake for thirty minutes. Serves four to six.

"A man's reach should exceed his grasp, or what's a heaven for?"
—Oswald Chambers

American Meatloaf

3 slices of fresh bread
1 carrot, cut small
1 rib of celery, cut small
1 onion, chopped
2–3 cloves of garlic, chopped
1/2 cup parsley, chopped (125 ml)
2/3 cup ketchup (150 ml)
2 1/2 tsp. dry mustard powder (12 ml)
1 lb. ground beef (448 g)
1/2 lb. ground pork (224 g)
2 eggs
2 tsp. salt (10 ml)
1 tsp. pepper (5 ml)
1 1/2 tsp. Tabasco sauce (7 ml)
1/2 tsp. dried rosemary (2 ml)

Heat oven to 400°F (200°C). Tear bread into tiny pieces and transfer to a large bowl. (Do not use breadcrumbs.) Add carrot, celery, onion, garlic, and parsley to bowl. Mix well. Add ketchup, mustard, beef, pork, eggs, salt, and pepper. Add Tabasco and rosemary. Mix thoroughly. Put mixture in nine-by-thirteen-inch baking pan (22x33 cm). Brush on topping. Bake for one hour. Serves six to eight.

Topping

In a small bowl whisk together:

1/3 cup ketchup (75 ml)
1/4 tsp. mustard powder (1 ml)
1 tsp. brown sugar (5 ml)
Pinch of rosemary
Spoon on top of meatloaf

"For a long time it had seemed to me that life was about to begin. Real life. But there was always some obstacle in the way, something to be got through first, some unfinished business, time still to be served; a debt to be paid. Then life would begin. At last it dawned on me that these obstacles were my life."
—Fr. Alfred D' Souza

Ratatouille

1 small eggplant chopped coarsely and drained of bitter juices
1 large zucchini, chopped
1 small yellow squash, chopped
1 large red pepper, chopped
1 large yellow pepper, chopped
1 large orange pepper, chopped
1 large onion, chopped
1/3 cup olive oil (75 ml)
1 tsp. rosemary (5 ml)
1/2 tsp. thyme (2 ml)
1/4 tsp. pepper (1 ml)
4 cloves of garlic, chopped
1 tsp. sea salt (5 ml)

Put eggplant, zucchini, squash, peppers, and onion in a large baking dish. Mix olive oil, rosemary, thyme, pepper, garlic, and salt together in a small bowl. Drizzle over vegetables and toss lightly. Heat oven to 425°F (220°C). Cover dish with lid or tinfoil. Put in the preheated oven and bake for fifteen minutes. Uncover and bake for twenty to twenty-five minutes more or until vegetables are crisp and tender. Serves six to eight.

Spaghetti Squash
(With Olives and Sundried Tomatoes)

1 large spaghetti squash
2/3 cup pitted and chopped Kalamata black olives (150 ml)
1/3 cup oil-packed sundried tomatoes, drained and chopped (75 ml)
1/3 cup fresh parsley, chopped (75 ml)
2 garlic cloves, minced
1/3 cup olive oil (75 ml)
2 tbsp. red wine vinegar (30 ml)
salt and pepper to taste

Preheat oven to 400°F (200°C). Cut spaghetti squash in half lengthwise. Scoop out seeds and discard. Place squash in a baking dish. Bake uncovered for forty-five minutes or until fork goes through squash easily. Scoop out flesh from the squash into a serving dish. In a medium bowl, mix olives, tomatoes, parsley, garlic, oil, vinegar, salt, and pepper. Taste and adjust seasonings as desired. Add to squash and toss gently. Serves two to three.

"Give what you have, for you never know—
to someone else it may be better than
you can even dare to think."
—Henry Wadsworth Longfellow

Lamb Patties
(with Broiled Tomatoes)

1 1/2 lbs. ground lamb (672 g)
4 tbsp. butter, divided (60 ml)
1/2 cup onion, diced (125 ml)
6 oz. breadcrumbs (180 ml)
4 tbsp. fresh dill, chopped (60 ml)
1 egg
Salt and pepper to taste
1/2 cup mushrooms, chopped (125 ml)
2 tbsp. green onion, minced (30 ml)
1/3 cup white wine (75 ml)
1/2 cup heavy cream (125 ml)
4 large vine-ripened tomatoes, sliced
10 slivers sliced garlic
2 tsp. marjoram (10 ml)
2 tsp. oregano (10 ml)
8 tsp. olive oil (10 ml)

Heat a teaspoon of butter in medium-hot skillet. Add onion and cook briefly, about three to four minutes. Remove from heat. Place ground lamb into a large mixing bowl. Add onion, bread cubes, dill, egg, and salt and pepper to taste. Blend well. Divide mixture into six patties. Heat two tablespoons of butter in a medium-hot skillet and cook patties for four minutes per side. Remove and wipe out the skillet. Add remaining butter to the skillet. Add mushrooms. Cook until lightly browned, around one to two minutes. Add green onions, wine, and cream. Simmer for five minutes. Pour over patties. Keep warm while preparing broiled tomatoes. Serves six.

Broiled Tomatoes

Mix garlic with marjoram, oregano, and olive oil. Brush over tomatoes. Place under broiler for five minutes.

"Today is the day I have been looking for. All my life has been spent in preparation for it. Yesterday and tomorrow are faraway nothings...the one a faint memory, the other a vague promise. But this is my day. It offers all that God has to give, and I am a laggard or a coward if I fail to make the most of it."
Anonymous

Curried Sweet Pepper Strips

2 1/4 lbs. orange, green, yellow, and red peppers (1 kg)
4 tbsp. olive oil (60 ml)
Salt and pepper to taste
2 tbsp. curry powder (30 ml)
Pinch of cayenne

De-seed the peppers. Cut into thin strips. Heat olive oil in a large skillet until hot but not smoking. Add pepper strips, salt and pepper to taste, curry powder, and cayenne. Cook for about four minutes or until crisp and tender. Serves six.

Cajun Stuffed Potatoes

6 large russet potatoes, uncooked
1 cup onion, chopped (250 ml)
6 thick slices of bacon, diced
4 tbsp. butter (60 ml)
1 tsp. smoky paprika (15 ml)
1 tsp. cayenne pepper (5 ml)
1/2 tsp. white pepper (2 ml)
1/2 tsp. onion powder (2 ml)
1/2 tsp. garlic powder (2 ml)
1/2 tsp. black pepper (2 ml)
1 cup green pepper (250 ml)
3 cups chicken stock (750 ml) divided

Slice ends off potatoes and scoop out insides with a sturdy spoon until hollowed out and only a thin shell remains. Reserve shavings. Cover potatoes with cold salt water until ready to use. In a large cast iron frying pan on medium heat, fry onions and bacon in butter until cooked through. Add potato shavings. Sprinkle with spices. Spread potato mixture evenly on bottom of pan until a crust forms. Stir with a wooden spoon. Spread evenly till another crust forms. Stir and then repeat. Stir well and add chopped green peppers and one cup of the chicken stock. Reduce heat. Simmer for five minutes. Remove from heat. Drain potato shells of salted water. Pack shells with shaving mixture until well mounded. Place stuffed potatoes upright, side by side in loaf pan. Pour remaining chicken stock over. Cover with tinfoil. Bake at 350°F (180°C) for one hour. Serves six.

"It is possible to hear the truth and not understand the truth, because of stubborn self-will, a deliberate closing of the ears, an unwillingness to be open. It is safe to hide in the dark."
Anonymous

Twice-Baked Potatoes

6 russet potatoes
2 cups cauliflower florets (500 ml)
4 tbsp. butter (60 ml)
4 tbsp. chicken broth (60 ml)
1/3 cup Parmesan cheese (75 ml)
1 tbsp. parsley (15 ml)
1/2 tsp. tarragon (2 ml)
Pinch of granulated garlic
Salt and pepper to taste
Paprika

Heat oven to 375°F (190°C). Prick potatoes with fork and bake until done, about one hour. Steam cauliflower florets in a bit of water until cooked through, for ten to fifteen minutes. Drain and set aside. Scoop out potato from shells and put in a medium bowl. Add cauliflower. Mash well. Add butter, chicken broth, Parmesan cheese, parsley, tarragon, garlic, and salt and pepper to taste. Mix well. Add more broth if needed for creamy consistency. Sprinkle with paprika. Heat broiler and place potatoes on a baking sheet. Broil for one minute or until potatoes are golden brown on top. Serves six.

Mediterranean Asparagus

1 lb. asparagus (448 g)
4 tbsp. olive oil (60 ml)
4 tbsp. white wine (60 ml)
4 oz. goat cheese (125 ml)
3 sundried tomatoes in oil, minced

Snap tough ends from asparagus stalks and discard. Rinse and drain asparagus and put in an eight-by-eight-inch baking dish (20x20 cm). In a small dish, mix the oil and wine. Sprinkle over asparagus. Dot with goat cheese and sundried tomatoes. Place under a preheated broiler. Broil until crisp and tender, about three minutes. Serves four.

"Do what you can, with what you have, where you are."
—Theodore Roosevelt

Scalloped Corn

1/3 cup green pepper, diced (75 ml)
1/3 cup red pepper, diced (75 ml)
1/3 cup onion, diced (75 ml)
2 tbsp. butter (30 ml)
1 large organic egg
1/3 cup whole milk (75 ml)
1/3 cup soda crackers, crushed (75 ml)
1/4 tsp. cardamom (1 ml)
1 can creamed corn (284 ml)
1 cup whole kernel corn, drained (250 ml)

Sauté peppers and onion in a medium-hot skillet with butter for three to four minutes. Remove from heat. In a medium bowl, combine egg, milk, crushed crackers, and cardamom. Stir into pepper and onion mix. Add corn and stir lightly. Pour into greased eight-by-eight-inch casserole dish (20x20 cm). Bake at 350°F (180°C) for thirty to thirty-five minutes or until knife inserted in center comes out clean. Serves four to six.

Antipasto Pizza

1 prepared thin-crust pizza crust, unbaked
1/2 cup sundried tomato pesto sauce (125 ml)
1 cup provolone or mozzarella cheese, shredded (250 ml)
1/2 cup in-jar roasted red peppers, sliced (125 ml)
1/3 cup marinated artichoke hearts, sliced (75 ml)
9 Kalamata olives, pitted and sliced
8 slices salami, cut in strips

Preheat oven to 450°F (230°C). Spread pesto sauce evenly over pizza crust to edges. Sprinkle with provolone or mozzarella cheese. Add peppers, artichoke hearts, and olives. Bake on top rack of oven for ten minutes until crisp. Take pizza out of oven. Scatter salami slices over it. Return to oven and then bake for another two minutes. Cut and serve. Serves four to six.

"You will only find truth if you are
willing to step into the light, to seek
light's truth with all your heart."
Anonymous

Asparagus Fritters

2 cups fresh trimmed asparagus (500 ml)
1 tbsp. lemon zest (15 ml)
1 large organic egg
1/4 cup whole milk (50 ml)
1/2 cup flour (125 ml)
1/2 tsp. baking powder (2 ml)
1/4 cup ricotta cheese (50 ml)
1/4 cup chives, chopped (50 ml)
1/4 cup fresh dill, chopped
Oil for frying
Salt and pepper to taste

Simmer asparagus in a small amount of water for four minutes. Remove from heat. Drain and chop. In a large bowl, mix zest, egg, milk, flour, baking powder, and cheese. Fold in chives and dill. Add asparagus. Heat oil in a large medium-hot skillet. Drop batter by tablespoons into hot oil. Fry until golden, two minutes per side. Season with salt and pepper to taste. Serves four.

Citrus Crepes
(With Chicken Salad)

2 cups flour (500 ml)
1/4 tsp. salt (1 ml)
2 large organic eggs
1 1/2 tsp. lime or lemon zest (7 ml)
2 cups coconut milk (500 ml)
4 tsp. orange juice
Pat of butter

Put flour and salt in a large bowl. Make well in center. Mix eggs, zest, coconut milk, and orange juice together and pour into well. Whisk until smooth. Lightly grease skillet with butter and heat skillet over medium heat. Drop enough batter into the skillet to form a very thin pancake. Fry for one minute per side. Remove from skillet. Repeat until all batter is used. Fill crepes with chicken salad and roll up. Makes six to eight.

Chicken Salad

1/2 cup lime juice (125 ml)
1 1/2 tsp. sesame oil (7 ml)
1 tbsp. sugar (15 ml)
1 tsp. fish sauce (5 ml)
1/2 tsp. red chili flakes (2 ml)
2 cups cooked chicken, sliced (500 ml)
1/2 cup mint leaves, chopped (125 ml)
1/3 cup cilantro, chopped (75 ml)

In a medium bowl, combine lime juice, oil, sugar, fish sauce, and chili flakes. Add chicken. Fold in mint and cilantro. Fill crepes.

Heavenly Hash Browns

1 tbsp. cumin seeds (15 ml)
3 tbsp. olive oil (45 ml)
2/3 cup chorizo sausage, diced (150 ml)
2 lbs. small potatoes, diced (900 g)
2 tbsp. oregano (30 ml)
Pinch of garlic powder
Pinch of chili powder
Salt and pepper to taste
1/2 bunch Italian parsley

Preheat oven to 375°F (190°C). Fry cumin seeds with oil in frying pan on medium-high heat for three minutes. Add chorizo sausage. Fry for two to three minutes. Add potatoes, oregano, garlic powder, chili powder, and salt and pepper to taste. Cook for five to ten more minutes. Transfer to an eight-by-eight-inch baking dish (20x20 cm). Bake for twenty minutes or until potatoes are cooked through. Remove and toss with parsley. Serves four to six.

Corned Beef Hash

6 large potatoes, peeled and diced
1 twelve-ounce can corned beef (336 g)
1 large onion, diced
1 cup beef stock (250 ml)
1/4 tsp. pepper (1 ml)
2 tbsp. parsley, chopped (30 ml)

In a large skillet over medium heat, combine potatoes, corned beef, onion, beef stock, and pepper. Cover and simmer for twenty minutes or until potatoes are cooked through and broth is almost gone. Stir thoroughly and then sprinkle with chopped parsley. Makes four to six servings.

"Jesus Christ cares absolutely nothing about anyone's moral case history. For when someone genuinely comes to Him He just forgives and starts from there as though the person had been born one minute before."
—A.W.Tozer

Beef Stroganoff

1 lb. fillet of beef, cut into julienne strips (448 g)
1 tbsp. smoky paprika (15 ml)
Salt and pepper to taste
2 tbsp. butter (30 ml)
1/2 cup onion, chopped (125 ml)
1/2 cup white wine (125 ml)
1 cup sour cream (250 ml)
1 tsp. ground mustard (5 ml)
1 cup canned mushrooms, sliced (250 ml)
Cooked broad egg noodles, enough for two portions

Sprinkle beef strips with paprika, salt, and pepper. Heat butter in a hot skillet. Add beef strips and fry until cooked through, about four to five minutes. Remove from skillet with a slotted spoon. Set aside. Add onion to skillet and fry for two to three minutes. Add wine. Cook until liquid is reduced by half. Lower heat. Add sour cream. Don't allow sauce to boil or it will curdle. Return beef to skillet. Heat through, cooking one to two more minutes. Serve over hot, cooked egg noodles. Serves two.

Tostadas

1 lb. ground beef (448 g)
1 cup sweet red pepper, chopped (250 ml)
1/2 cup chili sauce (125 ml)
1/2 tsp. chili powder (2 ml)
1/4 tsp. garlic powder (1 ml)
1/4 tsp. pepper (1 ml)
1/4 tsp. salt (1 ml)
1/4 tsp. onion salt (1 ml)
1/8 tsp. oregano (0.6 ml)
Dash of cayenne
2/3 cup sour cream (150 ml)
2 tbsp. chipotle sauce (30 ml)
6 corn or flour tortillas
3 cups of lettuce, shredded (750 ml)
1 1/2 cups guacamole (375 ml)
1 1/2 cups shredded Tex-Mex cheese blend (375 ml)

In a large skillet on medium heat, brown beef and red pepper until meat is no longer pink inside. Drain fat from pan. Stir in chili sauce, chili powder, garlic powder, pepper, salt, onion salt, oregano, and cayenne. Heat through. Taste and adjust seasonings as desired. Set aside. In a small bowl, combine sour cream and chipotle sauce. Set aside. Heat tortillas by warming in a dry skillet one minute per side. To assemble, layer each tostada with a portion of lettuce, meat mixture, guacamole, cheese, and sour cream chipotle mix. Serves six.

"If we could see the miracle of a single flower clearly, our whole life would change."
—Buddha

Picnic Chicken

6 lbs. chicken legs and thighs (3 kg)
3/4 cup unbleached white flour (175 ml)
4 dry envelopes of ranch salad dressing mix (8 tbsp.) or (120 g)
1 1/4 cups buttermilk (300 ml)
2 large organic eggs
6 cups ranch-flavored Dorito tortilla chips, crushed finely (1420 ml)
Pinch of cayenne
Pinch of chili powder
Cooking spray

Preheat oven to 400°F (200°C). In a shallow bowl, combine flour and half the dressing mix. In a separate shallow bowl, beat buttermilk with eggs. Place beside first bowl. In a third shallow bowl, stir remaining salad dressing mix with crushed Dorito chips. Sprinkle with cayenne and chili powder and mix lightly. Place beside the second bowl. Coat chicken in the flour mix, shaking off excess. Dip in buttermilk and egg mixture to coat. Press into Dorito chip mix, coating all sides generously. Line a large baking pan with tinfoil. Put wire racks atop and liberally spray with cooking spray. Place prepared chicken on racks. Spray chicken lightly with cooking oil. Bake for forty-five minutes. Serves eight to ten.

"This is the true joy in life: the being used for a purpose recognized by yourself as a mighty one; the being a force of nature instead of a feverish, selfish little clod of ailments and grievances complaining that the world will not devote itself to making you happy. I am of the opinion that my life belongs to the whole community, and as long as I live, it is my privilege to do for it whatever I can. I want to be thoroughly used up when I die, for the harder I work the more I live. I rejoice in life for its own sake. Life is no 'brief candle' to me. It is a sort of splendid torch which I have got hold of for the moment, and I want to make it burn as brightly as possible before handing it on to future generations."

–George Bernard Shaw

Soups & Stews

Fourteen-Carrot Gold Soup 142

Monastery Mushroom Soup 143

Pacific Salmon Corn Chowder 144

Pea and Barley Soup 145

French Garlic Soup. 146

Classic French Onion Soup. 147

Seafood Chowder. 148

Tortilla Soup 149

South of the Border Hot Pot Soup 150

Speedy Borscht. 151

Battensby Borscht 152

Tequila Crab Chowder 153

Fourteen-Carrot Gold Soup

2 tbsp. butter (30 ml)
1 leek, chopped
4 tbsp. gingerroot, sliced (60 ml)
4 cloves of garlic, chopped
1 tbsp. curry powder (15 ml)
4 cups good-quality chicken broth (1 L)
4 cups carrots, chopped (1 L)
1 large sweet potato, chopped
2/3 cup heavy cream (150 ml)
1 can of coconut milk (400 ml)
Salt and pepper to taste.

Heat a large soup pot to medium-hot. Add butter and melt it and then add the chopped leek. Sauté for three minutes. Add the ginger and garlic. Sauté for one minute. Add the curry powder, blending well. Add chicken broth, carrots, and sweet potato. Cook until tender, about fifteen minutes. Add cream and coconut milk. Add salt and pepper to taste. Pour into a blender in batches and puree until smooth. Return to the soup pot. Taste and adjust seasonings as desired. Reheat and serve. Makes six to eight servings

"The reason we are tried as with fire is in order that we come out of our trial as pure gold."

Monastery Mushroom Soup

2 tbsp. butter (30 ml)
1 tbsp. olive oil (15 ml)
1 1/2 cups dried mushrooms (375 ml)
1 1/2 cups oyster mushrooms (375 ml) or use any mushroom
selection of your choice to equal three cups (710 ml)
2 large onions, diced
1 large bay leaf
Pinch of thyme
3 cans of beer
1 egg
1/2 cup heavy cream (125 ml)
1 cup Gruyere cheese, grated (250 ml)
Salt and pepper to taste

In a large soup pot, sauté mushrooms and onions in butter and olive oil for five minutes. Add the bay leaf, thyme, and beer and then bring to boil. Lower heat and simmer for twenty minutes. Beat the egg with the cream and put a small amount into the soup and mix well. Add the rest of egg and cream mix slowly. Add salt and pepper to taste. Just before serving, sprinkle with cheese. Serves four to six.

Pacific Salmon Corn Chowder
(with White Sauce)

2 cups canned salmon (500 ml)
2 cups boiling water (500 ml)
1 twelve-ounce can of corn (375 ml)
2 cups potatoes, diced (500 ml)
1 cup onion, chopped (250 ml)
1 cup celery, chopped (250 ml)
1 nineteen-ounce can of stewing tomatoes (540 ml)
1/2 tsp. celery seed (2 ml)

Place salmon, water, corn, potatoes, onion, celery, stewing tomatoes, and celery seed in a large pot on medium heat. Boil gently for fifteen to twenty minutes or until vegetables are cooked through. Reduce heat. Gently mix in white sauce. Cover and keep warm until serving. Serves four to six.

White Sauce

3 tbsp. butter (45 ml)
3 tbsp. flour (45 ml)
2 cups milk (500 ml)
1 tsp. salt (5 ml)
1/2 tsp. pepper (2 ml)
1/4 tsp. cayenne (1 ml)
1 tbsp. curry powder (15 ml)

Melt butter in a medium-hot saucepan. Whisk in the flour. Add the milk slowly, stirring constantly until bubbly and thick. Add salt, pepper, cayenne, and curry powder. Add to chowder.

"It takes an awful lot before our 'ought' and 'should' worlds quit attempting to compel others to be what we want them to be, rather than what they are meant to be, by God's gift. If we die to our expectations, we just might discover to our delight, that what the other actually is, really and truly blesses our hearts."
Anonymous

Pea and Barley Soup
(with Ham Hock)

1 whole ham hock
2 cups split green peas (500 ml), washed and drained
8 cups water (2 L)
4 carrots, sliced
4 stalks of celery, diced
1 onion, diced
Pinch of thyme
1 large bay leaf
Salt and pepper to taste
1/2 cup barley (125 ml)

Put the ham hock in a large stockpot with water and bring to a boil. Add peas, carrots, celery, onion, thyme, bay leaf, salt, and pepper. Turn heat to simmer. Cover tightly and simmer for two hours. Add barley. Simmer for an additional two hours or until the peas are tender, adding more water as needed. Before serving, taste soup and adjust seasonings as desired. Cut the ham hock with a fork while still in the pot. It will be falling off bone. Discard bone before serving. Makes eight servings.

French Garlic Soup

5 slices of thick bacon, chopped
2 large onions, thinly sliced
20 cloves of garlic, coarsely chopped
6 cups chicken stock (1 1/2 L)
1/2 cup dry white wine (125 ml)
1 bay leaf
1/4 tsp. sea salt (1 ml)
1/4 tsp. fresh cracked pepper
6 pieces of day-old French bread
8 tbsp. fresh grated Parmesan cheese (120 ml)
2 tbsp. fresh chopped parsley (30 ml)

In a skillet, cook the bacon until crisp. Crumble and set aside. Don't drain the fat. Fry garlic and onions in the bacon fat on medium heat for five minutes or until tender. Remove from skillet. Put in a large soup pot with crumbled bacon. Add chicken stock, wine, bay leaf, salt, and pepper to the pot. Heat to bubbling. Lower heat and simmer for thirty minutes. Ladle into heat-proof bowls. Place a piece of French bread atop each bowl. Sprinkle with Parmesan cheese. Put on a large baking sheet and place under broiler. Broil until the cheese melts, about one to two minutes. Before serving, garnish with chopped parsley. Makes six servings.

"Happiness is not something you postpone for the future. It is something you design for the present."
–Jim Rohn

Classic French Onion Soup

1/2 cup butter (125 ml)
4 onions, sliced
1 cup dry red wine (250 ml)
8 cups beef stock (2 L)
2 cloves of garlic, chopped
1 bay leaf
2 fresh thyme sprigs
Pinch of rosemary
Sea salt to taste
Pepper to taste
1 cup Gruyere cheese, grated (250 ml)
8 slices of day-old French bread

Melt the butter in a soup pot at medium heat. Add the onions. Add the garlic, bay leaf, thyme sprigs, rosemary, salt, and pepper. Cook until the onions are very soft and caramelized, about ten to twenty minutes. Add wine and beef stock and then simmer for thirty minutes. Discard the bay leaf and thyme sprigs. Ladle into eight individual oven-proof bowls. Arrange bread slices atop. Sprinkle with grated cheese. Place under a broiler and broil until the cheese is bubbly, one to two minutes. Serves eight.

Seafood Chowder

1 fennel bulb cut into 6 wedges
1 large onion, chopped
4 cloves of garlic, minced
3 tbsp. olive oil (45 ml)
2 bay leaves
1 tsp. thyme (5 ml)
Pinch of red pepper flakes
Pinch of basil
Pinch of oregano
1 twenty-eight-ounce can of crushed tomatoes with juice (796 ml)
1 1/2 cups water (375 ml)
1 cup red wine (250 ml)
1 cup clam juice (250 ml)
1 lb. mild white fish (448 g)
1 lb. fresh mussels, scallops, shrimp, or combination of all three (448 g)

In a hot skillet, fry the fennel, onions, and garlic in olive oil for three minutes. Add bay leaves, thyme, pepper flakes, basil, and oregano. Stir well. Adjust seasonings to suit taste. Put the ingredients in a large soup pot. Add crushed tomatoes, water, wine, and clam juice. Simmer until heated through. Add white fish, mussels, scallops, and/or shrimp. Simmer for three to five minutes or until the fish is just opaque, being careful not to overcook or fish will be tough. Serves four.

```
"For a gallant spirit there can never be defeat."
                                    -W. Simpson
```

Tortilla Soup

1 tbsp. olive oil (15 ml)
2 cloves of garlic, minced
4 fresh tomatoes, diced
1 onion, diced
1 red pepper, diced
1 yellow pepper, diced
1 tsp. cumin (5 ml)
1 tsp. chili powder (5 ml)
Pinch of cayenne
Salt and pepper to taste
2 cups cooked and sliced chicken (500 ml)
4 cups chicken stock (1 L)
1 cup corn kernels (250 ml)
1 tbsp. lime juice (15 ml)
1 cup tortilla chips, crushed slightly (250 ml)
Fresh chopped cilantro

Add olive oil to medium-hot skillet. Add garlic. Sauté for half a minute. Add tomatoes and sauté until just warm and softened. Remove tomatoes and garlic from skillet and set aside. Add onion to skillet with red and yellow pepper. Sprinkle with cumin, chili powder, cayenne, and salt and pepper to taste. Cook until crisp and tender. Transfer to a soup pot, along with the garlic and tomatoes. Add chicken and stock. Simmer for ten to fifteen minutes. Add corn and lime juice. Sprinkle with cilantro and tortilla chips. Serves four.

"Drop a pebble in the water,
And its ripples reach out far;
And the sunbeams dancing on them
May reflect them to a star.
Give a smile to someone passing,
Thereby making his morning glad;
It may greet you in the evening
When your own heart may be sad.
Do a deed of simple kindness,
Though its end you may not see;
It may reach, like widening ripples,
Down a long eternity."
Anonymous

South of the Border Hot Pot Soup

1 lb. ground beef (448 g)
1/2 package taco seasoning mix
2 tbsp. olive oil (30 ml)
1 large onion, diced
4 cloves of garlic, minced
1 green pepper, diced
2 cups canned tomatoes in juice (500 ml)
2 cups kidney beans, drained (500 ml)
1 four-ounce can of green chilies (125 ml)
4 cups beef stock (1 L)
1 tbsp. chili powder (15 ml)
Pinch of cayenne
Dash of chipotle Tabasco sauce
Salt and pepper to taste
Sharp cheddar cheese, grated

In a large skillet, fry ground beef with taco seasoning mix until the meat is no longer pink inside. Remove from skillet and wipe the skillet clean with a paper towel. Heat the olive oil in the skillet and add onions, garlic, and green pepper. Cook for five minutes. Return the ground beef. Add the canned tomatoes, kidney beans, and green chilies. Stir briefly. Transfer to a soup pot. Add chicken stock, chili powder, cayenne, Tabasco, and salt and pepper to taste. Cover and simmer for thirty minutes. Ladle into bowls. Garnish with cheddar cheese. Serves four to six.

"Happiness is the flower of duty."
Anonymous

Speedy Borscht

2 ten-ounce cans prepared beets, drained (284 ml each)
2 ten-ounce cans good-quality beef stock (284 ml each)
Pinch of onion powder
Pinch of caraway seed
Pinch of sugar
Dash of lemon juice
Sour cream

Blend beets with beef stock in blender until smooth. Pour into saucepot. Season with onion powder and heat through. Add the caraway seed, sugar, and lemon juice. Taste and adjust seasonings as desired. Heat through. Serve garnished with sour cream. Serves four.

"We are the sum of our consenting thoughts."
Anonymous

Battensby Borscht

This recipe is simply delicious. I obtained it during a cold winter walk with my good friend Ms. Battensby. After divulging the secrets of this wonderful borscht in detail, I went home determined to remember all the steps in making it. But Ms. Battensby took the step further, one day appearing at my door with a steaming tureen of this homemade borscht! There is no tonic more pleasant to the spirit than when a friend appears to feed a hungry soul.

5 large raw beets, unpeeled
1 tbsp. butter (15 ml)
1 tbsp. olive oil (15 ml)
1 large onion, chopped
2 fennel bulbs, white part only, chopped
4 cups chicken stock (1 L)
1/2 tsp. sea salt (2 ml)
Fresh-ground black pepper
1/2 cup liquid whipping cream (125 ml)
1/2 cup feta cheese, crumbled (125 ml)
Fennel fronds, chopped

Preheat oven to 375°F (190°C). Roast the unpeeled beets in a covered roasting pan for forty-five to sixty minutes or until easily pierced through with a fork. Remove and let cool. Peel, chop finely, and set aside. Melt butter and oil in a hot skillet. Add onion and fennel and sauté for ten minutes. Add beets. Transfer to a soup pot. Add chicken stock, salt, and pepper. Simmer for twenty minutes. Remove soup from heat and pour in a blender. Puree until smooth. Return to soup pot. Just before serving, stir in whipping cream. Reheat gently. Serve soup topped with fennel fronds. Serves four.

"God sleeps in the minerals, awakens in plants,
walks in animals, and thinks in man."
—Arthur Young

Tequila Crab Chowder

1 cup grape tomatoes, cut in half (250 ml)
2 tbsp. olive oil (30 ml)
1/2 tsp. thyme (2 ml)
Salt and pepper to taste
6 strips bacon, diced
1 tbsp. butter (15 ml)
1 onion, chopped
1 carrot, chopped
2 celery stalks, chopped
1 small red pepper, chopped
4 cups chicken stock (1 L)
1/2 lb. Idaho potatoes, diced
2 cups corn kernels (500 ml)
1/2 cup tequila (125 ml)
1/4 lb. crabmeat (125 g)
1/4 cup cilantro, chopped (50 ml)
1 green onion, chopped

Roast tomatoes with olive oil, thyme, salt, and pepper in hot oven at 400°F (200°C) for twenty minutes. Remove and set aside. In a skillet, over medium-high heat, fry bacon until crisp. Remove bacon, set aside, and wipe out skillet with paper towel. Add butter to the skillet and melt it. Add onion, carrot, celery, and red pepper. Cook until softened but still crisp, about four to five minutes. Transfer to a soup pot. Add chicken stock, potatoes, and corn. Add bacon. Gently bring to a boil. Lower heat. Simmer for twenty minutes. Add tequila, crab, and cilantro. Ladle into soup bowls. Garnish with roasted tomatoes and chopped green onions. Serves four to six.

Symptoms of Inner Peace:

Be on the lookout for symptoms of inner peace. The hearts of a great many have already been exposed to inner peace and it is possible that people everywhere could come down with it in epidemic proportions. This could pose a serious threat to what has, up to now, been a fairly stable condition of conflict in the world.

Some signs and symptoms of inner peace:

- A tendency to think and act spontaneously rather than on fears based on past experiences.
- An unmistakable ability to enjoy each moment.
- A loss of interest in judging other people.
- A loss of interest in interpreting the actions of others.
- A loss of interest in conflict.
- A loss of the ability to worry. (This is a very serious symptom).
- Frequent, overwhelming episodes of appreciation.
- Contented feelings of connectedness with others and nature.
- Frequent attacks of smiling.
- An increasing tendency to let things happen rather than make them happen.
- An increased susceptibility to the love extended by others as well as the uncontrollable urge to extend it. Anonymous

Dressings

Basic Dressing 157
Ranch Dressing. 157
Honey Mustard Dressing. 158
Russian Poet Dressing 158
Mayonnaise. 159
Bleu Cheese Dressing. 159
Cranberry Balsamic Dressing. 160
Buttermilk Dressing 160
Fresh Herb Dressing 161
Italian Dressing. 161

Recipe for a Salad

To make this condiment your poet begs The pounded yellow of two boiled eggs; Two boiled potatoes, passed through kitchen sieve, Smoothness and softness to a salad give.

Let onion atoms lurk within the bowl, And, half suspected, animate the whole. Of mordant mustard just a single spoon, Distrust the condiment that bites too soon;

But deem it not, thou man of herbs, a fault, To add a double spoon of salt. Four spoons of oil from Lucca brown, And twice with vinegar procured from town;

And, lastly, in the flavoured compound toss A magic soupcon of anchovy sauce. O, green and glorious! O herbaceous treat! 'Twould tempt the dying anchorite to eat:

Back to the world he'd turn his fleeting soul, And plunge his fingers in the salad bowl! Serenely full, the epicure would say, 'Fate cannot harm me, I have dined to-day'.

—Sydney Smith poem (1771–1845)

Basic Dressing

1/4 cup lemon juice (50 ml)
1/4 cup balsamic vinegar (50 ml)
1/4 cup olive oil (50 ml)
1–2 cloves of garlic, minced
2 tsp. dried basil (10 ml)

Blend all the ingredients well in a bowl or shake in a jar. Adjust seasonings as desired. Refrigerate until ready to use. Makes about three-quarters of a cup (175 ml).

Ranch Dressing

1/3 cup mayonnaise (75 ml)
1/2 cup buttermilk (125 ml)
1 clove of garlic, minced
1/2 tsp. dill (2 ml)
1/2 tsp. sugar (2 ml)
1/4 tsp. dry mustard powder (1 ml)
Pepper to taste

Blend all the ingredients well in small bowl. Adjust seasonings as desired. Refrigerate until ready to use. Makes about one cup (250 ml).

Honey Mustard Dressing

1 1/4 cups mayonnaise (300 ml)
1/4 cup liquid honey (50 ml)
1/4 cup Dijon mustard (50 ml)
1/4 tsp. dry mustard powder (1 ml)
1/4 tsp. hot curry powder (1 ml)

Blend ingredients well in small bowl. If desired, substitute regular curry powder for hot curry. Refrigerate until ready to use. Makes about 1 3/4 cups (425 ml).

> "The light of God surrounds me;
> The love of God enfolds me;
> The power of God protects me;
> The presence of God watched over me.
> Wherever I am, God is!"
> Anonymous

Russian Poet Dressing

1/4 cup oil (50 ml)
1/4 cup ketchup (50 ml)
1 tbsp. sugar (15 ml)
1 tbsp. vinegar (15 ml)
1 tbsp. lemon juice (15 ml)
1 tsp. Worcestershire sauce (5 ml)
1/2 tsp. paprika (2 ml)
1/4 tsp. salt (1 ml)
1/4 tsp. pepper (1 ml)

Blend all the ingredients well in a small bowl and refrigerate until ready to use. Makes about 2/3 cup (150 ml).

Mayonnaise

In a blender put:

1/4 tsp. dry mustard (1 ml)
Dash of salt
Dash of white pepper
2 large organic eggs
2 tbsp. fresh lemon juice (30 ml)

Slowly add:

1 cup olive oil (250 ml)

Blend well. Refrigerate until ready to use. Makes just over a cup (255 ml).

"Do we really listen to others? Or honestly, are we too busy thinking of what we will say in return?"
Anonymous

Bleu Cheese Dressing

1 cup crumbled bleu cheese (250 ml)
1 cup mayonnaise (250 ml)
1 cup sour cream (250 ml)
1 cup buttermilk (250 ml)
1 tbsp. fresh lemon juice (15 ml)
Dash of Worcestershire sauce
1 garlic clove, mashed

Blend ingredients in blender. Refrigerate until ready to use. Note: If you like a chunky bleu cheese dressing, save some crumbled bleu cheese to add to the dressing after transferring to serving dish. Makes about 3 1/2 cups (829 ml).

Cranberry Balsamic Dressing

1/4 cup balsamic vinegar (50 ml)
2 tbsp. red wine vinegar (30 ml)
Small handful of dried cranberries
1/2 cup olive oil (125 ml)
Pinch of sugar

Mix ingredients in a small bowl. Taste and adjust the vinegar-oil ratio to your personal preference. Put the dressing in a small pot and bring to a boil. Turn heat to simmer and cook until thickened. Cool in fridge until ready to use. Makes about one cup (250 ml).

Buttermilk Dressing

1/2 cup buttermilk (125 ml)
1/2 cup plain yogurt (125 ml)
1 tbsp. dried dill (15 ml) or 3 tbsp. fresh dill, chopped (45 ml)
2 tsp. white vinegar (10 ml)
1 tsp. sugar (5 ml)

Mix all the ingredients well in a small bowl. Chill before using. Makes about 1 1/3 cups (325 ml).

"He that loves wealth loses much. He that loses friends loses more, but he that loses his spirits loses all."
—Spanish Proverb

Fresh Herb Dressing

1 garlic clove, minced
1/3 cup heavy cream (75 ml)
1/2 tsp. lemon zest (2 ml)
1 tsp. lemon juice (5 ml)
1/3 cup mayonnaise (75 ml)
1 tbsp. fresh parsley, chopped (15 ml)
1 tsp. fresh tarragon, chopped (5 ml)
2 tsp. fresh chives, chopped (10 ml)
Salt and pepper to taste

Mix all the ingredients well in a small bowl. Chill before using. Makes about 3/4 cup (175 ml).

"Love asks for everything one is."
Anonymous

Italian Dressing

1/3 cup olive oil (75 ml)
1/3 cup wine vinegar (75 ml)
2 tsp. basil (10 ml)
1 tsp. oregano (5 ml)
1/2 tsp. fresh cracked pepper (2 ml)
2 cloves of garlic, crushed

Mix all the ingredients in a small bowl or place in a jar and shake well. Taste and adjust seasonings as desired.

"People who used to be lights for us may flicker out. And those who used to stand with us may turn away. We must trust and build our faith not on fading lights, but on the Light that never fails."
—JR

Salads

Simply Salad 164
Maple Bacon Escarole Salad 165
Chicken Thai Salad 166
Prosciutto Goat Cheese Salad 167
Apple Cabbage Salad 168
Italian Pasta Salad 169
Wilted Spinach Salad 170
Three-Bean Salad 170
Hern Kale Salad 171
Red Salad 172
Teriyaki Salad 173
Cobb Salad 174
Classic Caesar Salad 175
Garlic Croutons 176
Mock Caesar Salad 176
Jan's Caesar Salad 177
Mexican Caesar Salad 178
Grilled Fusion Caesar Salad 179
Ray's Working Caesar Salad 180

Simply Salad

1 small head iceberg lettuce
1 small head endive lettuce
1 small head radicchio lettuce
3 large sun-ripened tomatoes, chopped
1 large cucumber, diced
1/2 cup fresh fennel, diced (125 ml)
1/2 cup red onion, sliced (125 ml)
1/3 cup sliced black olives (75 ml)
1/3 cup sliced green olives (75 ml)
1/2 cup cubed white cheese (125 ml)
Salad dressing of choice

Rinse and thoroughly dry salad greens or rinse and spin in a salad spinner. Tear lettuce into bite-sized pieces. Place in a large serving bowl.
Add tomatoes and cucumber. Add fennel, onion, and olives. Toss lightly and sprinkle with cheese. Serve with your salad dressing of choice. Serves eight.

Maple Bacon Escarole Salad
(with Apples)

4 thick slices of smoked maple bacon
8 cups salad greens of choice (2 L)
1 large apple, cored and chopped
2 tbsp. lemon juice (30 ml)
1/2 cup celery, thinly sliced (125 ml)
1/2 cup red onion, sliced thinly into rings
1/3 cup toasted pecans (75 ml)
1/3 cup dried cranberries (75 ml)

Cook bacon until crisp. Crumble and set aside. Wash and spin salad greens. Place in a serving bowl. Slice the apple and sprinkle with lemon juice to prevent browning. Add to the lettuce along with celery, onion, and toasted pecans. Add cranberries and crumbled bacon. Mix lightly. Drizzle with dressing. Toss to coat. Serves six to eight.

Maple Dressing

1/3 cup mayonnaise (75 ml)
2 tbsp. maple syrup (30 ml)
2 tbsp. apple cider vinegar (30 ml)
1 tsp. Dijon mustard (5 ml)
1 tbsp. green onion, minced (15 ml)

Mix well and add to salad.

Chicken Thai Salad

1 cup raspberry vinaigrette (250 ml)
1/3 cup French's hot sauce (75 ml)
2 tbsp. fresh grated ginger root (30 ml)
2 tbsp. sugar (30 ml)
2 garlic cloves, minced
2 tsp. dark soy sauce (10 ml)
2 cups cooked, sliced, and chilled chicken (500 ml)
1 cup fresh mint leaves, chopped (250 ml)
1 cup cucumber, sliced thin (250 ml)
6 cups mixed salad greens (283 g)
1/3 cup peanuts, unsalted (75 ml)

In a medium bowl, blend raspberry vinaigrette, French's hot sauce, ginger, sugar, garlic, and soy sauce. Set aside. Add chicken to separate bowl and drizzle with a bit of dressing to coat. Mix gently. Set aside.

Toss salad greens with mint leaves and cucumber. Arrange on a large platter. Drizzle lightly with remaining dressing. Top with sliced chicken. Sprinkle with peanuts. Serves four to six.

Prosciutto Goat Cheese Salad

6 cups salad greens (283 g)
Basil vinaigrette
8 slices prosciutto ham
1 cup goat cheese, crumbled (250 ml)
6 tbsp. sundried tomatoes in oil (90 ml)

Basil Vinaigrette

6 tbsp. olive oil (90 ml)
4 tbsp. balsamic vinegar (60 ml)
4 tbsp. prepared pesto sauce (60 ml)
1/8 tsp. salt (0.6 ml)
1/8 tsp. pepper (0.6 ml)

In a small bowl, mix olive oil, vinegar, pesto sauce, salt, and pepper until well blended. Lay slices of prosciutto ham on a working board. Top with a bit of goat cheese and a bit of sundried tomato. Fold end over end. Heat oven to 300°F (150°C). Arrange prosciutto folds on a baking sheet, seam side down. Cover with tinfoil. Bake for five minutes or until warmed. Divide salad greens on serving plates. Top with prosciutto folds. Drizzle with basil vinaigrette. Serves four.

```
"You can have no greater sign of confirmed pride
   than when you think you are humble enough."
                -C. S. Lewis
```

Apple Cabbage Salad

8 tsp. extra virgin olive oil (40 ml)
2 tbsp. white wine vinegar (30 ml)
4 tsp. natural liquid honey (20 ml)
1/2 tsp. sea salt (2 ml)
1/4 tsp. fresh-cracked pepper (1 ml)
3 crisp apples, chopped
2 1/4 cups red cabbage, sliced thin (550 ml)
1/3 cup red onion, sliced thin (75 ml)
1/2 cup bleu cheese, crumbled (125 ml)
1/3 cup toasted chopped walnuts (75 ml)

For dressing, mix oil, vinegar, honey, salt, and pepper in large bowl. Set aside. In a separate large bowl, toss apples, cabbage, and onion. Drizzle with dressing. Sprinkle with cheese and toasted walnuts. Serves four.

Note: To toast walnuts, put in a dry skillet on medium heat and shake the pan frequently, stirring lightly until aromatic, around two minutes.

"The first duty of love is to listen. Listening, not so much with your mind, but with your heart."
Anonymous

Italian Pasta Salad

1 cup tortellini, cooked and chilled (250 ml)
1 1/2 cups provolone cheese, cubed (375 ml)
3/4 cup salami, sliced (175 ml)
1 cup broccoli flowerets (250 ml)
2/3 cup red pepper, sliced (150 ml)
1 cup zucchini, sliced (250 ml)
1 onion, cut into rings
1/2 cup black olives, sliced (125 ml)
1/3 cup fresh parsley, chopped (75 ml)
1/3 cup Romano cheese (75 ml)
2 Roma tomatoes, cut in wedges

Place tortellini, cheese, salami, broccoli, red pepper, zucchini, onion, olives, parsley, Romano, and tomatoes in a large serving bowl. Drizzle with Italian dressing. Toss lightly. Serves six.

"A pencil and a dream can take you anywhere."
−Joyce Meyers

Wilted Spinach Salad

6 cups fresh spinach, washed and torn (283 g)
1/3 cup scallions, sliced (75 ml)
1 cup fresh mushrooms, sliced (250 ml)
Fresh ground pepper
4 slices thick bacon
1 tsp. sugar (5 ml)
2 tbsp. vinegar (30 ml)
Dash of salt
2 hardboiled eggs, chopped

Toss spinach, scallions, and mushrooms together in a large bowl. Sprinkle with pepper. Set aside. In a medium-hot skillet, fry bacon until crisp. Remove and reserving the drippings. Crumble bacon and set aside. Stir sugar, vinegar, and salt into bacon drippings in skillet. Heat to boiling. Remove from heat. Add spinach, scallions, and mushrooms. Toss until coated. Transfer to a serving dish. Top with chopped eggs. Sprinkle with bacon crumbles. Serves two.

Three-Bean Salad

2/3 cup onion, chopped (150 ml)
2/3 cup green pepper, chopped (150 ml)
1 cup canned lima beans (250 ml)
1 cup canned green beans (250 ml)
1 cup kidney beans (250 ml)
1/2 cup vinegar (125 ml)
1/4 cup olive oil (50 ml)
3 tbsp. sugar (45 ml)
1 tsp. celery seed (5 ml)
1 clove of garlic, minced

In a large bowl, combine onion and green pepper. Drain beans. Add to onions and pepper. In a separate bowl, combine vinegar, olive oil, sugar, celery seed, and garlic. Stir well. Pour over beans. Cover and chill for four hours. Serves six to eight.

"One of the peculiar sins of the twentieth century, which we've developed to a very high level, is the sin of credulity. It has been said that when human beings stop believing in God they believe in nothing. The truth is much worse: they believe in anything."
—Malcom Muggeridge

Hern Kale Salad

1 large bunch fresh kale
1/2 cup sunflower seeds (125 ml)
2/3 cup crumbled feta cheese (150 ml)

Rinse kale thoroughly and shake dry. Pat with a paper towel. Tear leaves from stalk and discard. Tear kale into bite-size pieces and place in large salad bowl. Add sunflower seeds and feta cheese. Prepare dressing. Pour over top. Toss lightly to coat. Add more sunflower seeds and feta cheese if desired. Makes four to six servings.

Dressing

2/3 cup olive oil (150 ml)
1/4 cup balsamic vinegar (50 ml)
1/8 cup water (25 ml)
4 cloves of garlic, minced

In a small bowl, mix ingredients well and drizzle over kale.

"My vision of God is determined by the condition of my character. My character determines whether or not truth can be revealed to me."
—Oswald Chambers

Red Salad

8 vine-ripened tomatoes, cut in wedges
3 tbsp. red wine vinegar (45 ml)
1 cup extra-virgin olive oil (250 ml)
4 cloves of garlic, minced
2 red onions, sliced
10 fresh basil leaves, torn
1/2 tsp. dried Italian oregano (2 ml)
1/2 tsp. marjoram (2 ml)
Salt and pepper to taste

Toss tomatoes, red wine vinegar, olive oil, garlic, red onions, fresh basil, oregano, marjoram, salt, and pepper in a large bowl. Mix lightly. Adjust seasonings as desired. Put in fridge. Chill well until serving. Serves six.

"If you cannot see beyond the visible, if you cannot touch that which is intangible, if you cannot hear that which is inaudible, if you cannot know that which is beyond knowing, then perhaps you should have serious doubts about your spiritual experiences."
Anonymous

Teriyaki Salad

2 cups cooked pork or beef, shredded (500 ml)
3 cups iceberg lettuce, shredded (750 ml)
2 cups bean sprouts (500 ml)
1 cup carrots, shredded (250 ml)
1/3 cup scallions, chopped (75 ml)
1/3 cup yellow pepper, chopped (75 ml)
1/3 cup cucumber, diced (75 ml)
1/3 cup roasted peanuts (75 ml)
Chopped fresh basil to taste
Chopped fresh cilantro to taste

In a large bowl, add shredded beef or pork. Add lettuce, sprouts, carrots, scallions, red pepper, and cucumber. Mix gently. Drizzle with dressing. Toss to coat. Sprinkle with peanuts, basil, and cilantro. Serves eight to ten.

Dressing

1/4 cup teriyaki sauce (50 ml)
1 tbsp. sesame oil (15 ml)
1 tbsp. chopped garlic (15 ml)
1 tbsp. grated fresh gingerroot (15 ml)
1 tsp. hot chili sauce (5 ml)
2 tbsp. salad oil (30 ml)

Put all the ingredients in a jar. Cover and shake well. Drizzle on salad.

Cobb Salad

2 tbsp. red wine vinegar (30 ml)
1/4 cup olive oil (50 ml)
1/4 tsp. each of salt and pepper (1 ml)
1 lb. cooked turkey or chicken breast, chopped (448 g)
1 tbsp. fresh dill, chopped (15 ml)
1 cup cherry tomatoes (225 g)
4 hardboiled eggs, quartered
1/2 tbsp. fresh oregano, chopped (7.5 ml)
1 head red leaf lettuce, rinsed and torn
4 slices bacon, cooked crisp and crumbled
2/3 cup bleu cheese, crumbled (150 ml)
2 avocados, sliced

In a large bowl, whisk vinegar, oil, salt, and pepper. Set aside. In a separate bowl, combine turkey or chicken breast with dill, tomatoes, pepper, eggs, and oregano. Arrange leaf lettuce on a large platter. Add bacon, cheese, and avocado. Top with turkey, dill, tomatoes, and eggs. Drizzle with vinegar, oil, salt, and pepper mixture. Serves four.

A Collection of Caesar Salads

Dealing with romaine lettuce: Cut the bottom core from a head of romaine lettuce and discard it. Wash the romaine under cold running water. Tear into bite-size pieces, removing ribs. Gently pat dry with a paper towel or put in salad spinner and spin until dry. Chill in fridge until ready to use

Classic Caesar Salad

1 large organic egg
2 cloves of garlic
3 anchovy fillets
3 tbsp. extra-virgin olive oil (45 ml)
1 tbsp. fresh lemon juice (15 ml)
Several dashes of Worcestershire sauce
1/3 cup fresh-grated Parmesan cheese (75 ml)
Pinch of dry mustard
1/2 cup garlic croutons (125 ml)
Fresh-ground black pepper
1 prepared head romaine lettuce

To coddle egg, place egg in a saucepan of boiling water. Remove from heat immediately. Let stand for one minute. Remove from water and cool slightly. Rub a large wooden salad bowl with an open-cut clove of garlic. Discard. In a bottom of salad bowl, mash remaining garlic with anchovies and olive oil until smooth. Add pinch of dry mustard. Squeeze fresh lemon juice over mixture. Blend in Worcestershire sauce. Break coddled egg into bowl and mix until creamy. Add prepared romaine lettuce. (Make sure lettuce is thoroughly dry or the dressing will not cling properly.) Toss lightly to coat. Sprinkle with croutons and grated Parmesan cheese. Grind fresh pepper over. Serves four.

"Give to Caesar what is Caesar's.
And to God, what is God's."
—Jesus Christ

Garlic Croutons

1/8 cup olive oil (25 ml)
1/8 cup butter (25 ml)
1 large clove of garlic, crushed
4 slices day-old French bread
Salt

Blend oil, butter, and garlic. Brush mixture on both sides of bread. Cut into half-inch cubes (1 cm). Spread on cookie sheet. Sprinkle with salt. Bake at 300°F (150°C) for twenty minutes or until bread is crisp. Let cool.

"A man never discloses his own character so clearly as when he describes another's."
–Jean Paul Richter

Mock Caesar Salad

1 large elephant clove of garlic, or 2 regular cloves of garlic, crushed
1/2 cup soy sauce (125 ml)
1/4 cup fresh squeezed lemon juice (50 ml)
1/2 tsp. fresh cracked pepper (2 ml)
1 prepared head romaine lettuce

In a small bowl, mix garlic, soy sauce, lemon, and pepper. Taste and adjust seasonings to suit your preference. Put the prepared romaine lettuce in a separate bowl. Drizzle with dressing and toss lightly. Sprinkle with croutons if desired. Serves four.

"We fulfill our purpose in life when we serve God."
Anonymous

Jan's Caesar Salad

3/4 cup mayonnaise (175 ml)
1/4 cup olive oil (50 ml)
1/8 cup chicken broth (30 ml)
3 tbsp. Parmesan cheese (45 ml)
1 tbsp. lemon juice (15 ml)
1 tsp. raspberry vinegar (5 ml)
1 hardboiled egg
1/8 tsp. hot mustard powder (0.6 ml)
1/2 tsp. Dijon mustard (2 ml)
1/2 tsp. Worcestershire sauce (2 ml)
1/4 tsp. black pepper (1 ml)
2 large garlic cloves, crushed
2 anchovy filets
1 head prepared romaine lettuce
Fresh-grated Parmesan cheese
Croutons

Put mayonnaise, oil, broth, Parmesan cheese, lemon, vinegar, egg, mustard, Worcestershire, pepper, garlic, and anchovy filets in a blender and blend well. Taste and adjust seasonings to suit personal preference. If dressing is a bit thick, thin with water. Put prepared romaine lettuce in a large serving bowl. Add enough dressing to coat and toss lightly. (Leftover dressing stores in the fridge for several days.) Sprinkle with croutons and fresh-grated Parmesan cheese. Serves four to six.

Mexican Caesar Salad

1 cup fresh cilantro, chopped (250 ml)
1 cup mayonnaise (250 ml)
1/2 cup extra-virgin olive oil (125 ml)
1/2 cup canned diced green chilies (125 ml)
1/4 cup red wine vinegar (50 ml)
2 cloves of garlic, crushed
2–3 dashes green Tabasco sauce
1/4 cup grated jalapeño cheese (50 ml)
1 head prepared romaine lettuce
Croutons

Put cilantro, mayonnaise, olive oil, green chilies, vinegar, garlic, and Tabasco sauce in a blender and blend until smooth. Put prepared romaine lettuce in large serving bowl. Coat with enough dressing to suit your taste. Sprinkle with jalapeño cheese and croutons.

"The heart of greed dies when one becomes a giver."
Anonymous

Grilled Fusion Caesar Salad

2 anchovy fillets, drained and chopped
2 garlic cloves, minced
1/2 cup olive oil (125 ml)
1/4 tsp. pepper (1 ml)
1/4 tsp. salt (1 ml)
12 slices baguette bread
1 large organic egg
2 tbsp. fresh lemon juice (30 ml)
3 hearts packaged romaine lettuce
Parmigiano-Reggiano cheese, grated

Mash anchovies, garlic, oil, salt, and pepper until smooth. Prepare gas grill on moderate heat. (Hot for charcoal.) Brush both sides of baguette slices with a bit of dressing. Grill each side for one to two minutes until toasted. Add egg and lemon juice to remaining dressing and blend well. Cut each romaine heart in half lengthwise. Grill romaine hearts for one minute or until slightly blackened at edges. Immediately remove from grill. Place on platter. Drizzle with dressing. Sprinkle with cheese. Arrange baguette slices around salad. Serves six.

"It is not the critic who counts; not the man who points out how the strong man stumbles, or where the doer of deeds could have done them better. The credit belongs to the man who is actually in the arena, whose face is marred by dust and sweat and blood, who strives valiantly; who errs and comes short again and again; because there is not effort without error and shortcomings; but who does actually strive to do the deed; who knows the great enthusiasm, the great devotion, who spends himself in a worthy cause, who at the best knows in the end the triumph of high achievement and who at the worst, if he fails, at least he fails while daring greatly. So that his place shall never be with those cold and timid souls who know neither victory nor defeat."
Anonymous

Ray's Working Caesar Salad

This recipe came through much cajoling. My friend Ray is as stubborn as they come where secrets are concerned. But I persevered, and eventually my cajoling found a loophole. We are both twins. I explained that should give me a special inroad to his Caesar salad recipe. Perseverance—a good virtue. Sacrifice—even better! A secret? No longer!

6 tbsp. olive oil (90 ml)
4 cloves of garlic, minced
Fresh-ground black pepper to taste
1 tbsp. Dijon mustard (15 ml)
1/2 tsp. mustard powder (2 ml)
4–5 drops Worcestershire sauce
1 large raw egg
1 entire tin anchovy filets, drained
1/2 cup fresh-grated Parmesan cheese (125 ml)
1 cup croutons (250 ml)
1 prepared head Romaine lettuce
1 1/2 tbsp. fresh-squeezed lemon juice (17 ml)

Put oil, garlic, and pepper in a large mason jar and let soak all day or for eight hours. Add Dijon mustard, mustard powder, Worcestershire sauce, and raw egg. Cover and shake until very creamy. Put drained anchovies on a paper towel to absorb extra oil. Remove to a chopping board and chop finely. Fill a serving salad bowl with prepared romaine lettuce. Sprinkle with chopped anchovies and fresh-cracked pepper. Add dressing from the jar after shaking well to reblend, and toss lightly. Sprinkle with fresh-grated Parmesan cheese and croutons. Sprinkle with fresh-squeezed lemon juice. Serves four to six.

```
"Tread in solitude your path quiet heart. Undismayed,
   you will know things, strange, mysterious, which
  to you no voice has said. While the crowd of petty
  hustlers grasp at vain and meager things, you will see
    a great world rising, where the sacred music sings."
                      Anonymous
```

Seafood & Fish

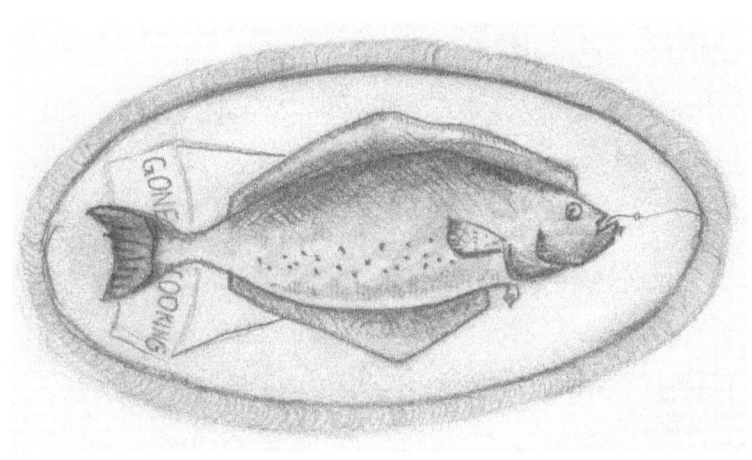

Basic Pan-Fried Fish 183
Salmon Cakes 184
Crab Cakes 185
Salmon Pie 187
Scallops in Cream 188
Stuffed Sole 189
Clams with Pesto Pasta 190
Mussels in White Wine 191
Shrimp in Creole Sauce 192
Shrimp in Cream 193
Indian Shrimp 194
Shrimp in Beer 195
Shrimp with Tequila 196
Almond-Crusted Salmon 197
Poached Salmon 198
Seafood Casserole 199
Fish Tacos 200
Baked Fish Tacos 202
Strawberry Salsa 202
Balsamic Fried Onions 203
Tuna Steaks 203
Easy Oyster Rockefeller 204
Fried Clams 205
Easy Lobster Thermidor 206
Salmon Wellington 207
Baked Fish 209
Provencal Halibut 210
Cuban-Style Red Snapper 211

Basic Pan-Fried Fish
(with Remoulade Sauce)

4 fish fillets: sole, flounder, or cod
Sea salt and pepper to taste
1/4 cup cream (50 ml)
1/4 cup flour (50 ml)
1/4 cup olive oil (50 ml)
4 tbsp. butter (60 ml)
2 tbsp. fresh lemon juice (30 ml)
4 slices lemon
4 tbsp. fresh parsley, chopped (60 ml)

Sprinkle fish with sea salt and pepper. Dip in cream. Dredge in flour. In a large skillet, heat oil to moderately hot. Add fish, keeping an even layer. Cook each side for one and a half minutes or until golden brown. Transfer fish to platter. Add butter to skillet and brown. Pour over fish. Sprinkle with lemon. Garnish with lemon slices and fresh-chopped parsley. Serve topped with remoulade. Serves four.

Remoulade

1 cup mayonnaise (250 ml)
2 tbsp. capers (30 ml)
2 tbsp. dill pickle, chopped (30 ml)
1/2 tsp. tarragon (2 ml)
1 tsp. Dijon mustard (5 ml)
1/2 tsp. sugar (2 ml)

Mix all the ingredients well and serve with fish.

"I believe that imagination is stronger than knowledge. That myth is more potent than history. That dreams are more powerful than facts. That hope always triumphs over experience. That laughter is the only cure for grief. And I believe that love is stronger than death."
—Robert Fulghum, *All I Really Need to Know I Learned in Kindergarten*

Salmon Cakes
(with Dill Sauce)

1 fifteen-ounce can of salmon (450 g)
1 large organic egg
1/2 cup green onions, diced (125 ml)
1/2 cup green pepper, diced (125 ml)
1/2 cup crushed breadcrumbs (125 ml)
1 tbsp. lemon juice (15 ml)
1 tsp. lemon rind, grated (5 ml)
1/2 tsp. rosemary (2 ml)
1/4 tsp. black pepper (1 ml)
1 tbsp. butter (15 ml)
Lemon wedges

Drain salmon and put in a large bowl. Stir in egg, onion, pepper, bread, lemon, rosemary, and pepper. Form into four patties. Melt butter in a hot frying pan. Cook salmon cakes in butter until golden brown on both sides, around two and a half minutes per side. Serve with lemon wedges and dill sauce. Serves two.

Dill Sauce

1 cup sour cream (250 ml)
1/4 cup mayonnaise (50 ml)
2 tbsp. chopped dill (30 ml)
1 tbsp. capers (15 ml)
1 tsp. lemon juice (5 ml)
1/2 tsp. sea salt (5 ml)
1/4 tsp. black pepper (1 ml)

In a small bowl, combine sour cream, mayonnaise, dill, capers, lemon juice, salt, and pepper until blended. Serve on the side with salmon cakes.

"The Chinese use two brush strokes to write the word 'crisis.' One brush stroke stands for danger; the other for opportunity. In a crisis, be aware of the danger—but recognize the opportunity."
—John F. Kennedy

Crab Cakes
(with Tartar Sauce)

2 cans of crab meat, about 2 cups (500 ml)
Fish stock or tomato juice to moisten
1 tsp. Old Bay Seasoning (5 ml)
1/4 tsp. salt (1 ml)
1/4 tsp. cayenne (1 ml)
2 tbsp. parsley (30 ml)
1/4 cup onion, minced (50 ml)
1/4 cup celery, minced (50 ml)
1/4 cup red pepper, minced (50 ml)
1/2 cup butter (125 ml)
1/4 cup flour (50 ml)
Flour for dredging
2 large eggs, beaten
1 cup crushed breadcrumbs (250 ml)
Butter for frying

In a medium bowl, moisten crab with several dashes of fish stock or tomato juice. Add Old Bay Seasoning, salt, cayenne, and parsley. Mix well and then set aside. Fry onions in butter with celery and red pepper in a hot skillet for three to five minutes. Mix in 1/4 cup flour (50 ml). Add crab mixture. Stir until combined. Add more stock or juice if mixture seems too thick. Remove from heat. Put in fridge and chill. When mixture is cool enough to handle, shape into small cakes. Pour flour for dredging on a large dinner plate, and dredge each crab cake in flour. On second plate beat eggs and dip each crab cake in egg. On third plate, pour crushed breadcrumbs and press each crab cake into breadcrumbs. Fry crab cakes in hot butter until golden on both sides, one to two minutes per side. Serve with tartar sauce. Serves four.

Tartar Sauce

1 cup mayonnaise (250 ml)
1/4 cup pickle, chopped (50 ml)
1/4 cup onion, chopped (50 ml)
1 tbsp. capers, chopped (15 ml)
2 tsp. vinegar (10 ml)
1 tbsp. ketchup (15 ml)
dash Tabasco sauce

Mix mayonnaise, pickle, onion, capers, vinegar, ketchup, and Tabasco sauce in medium bowl. Taste and adjust seasonings as desired. Makes about one and a half cups (375 ml).

"It is said an Eastern Monarch once charged his wise men to invent him a sentence which would be true and appropriate at all times. They presented him the words: 'And this too will pass.' How consoling is this in the depth of affliction, how reproving in the hour of pride."
—Abraham Lincoln

Salmon Pie

1 1/4 cups water (300 ml)
1 tsp. salt (5 ml)
1/2 cup long-grain rice (125 ml)
1 tbsp. butter (15 ml)
1 cup celery, diced (250 ml)
1/2 onion, chopped
2 eggs
Pinch of white pepper
1/2 cup Swiss cheese, grated and divided (125 ml)
1 cup canned salmon, un-drained and flaked (250 ml)
1/2 cup whole milk (125 ml)
Pinch of nutmeg
Pinch of curry powder
Pinch of cinnamon

In a saucepan, bring water and salt to a boil. Add rice. Cover tightly and reduce heat. Simmer for twenty minutes. Meanwhile grease a round pie pan with one teaspoon of the butter (5 ml). Set aside. Melt the remaining butter (10 ml) in medium-hot skillet. Add celery and onion. Sauté for three to five minutes. Beat one egg with a pinch of pepper and stir into cooked rice. Press rice onto the bottom and sides of prepared pie pan. Sprinkle with cheese. Spread with celery and onion. Top with salmon. Beat remaining egg with milk. Add nutmeg, curry, and cinnamon and pour the mixture over the pie. Bake at 375°F (190°C) for thirty to thirty-five minutes. Serves four.

Scallops in Cream

2 pints fresh scallops (900 g)
4 tbsp. butter (60 ml)
Salt and pepper to taste
4 tbsp. shallots, chopped (60 ml)
2 cups fresh mushrooms, sliced (500 ml)
10–14 grape tomatoes
1/3 cup white wine (75 ml)
1 cup heavy cream (250 ml)
Butter
2 tbsp. parsley, chopped (30 ml)
1/2 tsp. tarragon (2 ml)

Melt butter in a large medium-hot skillet. Add scallops, being careful not to overlap them. Cook, shaking the skillet lightly for one to two minutes or until scallops turn gold. Remove the scallops and set them aside. Add salt and pepper to taste. Add shallots, mushrooms, and tomatoes to skillet. Cook for one minute. Add wine and cream. Return scallops to skillet. Swirl in a dab of butter. Heat through. Sprinkle with tarragon and parsley. Add a bit more salt and pepper if desired. Serves four.

Stuffed Sole

4 sole fillets
1/3 cup celery, chopped (75 ml)
2 tbsp. pimento, diced (30 ml)
1/3 cup onion, chopped (75 ml)
4 tbsp. butter (60 ml)
2/3 cup breadcrumbs (150 ml)
Peel of 1 large orange, grated
1 large orange, chopped finely
Salt and pepper
Melted butter
Parsley

In a large skillet, fry celery, onion, and pimento in hot butter until tender, around four to five minutes. Add breadcrumbs, orange peel, and chopped orange. Add salt and pepper to taste. Arrange fillets on work surface. Spoon 1/4 cup (50 ml) of filling atop each fillet. Roll up the filled fillet, securing with a toothpick in center of each. Arrange fillets on an ungreased baking sheet. Bake uncovered in a 350°F (180°C) oven for twenty minutes. Remove from oven. Brush fillets with additional melted butter. Before serving, sprinkle with parsley. Serves four.

Clams with Pesto Pasta

(You can use mussels or cooked chicken in place of clams.)

3 cups fresh cilantro, chopped (750 ml)
3 tbsp. shallots, minced (45 ml)
1 jalapeño pepper, diced
2 tsp. lemon zest, grated (10 ml)
1/2 tsp. salt (2 ml)
1/2 cup almonds, chopped (125 ml)
6 tbsp. olive oil, divided (90 ml)
3/4 lb. linguini or fettuccini noodles (350 g)
1 onion, chopped
2 garlic cloves, minced
60 clams, scrubbed
1 cup white wine (250 ml)

To make pesto, in a food processor blend cilantro, shallots, jalapeño, lemon zest, salt, and almonds. Add a 1/4 cup (50 ml) olive oil in a slow stream. If pesto seems too thick, add a bit of cold water. Blend well. Set aside. Cook pasta according to package directions and drain. Set aside. In a large skillet, heat remaining olive oil. Add onion and garlic. Cook until lightly brown, about three to four minutes. Stir in clams. Increase heat to medium-high. Add wine. Cover and cook for three minutes or until clams open. Reduce heat to medium. Stir in pesto and pasta. Heat until warmed through. Serve immediately. Serves four.

Mussels in White Wine

1/2 cup onion, chopped (125 ml)
4 tbsp. shallots, chopped (60 ml)
1 bay leaf
1/2 tsp. dried thyme (2 ml)
Several sprigs fresh parsley
Fresh-cracked pepper
4 tbsp. butter (60 ml)
1 cup white wine (250 ml)
4 quarts fresh mussels (3.8 L)
12 slices day-old French bread
Olive oil
4–6 cloves of garlic

In a large sauce pot, combine onion, shallots, bay leaf, thyme, parsley, pepper, butter, and wine. Bring to a boil. Once boiling, add mussels. Immediately lower heat. Steam the mussels covered for three to four minutes or until mussels open. Remove to platter. Serve with garlic toast. Serves six.

Garlic Toast

Crush four to six garlic cloves in small bowl. Add enough olive oil to brush twelve pieces of French bread, both sides. Place bread under broiler and broil each side until warm and golden, one to two minutes.

Shrimp in Creole Sauce

1 1/2 lbs. raw shrimp (672 g)
4 tbsp. butter, divided (60 ml)
2 cups onion, chopped (500 ml)
1 tbsp. garlic, minced (15 ml)
3/4 cup celery, chopped (175 ml)
1 cup green pepper, chopped (250 ml)
1 cup sweet red pepper, chopped (250 ml)
Salt and pepper to taste
3 cups canned tomatoes (375 ml)
4 tbsp. parsley (60 ml)
1 bay leaf
1 tbsp. chipotle Tabasco sauce (15 ml)

Melt two tablespoons of the butter (30 ml) in a medium-hot skillet. Add onion and garlic. Sauté for two minutes. Add celery, green and red pepper, salt, and pepper. Cook until vegetables are crisp and tender, around three to five minutes. Add canned tomatoes, breaking tomatoes up gently with a fork. Add parsley, bay leaf, and Tabasco sauce. Cover and simmer for ten minutes. Melt remaining butter (30 ml) in a separate skillet on medium heat. Add shrimp. Cook until shrimp is no longer translucent, or about two minutes. Add the cooked shrimp to the first skillet. Serve immediately. Makes four servings.

Shrimp in Cream

2 tbsp. butter (30 ml)
1 1/2 lbs. raw shrimp (672 g)
1/2 tsp. pepper (2 ml)
1 tsp. smoky paprika (5 ml)
1/2 tsp. garlic salt (2 ml)
4 tbsp. green onions, chopped (60 ml)
1/3 cup white wine (75 ml)
1 1/2 cups heavy cream, divided (375 ml)
2 egg yolks

Melt butter in heavy skillet on medium-high heat. Add shrimp. Add pepper, smoky paprika, and garlic salt. Cook, shaking skillet, for one minute. Add chopped green onions. Add wine. Cook until green onions are lightly brown and shrimp is no longer translucent, about one minute.

Transfer to a warm platter. Add half the heavy cream to the skillet and cook for three to five minutes. Beat egg yolks with remaining cream. Add to skillet. Gently slide shrimp back into skillet. Reheat just until hot. Serves four.

Indian Shrimp

3 tbsp. butter (45 ml)
1/2 cup onion, chopped (125 ml)
1 tsp. hot chili flakes (5 ml)
1 1/2 lbs. raw fresh shrimp, shelled (672 g)
Salt and pepper to taste
1/4 tsp. cardamom (1 ml)
1 tsp. curry powder (5 ml)
1/4 tsp. cumin (1 ml)
Juice of 1 lime (2 ml)
1 cup sour cream (250 ml)
1/3 cup plain yogurt (75 ml)
1/3 cup cilantro, chopped (75 ml)

Heat butter in a hot skillet. Add onion, chili flakes, shrimp, salt, pepper, cardamom, curry, and cumin. Cook for two minutes or until shrimp is no longer translucent. Sprinkle with lime juice. Add sour cream and yogurt. Mix gently. Bring just to a boil. Reduce heat immediately and remove. Place in a serving dish. Sprinkle with chopped cilantro. Serves four.

"The secret of health is not to mourn for the past, nor worry about the future, but to live the present moment wisely and earnestly."
—Buddha

Shrimp in Beer

2 lbs. raw shrimp in shell (1 kg)
3 cloves of garlic, crushed
4 whole allspice buds
1/4 tsp. hot pepper flakes (1 ml)
Salt and pepper to taste
1 bay leaf
5 sprigs of fresh parsley
2 sprigs of fresh dill weed
1 can beer
Dash of Worcestershire sauce
Melted butter
Lemon wedges

Combine shrimp, garlic, allspice, hot pepper flakes, salt, pepper, bay leaf, parsley, dill, beer, and Worcestershire sauce in a large pot. Cover. Bring to a boil. Turn heat to simmer and simmer for two minutes or until shrimp is no longer translucent. Remove from heat. Remove shrimp with a slotted spoon and place in a serving dish. Drizzle with melted butter. Garnish with lemon wedges. Serves six.

Shrimp with Tequila

1 lb. raw shrimp (448 g)
1/3 cup fresh-squeezed lime juice (75 ml)
1/4 tsp. sea salt (1 ml)
1/4 tsp. fresh-cracked pepper (1 ml)
4 tbsp. butter (60 ml)
2 tbsp. green onions, chopped (30 ml)
1/3 cup tequila (75 ml)
1 cup liquid whipping cream (250 ml)
2 medium ripe avocadoes, sliced thin
1 large vine-ripened tomato, sliced
2 tbsp. cilantro, chopped (30 ml)

Shell shrimp and put in a medium bowl. Sprinkle with lime juice, salt, and pepper. Heat butter in a large medium-hot skillet. Add shrimp and cook for two minutes or until no longer translucent. Sprinkle with green onions. Add tequila and swirl pan gently. Mix in liquid whipping cream. Cook for one minute. Add avocado and tomato slices. Simmer until avocado and tomato are warm. Transfer to serving plates. Serves four.

"Creating without claiming. Doing without taking credit. Guiding without interference. This is primal virtue."
—Lao Tzu

Almond-Crusted Salmon

6 fillets of salmon
4 tbsp. butter (60 ml)
2 leeks, chopped
3 tbsp. lemon juice (45 ml)
1 cup liquid whipping cream (250 ml)
1 cup ground almonds (250 ml)
1/4 cup fresh parsley, chopped (50 ml)
1 tbsp. lemon peel, grated (15 ml)
1/2 tsp. salt (2 ml)
1/8 tsp. pepper (0.64 ml)
1/2 cup flour (125 ml)
2 large eggs, beaten
1 tbsp. butter (15 ml)
2 tbsp. olive oil (30 ml)

Fry leeks in butter in hot skillet until tender, about two to three minutes. Add lemon juice and cream. Set aside. Put three plates side by side on a working surface. Sprinkle the first plate with flour. On second plate, pour beaten eggs. On third plate, mix almonds, parsley, and lemon peel together. Sprinkle salmon fillets with salt and pepper. Dredge in flour, beaten egg, and almond mixture. Melt the butter with the olive oil in a moderately hot skillet. Add the salmon fillets and sear both sides until golden, about two minutes per side. Transfer fillets to baking sheet. Bake at 375°F (190°C) for five to six minutes or until salmon is just opaque. Gently reheat the leek mixture and spoon over salmon. Serves six.

Poached Salmon
(with Avocado Mayonnaise)

2 salmon fillets
1 cup white wine (250 ml)
1 cup water (250 ml)
1 onion, thinly sliced
2 fresh parsley sprigs
1 fresh tarragon sprig
1 lemon, cut in wedges
1 avocado, pitted and sliced

Combine wine, water, onion, parsley, and tarragon in shallow, wide skillet. Bring to a gentle boil. Add salmon fillets. Lower heat. Simmer for four minutes or until salmon is no longer translucent. Remove salmon from liquid with slotted spoon. Transfer to a serving platter. Top with avocado mayonnaise. Arrange lemon wedges around. Top with avocado slices. Serves two.

Avocado Mayonnaise

1 medium avocado, pitted
1 shallot, sliced finely
2 tbsp. lemon juice (30 ml)
2 tbsp. orange juice (30 ml)
1 tsp. mustard (5 ml)
1 egg
2/3 cup vegetable oil (150 ml)

Put all the ingredients in blender and blend until smooth, adding oil gradually until thick. Serve with salmon.

Seafood Casserole

1 lb. raw scallops (448 g)
1 cup dry white wine (250 ml)
1 onion, chopped
1 tbsp. parsley, chopped (15 ml)
2 tbsp. lemon juice (30 ml)
Salt to taste
4 tbsp. butter, divided (60 ml)
6 tbsp. flour (90 ml)
1 cup cream (250 ml)
4 oz. Gruyere cheese, cut up (120 g)
Dash of pepper
1 cup canned crabmeat, drained (250 ml)
1/2 cup canned shrimp, drained (125 ml)
1/2 cup mushrooms, sliced (125 ml)
1 1/2 cups crushed breadcrumbs (375 ml)
2 tbsp. melted butter (30 ml)

Combine scallops, wine, onion, parsley, lemon juice, and salt in medium saucepan. Bring to boil. Simmer for four minutes. Drain, reserving one cup of the liquid (250 ml). Set aside. In a separate saucepan, melt the butter. Whisk in flour. Add cream and reserved liquid all at once. Whisk briskly until mixture thickens and bubbles, and then remove from heat. Stir in Gruyere cheese and a dash of pepper. Add set aside scallop mixture. Add the drained crabmeat, drained shrimp, and the mushrooms. Spoon mixture into a nine-by-thirteen-inch buttered casserole dish (22x33 cm). Combine breadcrumbs with melted butter and spoon over casserole. Bake in preheated oven at 350°F (180°C) for twenty-five minutes or until heated through. Serves six.

"Our spiritual life should continually cause us to focus inwardly for the determined purpose of self-examination, because each of us has some qualities we have not yet added."
Anonymous

Fish Tacos
(in Beer Batter)

1 lb. fresh cod or halibut (448 g)
8 corn tortillas
1 cup unbleached white flour (250 ml)
1 can beer
1 tsp. salt (5 ml)
Pinch of baking powder
Oil for frying
2 cups packaged mixed coleslaw (500 ml) sprinkled
with commercially prepared citrus vinaigrette
1 lime, cut in wedges
Salt to taste
Prepared topping of choice.

In a large bowl, whisk flour with beer, salt, and a pinch of baking powder until smooth. If batter seems too thick, add a bit more beer. Set aside. Heat deep fryer with enough oil to cover fish completely, setting the temperature at 350–375°F (180–190°C). Cut fish into serving-size pieces. Sprinkle with lime and salt. Set aside.

Using tongs, drop each tortilla in hot oil in large skillet and fry on both sides until golden, about twenty seconds per side. Place on paper towel to absorb excess oil. (Keep warm on low temperature in oven until ready to fill.) Drop fish into beer batter and then into hot oil. Fry for three minutes or until golden. Drain on paper towels. Fill each tortilla with hot fried fish. Add topping of choice. Add coleslaw vinaigrette. Serves four.

Hot and Spicy Fish Taco Topping

1–2 dashes Habanero pepper sauce
2 large ripe mangos, pitted, peeled, and diced
2 avocados, pitted and diced
1 large onion, diced
Several dashes of lime juice
Several dashes of rice wine vinegar
1 cup fresh cilantro, chopped (250 ml)

In a blender, put mango, habanero, avocado, onion, lime, and vinegar. Blend well. Taste. Adjust seasonings as desired. Garnish with cilantro.

Mild Fish Taco Topping

1/3 cup mayonnaise (75 ml)
1/3 cup sour cream (75 ml)
1 tsp. grated lime (5 ml)
1 1/2 tsp. lime juice (7 ml)
1 garlic clove, minced
1/4 cup cilantro, chopped (50 ml)
1/4 cup green onion, chopped (50 ml)
Salt and pepper to taste

Blend all the ingredients well in a medium bowl. Taste and adjust seasonings as desired.

Baked Fish Tacos
(with Strawberry Salsa and Balsamic Fried Onions)

1 lb. catfish or cod fillets (448 g)
3 cups dark beer (750 ml)
2 tbsp. kosher salt
1 tbsp. brown sugar (15 ml)
8 large corn tortillas
Strawberry salsa (made ahead)
Balsamic fried onions (made ahead)

Rinse catfish or cod fillets. Cut in serving-size pieces and set aside on paper towel–lined plate. Prepare a brine by combining dark beer with kosher salt and brown sugar. Add fish to brine. Cover and put in fridge for six hours. Remove. Drain well. Pat fish dry with paper towel. Heat oven to 400°F (200°C). Place fish on parchment paper–lined baking sheet and bake for twenty minutes, turning once halfway through. Prepare corn tortillas according to package directions. Fill with baked fish. Top with raspberry salsa and balsamic fried onions. Serves four.

Strawberry Salsa

2 cups fresh strawberries (500 ml)
(if desired substitute with blackberries)
1 red bell pepper, chopped finely
1 jalapeño pepper, chopped finely
2 green onions, chopped finely
1/3 cup cilantro, chopped finely (75 ml)
1 tbsp. honey (15 ml)
1 tbsp. lime juice (15 ml)
1/2 tsp. lime zest (2 ml)
1 garlic clove, minced

Put all ingredients in blender and blend until smooth.

Balsamic Fried Onions

1 tbsp. butter (15 ml)
1 large white onion, sliced thinly
2 tsp. balsamic vinegar (10 ml)
1/2 tsp. smoky paprika (2 ml)
1 tsp. sugar (5 ml)
1 cup beer (250 ml).

Melt butter in skillet over medium heat. Add onion. Sauté for three to five minutes or until onion is softened. Add vinegar, paprika, sugar, and beer. Bring to boil. Reduce heat. Simmer for thirty minutes, stirring occasionally.

Tuna Steaks

4 tuna steaks one inch thick (2.54 cm)
2 tbsp. lemon rind (30 ml)
2 tsp. salt (5 ml)
2 tsp. coriander (10 ml)
1 1/2 tsp. pepper (7 ml)
1 1/2 tsp. ginger (7 ml)
1/4 tsp. cinnamon (1 ml)
4 tbsp. olive oil, divided (45 ml)
2 cups green salad mix (500 ml)
1 1/2 tsp. balsamic vinegar (7 ml)
Salt and pepper to taste

In a small bowl, combine lemon rind, salt, coriander, pepper, ginger, and cinnamon. Stir in two tablespoons of olive oil. Rub mixture into tuna steaks both sides. Heat one tablespoon of olive oil in medium-hot skillet. Add tuna steaks. Fry for three minutes on one side, until seared. Turn and fry for another three minutes or until seared. While steaks are frying, toss the salad greens with remaining olive oil and vinegar in a medium bowl. Add salt and pepper to taste. Place on platter. Remove steaks from skillet and slice thinly. Lay atop greens. Serves four.

Easy Oyster Rockefeller

1 pint fresh-shelled oysters (500 ml)
1 cup cooked chopped spinach (250 ml)
1/4 cup crushed breadcrumbs (50 ml)
2 tbsp. celery, finely chopped (30 ml)
2 tbsp. parsley, finely chopped (30 ml)
1 tbsp. green onion, minced (15 ml)
1/2 tsp. sea salt (2 ml)
1/2 tsp. black pepper (2 ml)
1/4 tsp. basil (1 ml)
1/4 tsp. paprika (1 ml)
3/4 cup softened butter (175 ml)
1/4 cup panko breadcrumbs (50 ml)
1 tbsp. melted butter (15 ml)
Rock salt (optional)

Divide oysters in bake-proof decorative shells. Arrange shells on a bed of rock salt in shallow baking pan. Set aside. In a medium bowl, combine spinach, breadcrumbs, celery, parsley, green onion, salt, pepper, basil, and paprika. Mix in softened butter. Set aside. In a separate bowl, toss panko breadcrumbs with melted butter. Spoon spinach mixture atop oysters in shell. Sprinkle with buttered panko crumbs. Bake in hot oven at 450°F (230°C) for ten minutes or until crumb mixture is lightly browned and edges of oysters begin to curl. Serve hot. Serves six.

"If a man takes no thought to what is distant
he will find sorrow near at hand."
—Confucius

Fried Clams

2 lbs. clam strips (900 g)
1 cup buttermilk (250 ml)
1 cup cornstarch (250 ml)
1/2 cup yellow cornmeal (125 ml)
1/3 cup flour (75 ml)
1 1/2 tsp. curry powder (7 ml)
1/2 tsp. celery salt ((2 ml)
1/4 tsp. cayenne (1 ml)
1/2 tsp. kosher salt (2 ml)
1 1/2 cups parsley sprigs, finely chopped (375 ml)
2 lemons, sliced
8 cups oil (2 L) for frying

Preheat oil in deep fryer to 400°F (200°C). Drain clams. Put in a large bowl and add buttermilk. Soak for five minutes. In a separate bowl, stir cornstarch with cornmeal, flour, curry powder, celery salt, cayenne, kosher salt, and parsley. Remove clams from buttermilk and dredge in the flour mixture. Shake to remove excess. Fry clams in hot oil until crisp and tender, about two minutes, or until golden. Place on paper towels to absorb excess oil. Sprinkle with additional salt if desired. Serves four.

Easy Lobster Thermidor

1 cup mushrooms, sliced (250 ml)
4 shallots, minced
2 tbsp. butter (30 ml)
4 tsp. flour (20 ml)
1/2 cup heavy cream (125 ml)
1/4 cup dry sherry (50 ml)
1/2 tsp. mustard powder (2 ml)
1/4 tsp. smoky paprika (1 ml)
Salt and pepper to taste
4 cups cooked lobster meat, broken up (900 g)
Lemon butter sauce

Fry mushrooms and shallots in a medium-hot skillet in butter until tender, around two to three minutes. Mix in flour. Stirring quickly, add cream and sherry. Lower heat. Add mustard powder, smoky paprika, and a dash of salt and pepper. Add lobster and stir gently. Remove from heat. Spoon mixture into decorative ovenproof shells. Place shells on broiling pan. Spoon lemon butter sauce atop. Broil for two minutes or until bubbly. Makes two servings.

Lemon Butter Sauce

2 egg yolks
Dash of salt
1/2 cup melted butter (125 ml)
1 tbsp. water (15 ml)
1 tbsp. lemon juice (15 ml)

Set egg yolks over boiling water in top of double boiler. Add salt, melted butter, water, and lemon juice. Stir until thickened.

Salmon Wellington

I got the idea for this dish from Jen, a quiet, devout beauty who owns Eagle Lodge Resort in spectacular Bella Coola, BC. When Jen presented this dish, I knew I had to have it again. Goodness is truly a virtue!

2 green onions, chopped finely
2 tbsp. butter (30 ml)
1/4 cup white wine (50 ml)
1/2 tsp. tarragon (2 ml)
1/2 tsp. sea salt (2 ml)
1/2 tsp. white pepper (2 ml)
1 cup liquid whipping cream (250 ml)
1 fourteen-ounce package of frozen puff pastry, thawed (398 g)
1 fourteen-ounce salmon fillet (400 g)
1 large organic egg, beaten

Melt butter in hot skillet. Add green onions. Sauté for two minutes. Add wine, tarragon, salt, and pepper. Reduce heat to simmer, stirring until wine is almost evaporated. Add cream. Simmer until reduced by half. Remove from heat. Preheat oven to 425°F (220°C). On floured surface, cut a block of puff pastry in half. Roll to twelve by ten inches (30 by 25 cm). Place pastry on a foil-lined baking sheet. Place salmon directly in center of pastry, leaving a two-inch border (5 cm) all around. Spoon sauce from skillet over salmon. Brush edges of pastry with beaten egg. Place second block of pastry on top of salmon. Press edges to seal. Thinly slit top for steam to escape while baking. Brush with leftover beaten egg. Bake for twenty-five minutes until golden. Let it sit for five minutes. Slice and drizzle with wine sauce. Serves four.

"Oh Great Spirit, Grant that I may not criticize my neighbor, until I have walked a mile in his moccasins."
Indian prayer

Wine Sauce

1/2 cup white wine (125 ml)
1 tsp. lemon juice (5 ml)
1/2 tsp. lemon zest (2 ml)
1/2 cup liquid whipping cream (125 ml)
1 tsp. dried tarragon (5 ml)
Salt and pepper to taste

In a small saucepot, bring wine, lemon juice, and zest just to a boil. Turn heat to simmer. Simmer for five minutes or until almost evaporated. Add cream, stirring until slightly thickened. Do not let it boil. Spoon over salmon.

Baked Fish

8 boneless fillets, flounder or sole
Salt and pepper to taste
4 tbsp. shallots, finely chopped, divided (60 ml)
1/3 cup white wine (75 ml)
1/3 cup heavy cream (75 ml)
1/3 cup crushed breadcrumbs (75 ml)
2 tbsp. parsley, chopped (30 ml)
4 tbsp. butter, melted (60 ml)

Preheat oven to 400°F (200°C). Sprinkle fillets with salt and pepper. Roll fillets tightly. Grease a nine-by-thirteen-inch baking dish (22x33 cm) with butter. Sprinkle bottom of dish with one tablespoon of shallots (15 ml). Arrange filets in dish, seam side down. Mix wine and cream together and pour over fillets. Sprinkle with breadcrumbs, parsley, and remaining shallots. Melt butter. Pour on top. Bake for twenty minutes. Serves four.

```
If we think only good thoughts, feel only good
   emotions, and see only good in nature and
    people, we will have only good memories."
Anonymous
```

Provencal Halibut

4–6 Halibut steaks
1 cup white wine (250 ml)
6 cups vine-ripened tomatoes, chopped (1 1/2 L)
2 cups onions, chopped (500 ml)
1/3 cup fresh parsley, chopped (75 ml)
1/3 cup fresh basil, chopped (75 ml)
2 tbsp. olive oil (30 ml)
1 scant tsp. salt (5 ml)
1 tsp. anchovy paste (5 ml)
1/4 tsp. black pepper (1 ml)
2 large garlic cloves, minced
1/3 cup panko breadcrumbs (75 ml)
3 tbsp. Parmesan cheese (45 ml)
1 tsp. melted butter

Preheat oven to 350°F (180°C). In a large bowl, combine tomatoes, onions, parsley, basil, olive oil, salt, anchovy paste, pepper, and garlic.
Oil a nine-by-thirteen-inch baking pan (22x33 cm). Arrange halibut steaks in pan. Pour wine over. Spoon tomato mixture atop. Bake for thirty-five minutes. Remove halibut from oven. Heat broiler. In a small bowl, combine panko breadcrumbs with Parmesan cheese and melted butter. Sprinkle over halibut. Place halibut under broiler. Broil for one to two minutes or until breadcrumbs on top are toasted. Serves four to six.

Cuban-Style Red Snapper

6 red snapper fillets
1 1/2 tbsp. fresh lemon juice (22 ml)
1/2 tsp. salt (2 ml)
1 tbsp. olive oil (15 ml)
2 cups onion, chopped (500 ml)
2 1/2 cups tomatoes, chopped (625 ml)
1/2 cup parsley, chopped (125 ml)
2/3 cup white wine (150 ml)
1/4 tsp. pepper (1 ml)
4 bay leaves
2 cloves of garlic, minced
6 baking potatoes, peeled and cut into wedges

Preheat oven to 350°F (180°C). Arrange fillets in a nine-by-thirteen-inch baking pan (22x33 cm) coated with cooking spray. Sprinkle fillets with lemon juice and salt. Set aside. Heat oil in medium-hot skillet. Add onion. Sauté until softened, around four to five minutes. Add tomatoes, parsley, wine, pepper, bay leaves, and garlic. Lower heat. Simmer for fifteen minutes. Pour sauce over fillets. Top with potato wedges. Bake, uncovered, for one hour and twenty minutes or until potatoes are tender. Serves six.

Meats & Marinades

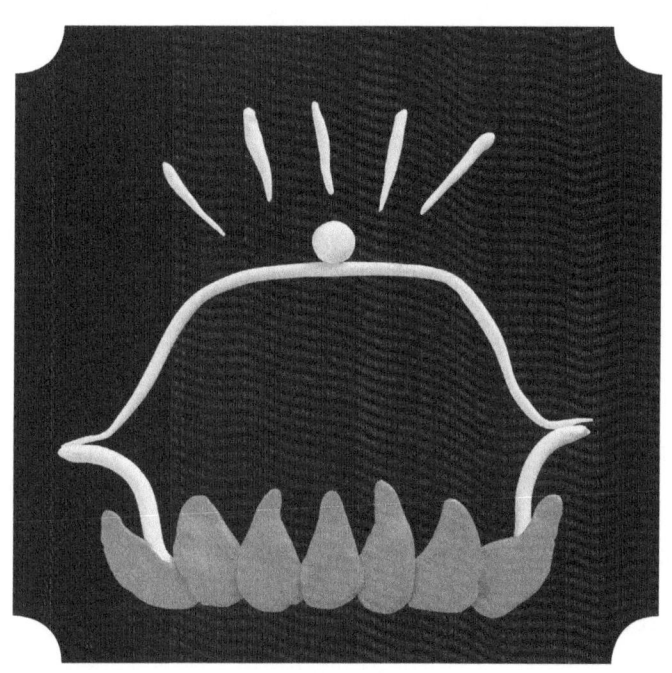

Soulful Steaks. 215
Beer Marinade 216
Jack Daniels Marinade 217
Red Wine Marinade 217
Balsamic Tequila Marinade 218
Rosemary Marinade 219
Graham's Marinade. 219
Bleu Cheese Steaks 220
Jalapeño Steaks 221
Cognac Pepper Steak 222
Argentina Flank Steak 223
Filet Mignon 224
Steak Diane. 225
Pot Roast 226
Beer Pot Roast 227
Prime Rib 228
Yorkshire Pudding 229
Cajun Prime Rib Steaks 230
Mustard Herb-Crusted Roast Pork 231
Cranberry Ginger Pork Roast. 232
Pork Tenderloin 233
Wiener Schnitzel 234
Scalloped Pork Chops 235
Tequila-Glazed Ribs 236
Barbecued Ribs. 237

Soulful Steaks

About steaks: Buy as good a steak as you can to ensure a truly great eating experience. Cheaper cuts can do well if you pierce the steak with a fork on both sides and use a good marinade. Marinate for several hours or overnight to soften tough fibers. Marinating with alcohol or citrus not only softens meat but also adds a lot of flavor and spirit to whatever cut you choose!

Broiling Time for Steaks

One-inch thick cut (2.54 cm)
8–10 minutes, rare
12–14 minutes, medium
18–20 minutes, well done

One-and-a-half-inch thick cut (4 cm)
14–16 minutes, rare
18–20 minutes, medium
25–30 minutes, well done

Two-inch thick cut (5 cm)
20–25 minutes, rare
30–35 minutes, medium
40–45 minutes, well done

"I sought my soul,
But my soul I could not see.
I sought my God,
But my God eluded me.
I sought my brother,
And I found all three."
Anonymous

Beer Marinade

1 onion, sliced
3 tbsp. vinegar (45 ml)
1/2 cup brown sugar (125 ml)
2 tbsp. olive oil (30 ml)
1/2 cup soy sauce (125 ml)
2 tbsp. Worcestershire sauce (30 ml)
1 tsp. garlic powder (5 ml)
1 tsp. mustard powder (5 ml)
2 tsp. minced garlic (10 ml)
1/2 tsp. salt (2 ml)
1/2 tsp. pepper (2 ml)
1 twelve-ounce bottle of beer (375 ml)

Mix onion, vinegar, sugar, olive oil, soy sauce, Worcestershire sauce, garlic powder, mustard powder, minced garlic, salt, pepper, and beer in a blender until smooth. Pour ingredients into a saucepan. Heat and bring to a boil. Lower heat and simmer for five minutes. Remove and let cool. When cool, pour marinade over steaks and marinate overnight or all day as you head off to work. Drain marinade and grill steaks according to preference level. Good for two to four steaks.

```
"We do not see things as they are;
    we see things as we are."
            —Talmud
```

Jack Daniels Marinade

1 clove of garlic, minced
2 tsp. dry mustard (10 ml)
1/4 cup Jack Daniels or other whiskey (50 ml)
2 tbsp. butter (30 ml)
Salt and pepper to taste

Score steaks of your choice. Mix garlic, mustard, and whiskey together and pour over steaks. Place steaks in a plastic bag and marinate overnight in fridge. Drain marinade before grilling. Grill according to your preference level. Good for two steaks.

"And what is as important as knowledge?" asked the mind. "Caring, and seeing with the heart" answered the soul.
Anonymous

Red Wine Marinade

1/2 cup red wine (125 ml)
1/4 cup balsamic vinegar (50 ml)
2–3 cloves of garlic, minced
2 tbsp. Worcestershire sauce (30 ml)
1 tsp. salt (5 ml)
1/2 tsp. pepper (2 ml)

Mix all the ingredients together and pour marinade over steaks and marinate for several hours. Pour marinade off steaks before grilling. Good for two to four steaks.

"They must often change, who would be constant in happiness or wisdom."
–Confucius

Balsamic Tequila Marinade

1/2 cup tequila (125 ml)
1/2 cup lime juice (125 ml)
1/4 cup olive oil (50 ml)
5 cloves of garlic, peeled and thinly sliced
1 tsp. kosher salt (5 ml)
1/2 tsp. fresh-cracked pepper (2 ml)
1–2 jalapeños, minced
1 shallot, chopped
2 cups cilantro, chopped (500 ml)
2 tsp. toasted cumin seeds (10 ml)
Lime wedges

In a medium bowl, combine tequila, lime juice, olive oil, garlic, salt, pepper, jalapeños, shallot, cilantro, and cumin. Pour over steaks. Put in fridge and marinate for four hours. Pour marinade into a small sauce pot. Heat to boiling. Lower heat. Simmer for fifteen minutes. Grill steaks to desired doneness, brushing with marinade as you grill. Garnish with lime wedges before serving. Good for two steaks.

"Go to your bosom: Knock there, and ask
your heart what it doth know."
—William Shakespeare

Rosemary Marinade

1/2 onion, minced
2–3 cloves of garlic, minced
1/4 cup balsamic vinegar (50 ml)
1/8 cup light soy sauce (25 ml)
1 tbsp. Dijon mustard (15 ml)
1 1/4 tbsp. rosemary leaves (16 ml)
1/2 tsp. salt (2 ml)
1/2 tsp. black pepper (2 ml)

Mix marinade ingredients together. Pour in a plastic bag. Add steaks. Marinate the steaks in the fridge, turning frequently until ready to grill. Good for two steaks.

Graham's Marinade

2 tbsp. lemon juice (30 ml)
2 tbsp. olive oil (30 ml)
1/4 tsp. garlic powder (1 ml)
1/4 tsp. fresh-cracked pepper (1 ml)
1/4 tsp. sea salt (1 ml)

Pierce steaks through with a fork. Combine marinade ingredients in a small bowl. Brush marinade on steaks on both sides. Let stand for fifteen minutes before grilling. Good for two steaks.

Bleu Cheese Steaks
(with Red Wine)

4 sirloin or filet mignon steaks wrapped with bacon
4 tbsp. butter
3 cloves of garlic, crushed
1 shallot, chopped
1 tbsp. fresh thyme, chopped (15 ml)
1 cup beef broth (250 ml)
1/4 cup red wine (50 ml)
1/2 cup bleu cheese, crumbled (125 ml)
1/4 cup crushed breadcrumbs (50 ml)
1 tbsp. parsley (15 ml)
Salt and pepper to taste

For wine sauce, melt butter in a hot skillet. Add shallot and thyme. Sauté for three to four minutes. Add beef broth and wine. Gently boil for ten minutes. Turn off heat. Set aside. In a small bowl, blend blue cheese, breadcrumbs, and parsley. Set aside. Sprinkle steaks with salt and pepper. Place on preheated broiling pan and place under broiler. Broil until desired doneness. Press cheese mixture atop steaks. Broil for two minutes more. Spoon wine sauce over. Serves four

Jalapeño Steaks
(with Tequila)

2 good-quality steaks of your choice
2/3 cup frozen orange juice concentrate (150 ml)
1/2 cup tequila (125 ml)
1/3 cup lime juice (75 ml)
2 tbsp. olive oil (30 ml)
2 tbsp. fresh ginger, grated (30 ml)
3–4 garlic cloves, minced
1 tsp. salt (5 ml)
1 tsp. Mexican oregano (5 ml)
1 tsp. hot chili powder (5 ml)
2–3 jalapeño peppers, minced
Cilantro sprigs
Lime wedges

In a medium bowl, combine orange juice, tequila, lime juice, olive oil, ginger, garlic, salt, oregano, chili powder, and jalapeño peppers. Pour over steaks and marinate for four hours, turning often. Drain marinade from steaks. Reserve. Place steaks on hot grill. Grill until desired doneness, brushing with reserved marinade. Garnish with cilantro sprigs and lime wedges. Serves two.

Cognac Pepper Steak

4 top loin steaks cut one inch thick (2.54 cm)
4 tsp. peppercorns, coarsely cracked (20 ml)
1 garlic clove, crushed
2 tbsp. butter (30 ml)
1 tbsp. olive oil (15 ml)
1/3 cup cognac (75 ml)
1/3 cup liquid whipping cream (75 ml)

Press peppercorns into both sides of steaks. Let stand for thirty minutes. Heat butter and olive oil in medium-hot flameproof skillet. Add steaks. Grill to desired doneness. Sprinkle with salt. Add cognac and ignite, allowing flames to subside. Remove steaks to a hot platter. Add cream and garlic to skillet. Bring to boiling. Pour over steaks. If desired, use beef stock instead of cream. If using beef stock, omit garlic. Serves four.

"We would be able to live in this world more peacefully if our spirituality closely looked at the world around us, appreciating its depth and divinity."
Anonymous

Argentina Flank Steak

2 flank steaks
1 cup parsley, chopped, solidly packed (250 ml)
1/2 cup virgin olive oil (125 ml)
1/4 cup red wine vinegar (50 ml)
6 cloves of garlic, minced
3 tbsp. fresh cilantro, chopped (45 ml)
1 tsp. oregano (5 ml)
1/2 tsp. chili flakes (2 ml)
1/2 tsp. salt (2 ml)
1/4 tsp. black pepper (1 ml)

In a medium bowl, combine parsley, oil, vinegar, garlic, cilantro, oregano, chili flakes, salt, and pepper. Pour into plastic bag. Pierce steaks well with fork and put in bag with marinade. Marinate overnight or up to twenty-four hours. Preheat barbecue grill to medium-high. Remove steaks from marinade. Grill to desired doneness. Remove from heat. Let stand a few minutes. Slice across grain. Serves two.

Filet Mignon
(with Brown Sauce)

4 filet mignon steaks cut one inch thick (2.54 cm)
Salt and pepper to taste
1 tbsp. oil (15 ml)
2 tbsp. butter, divided (30 ml)
2 tbsp. shallots, chopped (30 ml)
1/2 cup dry red wine (125 ml)
1/2 cup prepared brown sauce (125 ml)

Heat oil and one tablespoon of butter in heavy skillet on medium-high. Sprinkle steaks with salt and pepper. Add to skillet and cook to desired doneness. Transfer to warm serving platter. Add shallots and one tablespoon of the butter to skillet and sauté briefly. Pour wine over. Cook until almost reduced by half. Add brown sauce. Cook for two more minutes. Spoon sauce over steaks. Serves four.

Brown Sauce

2 tbsp. butter (30 ml)
1 tbsp. flour (15 ml)
1 cup beef stock (250 ml)

Melt butter in a heavy sauce pot. Add flour and mix vigorously. Slowly add beef stock and cook until thick and bubbly. Pour over steaks.

"I do not feel obliged to believe that the same God who has endowed us with sense, reason, and intellect has intended us to forgo their use."
—Galileo Galilei

Steak Diane

4 boneless sirloin steaks
Salt and pepper to taste
2 tbsp. olive oil (30 ml)
2 tbsp. butter, divided (30 ml)
4 tbsp. chives, chopped (60 ml)
3 tbsp. cognac (45 ml)
3 tbsp. parsley, chopped (45 ml)
1 1/4 tsp. Dijon mustard (6 ml)
1/2 tsp. Worcestershire sauce (2 ml)
1 tbsp. beef broth (15 ml)
1 tbsp. butter (15 ml)

Pound steaks with mallet to quarter-inch (6.35 mm) thickness to soften fibers. Sprinkle with salt and pepper on both sides. Add olive oil and butter to a large skillet. Heat to medium-hot. Add steaks and fry until desired doneness. Transfer to hot serving platter. Add shallots to skillet and briefly sauté. Add cognac, parsley, mustard, and Worcestershire sauce. Add beef broth. Swirl in remaining butter. Pour over steaks. Serves four.

Pot Roast
(with Apple Cider and Gravy)

3 1/2-lb. beef chuck pot roast (1 1/2 kg)
Salt and pepper to taste
2 tbsp. oil (30 ml)
2 onions, chopped
2 tsp. gingerroot, grated (10 ml)
2 cups apple cider (500 ml)
2 cups carrots, sliced (500 ml)
2 cloves of garlic, minced

Sprinkle roast with salt and pepper. In a heavy-bottomed pot, brown roast on all sides in hot oil. Drain fat from pot. Add onion, apple cider, carrots, garlic, and ginger. Bring to boil. Immediately lower heat. Cover pot and simmer for one and a half hours on the stove top until pot roast is fork tender. Remove roast and vegetables to a platter. Reserve liquid for gravy. Serves six.

Gravy

1 cup sour cream (250 ml)
2 tbsp. cornstarch (30 ml)
Salt and pepper

In a small bowl, combine sour cream with cornstarch. Stir into pot roast liquids. Cook on medium-high until thickened. Season to taste with additional salt and pepper if desired.

Beer Pot Roast

3-lb. boneless beef roast (1.5 kg)
1 tsp. thyme (5 ml)
1 tsp. salt (5 ml)
1/2 tsp. pepper (2 ml)
2 tbsp. oil (30 ml)
1 onion, chopped
3 cloves of garlic, minced
2 tbsp. flour (30 ml)
1 bottle beer
1 cup beef both (250 ml)
2 tbsp. ketchup (30 ml)
1 1/2 tsp. Worcestershire sauce (7 ml)
1 lb. sweet potatoes, peeled and chopped (448 g)
1 lb. new potatoes (448 g)
4 carrots, chopped
1 cup frozen peas (250 ml)
1 tbsp. balsamic vinegar (15 ml)
1 tbsp. brown sugar (15 ml)

Rub thyme, salt, and pepper over roast. Set aside. Heat oil in a heavy-bottomed pot over medium heat. Cook onion and garlic in oil until softened, about three to five minutes. Add flour. Gradually whisk in beer, broth, ketchup, and Worcestershire sauce. Add sweet potatoes, potatoes and carrots. Place roast atop vegetables. Cover. Lower heat and simmer on stove top or bake at 325°F (165°C) for two and a half to three hours, or until beef is fork tender, basting occasionally. Add frozen peas, vinegar, brown sugar, salt, and pepper. Transfer beef to cutting board to sit for a few minutes before slicing. Serves six.

"In the end, coming to faith remains for all
a sense of homecoming, of picking up the
threads of a lost life, of responding to a bell
that had long been ringing, of taking a place
at a table that had long been vacant."
—Malcolm Muggeridge

Prime Rib
(with Garlic Peppercorn Crust and Yorkshire Pudding)

1 ten-pound standing rib roast
6 garlic cloves, crushed
1 1/2 tbsp. coarse sea salt (22 ml)
1 tbsp. peppercorns, crushed (15 ml)
1 tsp. black pepper (5 ml)
1 tbsp. thyme, chopped (15 ml)
2 tsp. paprika (10 ml)
3 tsp. olive oil (15 ml)
1 cup dry red wine (250 ml)
1/2 cup port (125 ml)
1 cup beef stock (250 ml)

In a small bowl, make a thick paste of garlic, salt, peppercorns, pepper, thyme, paprika, and olive oil. Rub into roast on all sides. Place roast bone side down in a large roasting pan. Cover loosely with tinfoil. Let stand at room temperature for thirty minutes. Preheat oven to 450°F (230°C). Remove foil and put roast in hot oven for thirty minutes. Reduce oven temperature to 350°F (180°C). Continue roasting for sixty minutes for rare up to seventy-five minutes for medium rare. Remove and tent loosely with foil. Let sit for twenty minutes before carving. Serves ten to twelve.

Meanwhile, for gravy, drain meat juices from roasting pan and reserve.
Add wine, port, and beef stock to roasting pan. Stir briskly. Bring to boil. Remove from heat and strain into serving dish. Keep warm while making Yorkshire pudding. Serve with roast and pudding.

Yorkshire Pudding
(You can make batter ahead of time. Just keep it in the blender.)

1 cup unbleached white flour (250 ml)
1 cup whole milk (250 ml)
4 large organic eggs
1/2 tsp. salt (2 ml)
3 tbsp. melted butter (45 ml)
Oil
Reserved meat juices from roast

Put flour, milk, eggs, salt, and melted butter in blender. Blend well. Touch blend button every few seconds. The more you blend, the more air gets into the batter to create very light and fluffy Yorkshires. Pour batter into a very hot preheated 400°F (200°C) heavily oiled muffin tins filled a quarter of the way up with oil and reserved meat juices. Bake for twenty-five minutes without opening the oven. Serve with butter and gravy. Makes twelve. Note: Yorkshires are like the classic popovers. If you like, you can eliminate the meat juices altogether and just use oil.

"Not all of us can do great things. But we
can do small things with great love."
—Mother Theresa

Cajun Prime Rib Steaks

After completing a run of A Streetcar Named Desire *(set in Louisiana) in which my director cast me in the role of Blanche Du Bois, I served this recipe as a thank-you gift. This recipe has heat, so if you're not too fond of spice, tone down the amount of rub.*

(Preparation one day ahead.)

10-lb. prime rib roast (4 1/2 kg) (have your butcher crack the ribs)
1/4 cup black pepper (50 ml)
1/4 cup garlic powder (50 ml)
1/4 cup salt (50 ml)
2 medium onions, thinly sliced

Additional seasonings. Combine in a small dish and store for next day's use.

1 tbsp. salt (15 ml)
1 tbsp. white pepper (15 ml)
1 tbsp. black pepper (15 ml)
2 1/2 tsp. dry mustard (12 ml)
2 tsp. cayenne pepper (10 ml)

Remove fat cap off prime rib and save. Place the roast, standing on bones, in a large roasting pan. With sharp knife, make several deep slashes in roast so seasoning can get through. Sprinkle roast generously with black pepper, garlic powder, and salt. Carefully arrange onions on top. Replace fat cap. Put in fridge. Refrigerate for twenty-four hours. Next day put roast in oven at 550°F (290°C) for thirty-five minutes. Remove. Put back in in fridge for three hours. After three hours remove from fridge and discard fat cap. Scrape onions off roast, along with the seasonings, and discard. With a long knife, slice between the ribs of the roast into six steaks (four of the steaks will have bones). Sprinkle both sides of each steak with additional seasonings. Grill on medium-hot grill until desired doneness. Serves six.

"If you want to better yourself, better your fellow being. If you want to feel the richness and warmth of unfailing love, give it. If you want to make a difference and leave your world a better place, let others know how important they are as you put their needs above yours."
–Jaren L. Davis

Mustard Herb-Crusted Roast Pork

4-lb. boneless pork roast (2 kg)
1/2 cup Dijon mustard (125 ml)
1/4 cup stoneground mustard (50 ml)
2 tbsp. lemon juice (30 ml)
1 tbsp. lemon zest (15 ml)
2 tbsp. rosemary, chopped (30 ml)
2 tbsp. sage, chopped (30 ml)
4 tbsp. fresh garlic, minced
1 1/2 tsp. salt (7 ml)
1 1/2 tsp. fresh-cracked pepper (7 ml)

Preheat oven to 425°F (220°C). Spray medium-sized roasting pan with cooking oil. Set aside. In a small bowl, whisk Dijon mustard, stoneground mustard, lemon juice, and lemon zest. Make gashes in pork with sharp knife and rub mixture over pork. Place in roasting pan. Roast for forty-five minutes. Meanwhile, in small bowl, mix rosemary, sage, garlic, salt, and fresh-cracked pepper together. Set aside. Remove pork from oven. Pat herb mixture on top and sides until well coated. Return to oven. Reduce temperature to 350°F (180°C). Roast for forty-five more minutes. Let rest a few minutes to firm before carving. Serves six to eight.

Cranberry Ginger Pork Roast

4-lb. pork roast (2 kg)
1 cup frozen chopped cranberries (250 ml)
1/4 cup pure maple syrup (50 ml)
1-2 canned chipotle peppers, chopped
2 tablespoons ginger, grated (30 ml)
1/4 cup dark soy sauce (50 ml)
1/8 cup water (25 ml)
1/4 tsp. salt (1 ml)
1/4 tsp. fresh cracked pepper (1 ml)

Put cranberries, syrup, chipotle peppers, ginger, soy sauce, water, and salt in blender and blend well. Rub well into roast on all sides. Roast in hot 350°F oven (180°C) for ninety minutes. Let stand a few minutes before carving. Serves six to eight.

"Any good work, kindness, or service, I can render to any person or animal, let me do it now. Let me not neglect, or delay, to do it, for I will not pass this way again."
—Old Quaker saying

Pork Tenderloin
(with Brandied Apples)

1-lb. pork tenderloin (448 g)
2 tbsp. Dijon mustard (30 ml)
1/4 tsp. salt (1 ml)
1 tbsp. olive oil (15 ml)
2 tbsp. butter (30 ml)
2 red apples, cored and thinly sliced
1 tbsp. sugar (15 ml)
Dash of white pepper
1 tbsp. chopped rosemary (15 ml)
1/3 cup brandy (75 ml)

Preheat oven to 375°F (190°C). Brush both sides of the tenderloin with mustard. Sprinkle with salt and pepper. Heat oil in a medium-hot skillet. Add tenderloin and sear, turning often until golden, about 1 minute per side. Transfer to the roasting pan. Roast for twenty-five to thirty minutes or until cooked through and no longer pink inside. Remove from oven and place on cutting board. Let stand for five minutes before slicing into medallions. Serves two.

Meanwhile, in medium-hot skillet, melt butter. Add apples, sugar, pepper, and rosemary. Simmer for four minutes or until apples are tender. Add brandy. Bring to a boil. Boil for one minute. Remove from heat. Serve over tenderloin.

Wiener Schnitzel

4 veal scaloppini or 4 boneless pork chops
Salt and pepper to taste
2 eggs, lightly beaten
3 tbsp. water (45 ml)
1/2 cup flour for dredging (125 ml)
1 cup crushed breadcrumbs (250 ml)
1/4 cup vegetable oil (50 ml)
1 lemon, cut up
6 tbsp. butter (90 ml)
1/4 cup capers, drained (optional) (50 ml)

Place veal or pork chops between sheets of plastic wrap. Pound thin with a mallet until doubled in size and almost transparent. Sprinkle with salt and pepper. Pour flour onto a plate. On a separate plate, whisk eggs and water and put beside the first plate. Pour breadcrumbs onto a third plate. Line plates side by side. Coat veal or pork chops with flour. Dip in egg. Dip in breadcrumbs. Heat oil in a large skillet to medium-hot. Add veal or pork. Fry for three to four minutes per side or until golden. Remove from skillet. Keep warm. Heat butter in skillet until it foams. When foam subsides, pour the butter evenly over schnitzel. Squeeze lemon over it. Garnish with capers if desired. Serves four.

Scalloped Pork Chops

6–8 pork chops
1 tbsp. stoneground mustard (15 ml)
1 tbsp. cooking oil (15 ml)
6–8 russet potatoes, peeled and sliced thin
2 large onions, sliced into rings
2 cans cream of mushroom soup, undiluted (568 ml)
1 soup can of milk (284 ml)
1/2 tsp. salt (2 ml)
1/2 tsp. pepper (2 ml)
1/2 tsp. marjoram (2 ml)
1/2 tsp. sage (2 ml)

Brush the pork chops with mustard on both sides. Heat the cooking oil in a medium-hot skillet. Add pork chops. Fry until golden, about one minute per side. Remove from the skillet. Layer potatoes, onion, and chops in nine-by-thirteen-inch baking pan (22x33 cm). Blend the mushroom soup with milk, salt, pepper, marjoram, and sage. Pour over chops. Bake covered at 350°F (180°C) for ninety minutes, removing foil for the last few minutes. Serves three to four.

Tequila-Glazed Ribs

4 lbs. spareribs (2 kg)
Salt and pepper
1 tbsp. hot chili garlic sauce (15 ml)
2 tbsp. soy sauce (30 ml)
1/3 cup frozen concentrated orange juice (75 ml)
1/4 cup frozen concentrated lime juice (50 ml)
2/3 cup tequila (150 ml)
4 cloves of garlic, minced
Pinch each of lemon and lime zest
3/4 cup brown sugar (175 ml)

Preheat oven to 350°F (180°C). Place ribs on a large baking sheet and sprinkle with salt and pepper. Cover with tinfoil. Bake for ninety minutes. While baking, combine hot chili garlic sauce, soy sauce, orange and lime concentrate, tequila, garlic, zest, and brown sugar in a medium saucepot. Bring just to a boil. Lower heat and simmer for twenty minutes. Set aside. Remove ribs from the oven and liberally coat with sauce. Return to the oven. Do not cover. Bake for thirty minutes more or until crispy. Serves six to eight.

```
"As thy days, so shall thy strength be."
             Deuteronomy 33:25
```

Barbecued Ribs

4 lbs. beef ribs (2 kg)
4 cups ketchup (1 L)
4 garlic cloves, minced
1 tsp. pepper (5 ml)
1 tbsp. smoky paprika (15 ml)
4 tbsp. chili powder (60 ml)
Dash of liquid smoke
Dash of Worcestershire sauce
1/2 tsp. dry mustard powder (5 ml)
1/2 cup white vinegar (125 ml)
1/4 cup brown sugar (50 ml)

To a large saucepan add ketchup, garlic, pepper, paprika, chili powder, liquid smoke, Worcestershire sauce, mustard powder, vinegar, and sugar. Stir well. Bring to boil. Reduce heat and simmer for twenty minutes. Taste and adjust seasonings as desired. Remove from heat and set aside. Place ribs on a roasting rack and roast in a hot oven at 350°F (180°C) for ninety minutes. Remove from oven. Pour half the sauce the on ribs. Return to the oven and bake another thirty minutes, basting frequently with remaining sauce, until ribs are crisp and tender. Serves six to eight. Note: If desired, use baby back ribs in place of beef ribs. Cook for same amount of time.

"May
God's smile shine
On every path
You take
And may every
Turn in the
Road bring new
Blessings."
-A Celtic blessing

Seventeen most important things to remember in life:

1. Never give up on anybody; miracles happen every day.
2. Be brave. Even if you're not, pretend to be. No one can tell the difference.
3. Think big thoughts, relish small pleasures.
4. Learn to listen. Opportunity sometimes knocks very softly.
5. Never deprive someone of hope; it might be all they have.
6. Strive for excellence, not perfection.
7. Don't waste time grieving over past mistakes. Learn from them and move on.
8. When someone hugs you, let them be the first to let go.
9. Never cut what can be untied.
10. Don't expect life to be fair.
11. Remember: Success comes to the one who acts first.
12. Never waste an opportunity to tell someone you love them.
13. Remember that nobody makes it alone. Have a grateful heart, and be quick to acknowledge those who help you.
14. Never underestimate the power of a kind word or deed.
15. Laugh a lot. A good sense of humor cures almost all life's ills.
16. Don't miss the magic of the moment by focusing on what's to come.
17. Watch for big problems. They disguise big opportunities.

—Kelsey, *Board of Wisdom*

Poultry

Coq Au Vin 240
Roasted Herb Chicken 241
Judy's Chicken Picatta 242
Bourbon Street Chicken 243
Chicken Casserole 244
Beer Can Chicken 245
Chicken Bella. 246
Chicken Parmesan 247
Orange Pheasant 248
Chicken Cacciatora. 249
Indian Chicken. 250

Coq Au Vin

6 slices of bacon, cooked and crumbled (save drippings)
3 1/2 lbs. chicken thighs and breasts (1 1/2 kg)
Salt and pepper
3 tbsp. brandy (45 ml)
2 tbsp. flour (30 ml)
1 cup dry red wine (250 ml)
2 cloves of garlic, minced
1 bay leaf
1/2 tsp. rosemary (2 ml)
1/4 tsp. thyme (1 ml)
1 cup pearl onions (250 ml)
1 cup whole mushrooms (250 ml)
1/2 cup carrots, sliced (125 ml)
1 stick celery, sliced

In a large skillet over medium heat, brown chicken in bacon drippings for fifteen minutes or until golden brown on all sides. Pour brandy over it. Carefully ignite brandy. When flame subsides, remove chicken from skillet and place on platter. Add flour to the skillet drippings, along with wine. Stir well. Add bay leaf, rosemary, thyme, onions, mushrooms, carrots, and celery. Return chicken. Cover and simmer for thirty minutes or until chicken is cooked through. Serves four.

Roasted Herb Chicken

My mother, Angela, inspired this herb-roasted chicken recipe. A fabulous hostess, Mom always pulled out chairs and set out extra plates with a welcoming smile for whoever came to her door. Over time, as the size of the guests grew, so did the size of her tables. It is said God loves a generous giver. If so, God must really love my mother, who is ever so generous in hospitality to the hungry and thirsty. This dish is fast and easy to prepare, a byword my busy mom is always looking for. (If cooking for a crowd, use two roasting chickens. Double oil and spice as needed to coat.)

> 3-lb. whole roasting chicken (1350 g)
> 3 tbsp. olive oil (45 ml)
> 2 cloves of garlic, crushed
> 1/2 tsp. rosemary (2 ml)
> 1/4 tsp. thyme (1 ml)
> 1/2 tsp. onion powder (2 ml)
> 1/4 tsp. salt (1 ml)
> 1/4 tsp. pepper (1 ml)
> 1/4 tsp. paprika (1 ml)
> 2 tbsp. lemon juice (30 ml)
> 1 whole lemon
> Sprig each/thyme, rosemary

Pour oil in a small dish. Add garlic, rosemary, thyme, onion powder, salt, pepper, paprika, and lemon juice. Mix well. Raise skin from chicken breast and rub mixture well into the breast. Release skin. Rub top and sides until chicken is entirely coated. Roll whole lemon between the palms of your hands to release its fragrance, slightly bruising the lemon. Place inside the cavity of the chicken. Place sprig of thyme inside the cavity. Lay the chicken on the rosemary sprig. Bake uncovered in preheated oven at 350°F (180°C) for ninety minutes. Serves four.

Judy's Chicken Picatta

4 chicken cutlets
Salt and pepper
All-purpose flour
2 tbsp. cooking oil (30 ml)
1/3 cup white wine (75 ml)
1 garlic clove, minced
1/2 cup chicken stock (125 ml)
2 tbsp. lemon juice (30 ml)
1 tbsp. capers (15 ml)
2 tbsp. butter (30 ml)
1 whole lemon, sliced
2 tbsp. fresh chopped parsley (30 ml)

Season cutlets on both sides with salt and pepper. Dust with flour. Heat oil on medium heat in a large skillet. Add cutlets. Sauté for two to three minutes on one side. Turn and cook the other side for two minutes with skillet covered. Transfer cutlets to a warm platter. Pour fat from the skillet. Add wine and deglaze. Add minced garlic. Cook for two minutes. Add chicken broth, lemon juice, and capers. Return cutlets to skillet and cook each side for one minute. Transfer to a warm platter. Add butter to skillet and melt. Add lemon slices. Pour over cutlets. Garnish with fresh-chopped parsley. Serves two.

Bourbon Street Chicken

6 skinless chicken breasts
1 1/2 tsp. ginger (7 ml)
Pinch of cayenne
1/2 tsp. garlic powder (2 ml)
1/2 cup soy sauce (125 ml)
1/2 cup onion, minced (125 ml)
1/2 cup brown sugar (125 ml)
1/3 cup bourbon (75 ml)

In a medium bowl, make a marinade by combining ginger, cayenne, garlic powder, soy sauce, onion, brown sugar, and bourbon. Whisk until blended. Pour marinade over chicken and place in fridge for several hours or overnight. Preheat oven to 350°F (180°C). Remove chicken from marinade, reserving the marinade, and place side by side in a nine-by-thirteen-inch baking dish (22x33 cm). Cover dish in tinfoil. Place in the preheated oven. Pour reserved marinade into a small pot and simmer for ten minutes. Baste chicken frequently with the marinade until chicken is cooked through, thirty to thirty-five minutes. Serves six. Note: if desired, grill chicken breasts on barbecue on medium-hot heat for twenty-five minutes or until no longer pink inside, turning frequently.

Chicken Casserole

1 lb. skinless chicken breasts (448 g)
1 tbsp. butter (15 ml)
1 ten-ounce can of cream of chicken soup (284 ml)
1/3 cup roasted red peppers (75 ml)
1/3 cup apple cider (75 ml)
4 tbsp. tomato sauce (60 ml)
2 garlic cloves, chopped
1/2 tsp. fresh-cracked pepper (2 ml)
2 tbsp. fresh basil leaves, chopped (30 ml)
1/3 cup grated mozzarella cheese (75 ml)

Brown chicken breasts in butter in a large skillet on medium heat for five minutes. Add to skillet cream of chicken soup, roasted red pepper, apple cider, tomato sauce, garlic, and pepper. Bring to a boil and then reduce heat. Cover and simmer for twenty to thirty minutes or until chicken is no longer pink inside. Sprinkle with chopped basil and mozzarella cheese. Serves four.

Beer Can Chicken

1 four-pound whole chicken (2 kg)
2 tbsp. vegetable oil (30 ml)
Dry spice rub, as much as needed
1 can beer
1 large russet potato, raw

Rinse chicken. Remove giblets and neck and discard. Pat the chicken dry with a paper towel. Rub with oil. Snap open the beer can's tab and drain a little beer out. With a can opener, make two holes beside the open tab. Spoon a little dry rub into the beer can. Then sprinkle a little rub inside the chicken cavity. Smooth remaining rub over entire chicken to coat. Place the beer can on a hard surface, and push the chicken, cavity side down, onto the can so that the can almost disappears. Put a potato in the neck cavity of the chicken to seal it tightly. Transfer chicken to a barbeque, placing in center of grate. Cover the grill and cook the chicken over medium-high indirect heat (no direct burners under chicken) for ninety minutes or until juice from chicken runs clear. Remove and rest for ten minutes before carving. Serves four to six.

Dry Rub

1/4 cup brown sugar (50 ml)
4 tbsp. chili powder (60 ml)
3/4 tsp. cayenne (4 ml)
1 level tbsp. garlic powder (15 ml)
2 tsp. dry mustard powder (10 ml)
2 tsp. each salt and pepper (10 ml)

Mix ingredients well in a small bowl.

Chicken Bella

12 chicken thighs
12 cloves of garlic, chopped
1 onion, chopped
1 1/2 tbsp. oregano (22 ml)
1 tbsp. rosemary (15 ml)
1/2 tsp. thyme (2 ml)
Salt and pepper to taste
1/4 cup wine vinegar (50 ml)
1/4 cup olive oil (50 ml)
1 cup dried apricots, chopped (250 ml)
1/2 cup pitted black olives (125 ml)
1/4 cup capers, drained (50 ml)
2 tbsp. caper brine (30 ml)
4 bay leaves
1/3 cup brown sugar (75 ml)
1 cup white wine (250 ml)
1/4 cup fresh chopped parsley (50 ml)

In a large mixing bowl, combine garlic, onion, oregano, rosemary, thyme, salt, pepper, vinegar, oil, chopped apricots, olives, capers, brine, and bay leaves. Add chicken pieces and coat well. Cover bowl with plastic wrap and marinate for several hours or overnight in fridge. Preheat oven to 350°F (180°C). Put the chicken in a thirteen-by-nine-inch baking dish (22x33 cm) or larger so as not to crowd it. Stir brown sugar into marinade and pour over chicken. Pour wine around the sides. Bake for sixty minutes, basting occasionally. Serves six.

Chicken Parmesan
(with Wine)

4 skinless chicken breasts
Salt and pepper to taste
1/2 cup butter, divided (125 ml)
1 cup panko breadcrumbs (250 ml)
2/3 cup fresh Parmesan cheese, grated (150 ml)
4 tablespoons shallots (60 ml)
1/2 tsp. tarragon (2 ml)
1/3 cup white wine (75 ml)

Salt and pepper the chicken breasts. Melt half the butter in a heavy bottomed medium-hot skillet. Add chicken breasts to skillet. Fry for two to three minutes per side. Remove. Transfer to a warm platter. Add shallots to the skillet and sauté for one minute. Remove and set aside. In a medium bowl, blend breadcrumbs with Parmesan cheese and remaining butter. Divide into four portions. Press a portion to both sides of chicken breasts. Transfer chicken to baking sheet. Carefully pour wine around chicken. Sprinkle with shallots and tarragon. Bake uncovered at 400°F (200°C) for ten minutes, or until golden. Cover with lid. Continue baking for twenty-five minutes or until chicken is no longer pink inside. Serves four.

Orange Pheasant

2 pheasants or roasting chickens, 3 lbs. each (1350 g)
2 tsp. fresh-chopped sage (10 ml)
1/2 tsp. salt (2 ml)
1/4 tsp. pepper (1 ml)
2 oranges, peeled and chopped
1/2 cup orange juice (125 ml)
1/2 cup white wine (125 ml)
2 tbsp. brown sugar (30 ml)
2 tbsp. cider vinegar (30 ml)
2 whole cloves
1/4 tsp. ginger (1 ml)
4 tsp. cornstarch (20 ml)
2 tbsp. orange liqueur (30 ml)
2 tsp. grated orange rind (10 ml)

In a small bowl, mix sage with salt and pepper and sprinkle inside the cavity of the birds. Fill cavity with chopped orange. Place birds, breast side up, in a roasting pan. In a medium bowl, combine orange juice, wine, sugar, vinegar, cloves, and ginger. Pour over birds. Place birds in cold oven. Turn oven to 400°F (200°C). Bake for ninety minutes. Remove the birds from the oven and transfer to a warm serving platter. Remove chopped orange from cavity and discard. Make sauce and spoon over birds. Serves six.

Sauce

Skim fat from pan juices and discard. Strain juices, reserving 1 1/2 cups (375 ml). In a small saucepan, mix cornstarch with orange liqueur. Slowly add pan juices to mixture. Add orange rind. Cook until thickened and bubbly.

"Don't keep the boxes of your love and tenderness sealed until your friends are gone. Fill their lives with sweetness. Speak approving, cheering words while their ears can hear them and while their hearts can be thrilled by them."
—George W. Childs

Chicken Cacciatora

2 whole roasting chickens, 3 lbs. each, cut in pieces (2700 g)
1/2 cup sunflower oil (125 ml)
2 large green peppers, diced
1 large red pepper, diced
1 1/2 cups fresh mushrooms, diced (375 ml)
1 cup onion, diced (250 ml)
1 cup dry white wine (250 ml)
2 cups chicken stock (500 ml)
4 cups, fresh or canned, Italian plum tomatoes (900 g)
1 tsp. oregano (5 ml)
Pinch of chili pepper flakes
Salt and pepper to taste

Pour oil into heavy skillet and heat to medium-hot. Add chicken pieces in batches, careful not to crowd. Fry for ten minutes or until all sides are golden, turning chicken frequently with tongs. Remove from skillet. Drain excess oil from skillet. Add green and red peppers, mushrooms, and onion. Sauté for five minutes. Add white wine. Add chicken broth and plum tomatoes. Sprinkle with oregano and chili pepper flakes. Add salt and pepper to taste. Simmer for thirty minutes or until chicken is tender and sauce thickened. Serves six.

Indian Chicken

3 lbs. chicken pieces (1350 g)
Salt and pepper to taste
2 tbsp. butter (30 ml)
3/4 cup onion, minced (175 ml)
1/3 cup celery, minced (75 ml)
1/2 tsp. garlic powder (2 ml)
2 tbsp. curry powder (30 ml)
1/2 tsp. turmeric (2 ml)
1/2 tsp. chili powder (2 ml)
1 cup tart apple cut small (250 ml)
1/2 cup bananas cut small (125 ml)
1 cup chicken broth 375 ml)
1 cup heavy cream (250 ml)

Sprinkle chicken with salt and pepper. Heat butter in medium-hot skillet and add chicken pieces, skin side down. Cook until golden, about five minutes. Add onion, celery, and garlic. Sprinkle with curry powder, turmeric, and chili. Sauté briefly. Add apples and banana. Simmer for five minutes. Add chicken broth and stir gently. Cover skillet. Simmer for twenty-five minutes or until chicken is tender and no longer pink through. Remove chicken to platter. Pour skillet contents into blender and puree. Return contents to skillet. Add cream. Add chicken. Heat through. Serves four.

Sauces

To Sauce the Dish

Basic Béchamel Sauce 252

Cheese Sauce 252

Herb Garlic Sauce 252

Lemon Chive Sauce 252

Mornay Sauce 253

Blender Hollandaise Sauce 253

Classic Hollandaise 254

Béarnaise Sauce 255

Quick Alfredo Sauce 255

Garlic Cream Sauce 256

Basic Béchamel Sauce

2 tbsp. butter (30 ml)
2 tbsp. flour (30 ml)
1/4 tsp. salt (1 ml)
dash pepper
1 cup whole milk (250 ml)

Melt butter in a small saucepan. Whisk in flour, salt, and pepper. Add milk all at once and stir till thick and bubbly. Keep warm till use. Good with steamed vegetables or with fish. Makes one cup (250 ml).

Cheese Sauce

Make basic béchamel sauce, but increase milk to 1 1/4 cups (300 ml). Stir in one cup of shredded cheddar cheese (250 ml). Serve over cooked vegetables.

Herb Garlic Sauce

Make basic béchamel sauce, but add one clove of minced garlic, 1/2 tsp. basil (2 ml), and 1/4 tsp. tarragon (1 ml). Serve with carrots, broccoli, or green beans.

Lemon Chive Sauce

Make basic béchamel sauce, but add 1 tbsp. chives (15 ml) and 2 tsp. lemon juice (10 ml). Serve with potatoes, asparagus, or fish.

Mornay Sauce

3 tbsp. butter (45 ml)
3 tbsp. flour (45 ml)
1/2 tsp. salt (2 ml)
1/4 tsp. nutmeg 1 ml)
Dash of pepper
1 1/4 cups cream (300 ml)
1/4 cup dry white wine (50 ml)
1/3 cup shredded cheese (75 ml)

Melt butter in a medium-hot saucepan. Add flour, salt, nutmeg, and pepper. Add cream all at once. Stir constantly for one minute. Stir in wine and cheese. Cook till cheese melts. Remove from heat. Serve with chicken, fish, or poached eggs. Makes 1 3/4 cups (425 ml).

"Health is the greatest gift. Contentment the greatest wealth. Faithfulness the best relationship."
—Buddha

Blender Hollandaise Sauce

3 egg yolks
1/2 cup melted butter (125 ml)
2 tbsp. lemon juice (30 ml)
1/4 tsp. salt (1 ml)
Pinch of black pepper
Pinch of cayenne (optional)

Put egg yolks in a blender. Very slowly, blending on low speed, pour in melted butter. Blend until thickened. Add lemon juice and black pepper. Add pinch of cayenne if desired. Serve hot over vegetables, poultry, fish, or eggs. Makes ten ounces (155 ml).

Classic Hollandaise

4 egg yolks
1/2 cup butter, softened (125 ml)
2 tbsp. lemon juice (30 ml)
Dash of salt
Dash of white pepper

Place egg yolks and one third of the butter in top of double boiler set to briskly boiling water. Stir rapidly. Add another third of butter and continue stirring rapidly. As butter melts, add remaining butter, stirring rapidly. Remove from heat. Stir in lemon juice, one teaspoon at a time. Season with salt and pepper as desired. Replace over boiling water and stir for two to three minutes until thickened. Sauce should be thick but pourable. If sauce curdles, immediately beat in two tablespoons of boiling water (30 ml) to smooth. Remove from heat. Serve hot over vegetables, poultry, fish, or eggs. Makes one cup (250 ml).

"Human beings must be known to be loved; but
Divine beings must be loved to be known."
-Blaise Pascal

Béarnaise Sauce

1/2 cup white vinegar (125 ml)
2 shallots, chopped
3–4 whole black peppercorns
1 bay leaf
1/3 tsp. dried tarragon (75 ml)
4 egg yolks
1 cup butter (250 ml)

Combine vinegar, shallots, peppercorns, bay leaf, and tarragon in a small saucepan. Bring to a boil. Reduce heat. Simmer, uncovered, until mixture is reduced by half. Strain. Reserve liquid. Place egg yolks in top of simmering double boiler, and stir until combined. Gradually stir in reserved liquid. Cut butter into small cubes and drop in liquid, one cube at a time, until all cubes are added. Stir gently and thoroughly. Remove sauce from simmering water. Pour in serving dish and let stand, covered, until ready to use. Serve over meat, poultry, or fish. Makes 3/4 cup (175 ml).

Quick Alfredo Sauce

1/2 cup butter (125 ml)
1 eight-ounce package cream cheese (250 ml)
2 tsp. garlic powder (10 ml)
2 cups whole milk or cream (500 ml)
1 cup fresh grated Parmesan cheese (250 ml)
1/4 tsp. white pepper (1 ml)

Melt butter in a nonstick saucepan over medium heat. Add cream cheese and garlic powder, stirring constantly until smooth. Add milk or cream a little at a time, whisking rapidly to smooth out any lumps. Stir in the Parmesan cheese and pepper. Remove from heat when sauce reaches desired consistency. (Sauce will thicken rapidly.) Thin sauce with additional milk or cream if it gets too thick. Good with pasta, steamed vegetables, or spaghetti squash. Makes four servings.

"Wise sayings often fall on barren ground;
but a kind word is never thrown away."
–Sir Arthur Helps

Garlic Cream Sauce

2 tbsp. butter
2 cloves of garlic, minced
3 tbsp. unbleached white flour
1 1/4 cups chicken broth
1/2 cup full fat sour cream

Melt butter in a medium-hot saucepan. Add garlic and sauté to brown., about thirty seconds. Whisk in flour. Add chicken broth slowly, continuing to whisk until smooth. Reduce heat. Cook till bubbly and thickened. Add sour cream. Heat through. Good on chicken, seafood, or pasta. Makes about 1 1/2 cups (375 ml).

"What we choose changes us.
Who we love transforms us.
How we create reshapes us.
What we do remakes us."
–Dr. Eugene Callender

Pasta

Pasta Primavera	260
Classic Lasagna	261
Pasta Verde	262
Basil Pesto Pasta	263
Spinach Pesto with Pasta	263
Parsley Almond Pesto Pasta	264
Sundried Tomato Pesto Pasta	265
Herb Butter Pasta	265
Penne with Tomato Eggplant Sauce	266
Spaghettini with Vodka Tomato Sauce	267
Italian Spaghetti	268
Bronwyn's Favorite Tuna Casserole	269
Chili Eggplant Noodles	270
Greek Pasta with Shrimp	271

Cooking Perfect Pasta

To get perfect pasta, follow these tips below:

- Fill a large stock pot with a gallon of water (approx. 4 L).
- Add one teaspoon of salt. Salt prevents sticking.
- Bring water to a rolling boil.
- Slowly add pasta of your choice and stir hardily so pasta will not stick.
- One part raw pasta will equal two parts cooked.
- Do not add oil. Oil makes pasta slippery and the sauce won't stick to it properly when done.
- Time the pasta. Most pasta cooks in eight to twelve minutes. Pasta should be al dente—firm yet tender, with a tiny core in the middle.
- Drain pasta in a colander, reserving a small amount of pasta water in a dish below the colander to add back later.
- Rinse the pasta (optional). If you like a starchier taste, don't rinse it. Rinsing does remove starch that helps cling the sauce to pasta.
- Add some reserved pasta water to pasta if pasta seems sticky or dry. Stir gently.
- Serve immediately, or keep covered and warm until ready for use, by placing over a pot of barely simmering water.

"Happiness is not an individual matter. When you are able to bring relief, or bring back the smile to one person, not only that person profits, but you also profit. The deepest happiness you can have comes from that capacity to help relieve the suffering of others. So if we have the habit of being peace, then there is a natural tendency for us to go in the direction of service. Nothing compels us, except the joy of sharing peace, the joy of sharing freedom from afflictions, freedom from worries, freedom from craving, which are the true foundations for happiness. And once we have the condition of peace and joy in us, we can afford to be in any situation. Even in the situation of hell, we will be able to contribute our peace and serenity. The most important thing is for each of us to have some freedom in our heart, some stability in our heart, some peace in our heart. Only then will we be able to relieve the suffering around us."

—Thich Nhat Hanh, Vietnamese Buddhist teacher

Pasta Primavera

1/2 lb linguini or fettuccini (250 g)
4 tbsp. butter, divided (60 ml)
2 cups broccoli florets (500 ml)
1 cup carrots, sliced (250 ml)
1 onion, thinly cut
2 cloves of garlic, crushed
1 cup fresh peas (250 ml)
1/2 cup almonds, sliced (125 ml)
1/2 tsp. thyme (2 ml)
1/4 tsp. sweet basil (1 ml)
Salt and pepper to taste
1/3 cup white wine (75 ml)

Cook pasta according to directions. While cooking, melt two tablespoons of butter in a medium-hot skillet. Stir in broccoli, carrots, onion, and garlic. Cook for three minutes. Stir in peas. Cook for one minute longer. Drain pasta. Stir into skillet with the remaining butter. Mix gently. Add sliced almonds, thyme, basil., and salt and pepper to taste. Add wine. Taste. Cover. Cook one to two more minutes. Arrange on two plates. Sprinkle with Parmesan cheese. Serves two.

Classic Lasagna

1 lb. lean ground beef (448 g)
2 cloves of garlic, minced
1 onion, chopped
1 1/2 cups can sliced mushrooms (300 ml)
1 tsp. oregano (5 ml)
1 tsp. salt (5 ml)
1/2 tsp. marjoram
1/2 tsp. basil (2 ml)
1/2 tsp. pepper (2 ml)
2 jars pasta sauce (796 ml each)
1/3 cup red wine (75 ml)
2 cups ricotta cheese (500 ml)
2 large eggs
1/3 cup Parmesan cheese (75 ml)
1/4 cup finely chopped parsley (50 ml)
3 cups shredded mozzarella cheese (750 ml)
8–10 no-boil lasagna noodles

Preheat oven to 375°F (190°C). Spread a cup of pasta sauce onto the bottom of a nine-by-thirteen-inch pan (22x33cm). In a skillet, over medium heat fry beef with garlic, onions, mushrooms, oregano, salt, marjoram, basil, and pepper until beef is cooked through, five to ten. minutes. Add remaining pasta sauce and wine. In a small bowl, mix ricotta cheese with eggs, Parmesan cheese, and parsley. Lay lasagna noodles side by side in pan. Spoon half the meat sauce on top. Spoon with half cheese sauce. Add another layer of noodles. Repeat layers. Sprinkle liberally with mozzarella cheese. Cover with tinfoil. Bake for forty-five minutes. Let rest for five to ten minutes before serving in order to firm. Serves eight.

Pasta Verde

4 eggs
1/3 cup heavy cream (75 ml)
1 1/2 cups mushrooms, sliced (375 ml)
1/3 cup onion, chopped (75 ml)
3 tbsp. butter (45 ml)
1 1/2 cups spinach, cooked and drained (375 ml)
2 cups hot cooked linguine or fettuccini (500 ml)
1 tbsp. butter (15 ml)
1 cup fresh-grated Parmesan cheese (250 ml)
Pinch of nutmeg
Pinch of cayenne (optional)
Pinch of salt
Pinch of pepper

Combine eggs with cream and let sit at room temperature for several minutes. In a hot skillet, cook mushrooms and onion in butter for four to five minutes. Stir in spinach. Toss pasta with butter. Add egg and cream and stir gently. Add nutmeg and cayenne if desired. Sprinkle with salt and pepper. Add mushrooms, onion, and spinach mixture. Sprinkle with cheese. Toss gently. Serves two.

"True greatness is inner self-emptying that manifests itself in service to others."
Anonymous

Basil Pesto Pasta

1 1/2 cups fresh basil leaves (375 ml)
4 cloves of garlic, crushed
1/3 cup pine nuts, toasted (75 ml)
1/4 cup Parmesan cheese, grated (50 ml)
1/4 cup lemon juice (50 ml)
1/4 cup olive oil (50 ml)
salt and pepper to taste

Blend all ingredients well in a food processor or blender. Cook pasta of choice according to directions. Top with pesto. Serves two.

"God honors faith. Not rightness in externals. Every thing and living being in creation is to be met, not used. All of God's creation has spirit in and through it."
Anonymous

Spinach Pesto with Pasta

1 1/2 cups fresh spinach, torn (375 ml)
1/2 cup Parmesan cheese, grated (125 ml)
1/4 cup almonds (50 ml)
2 cloves of garlic, crushed
1/4 cup olive oil (50 ml)
1 tsp. dried basil (5 ml)
Salt and pepper to taste

Blend ingredients in a food processor or blender. Cook pasta of choice according to directions. Top with pesto. Serves two.

Parsley Almond Pesto Pasta

1 clove of garlic, crushed
1 1/2 cups flat-leaf parsley, thick stems removed (375 ml)
3/4 tsp. salt (4 ml)
Dash of pepper
1/3 cup olive oil (75 ml)
1/3 cup almonds, unsalted and blanched (75 ml)
1/4 cup Parmesan cheese, grated (50 ml)
2 plum tomatoes, chopped

Blend garlic, parsley, salt, pepper, olive oil, almonds, and Parmesan cheese in food processor or blender. Cook pasta of choice according to directions. Toss with pesto. Add chopped plum tomatoes just before serving. Serves two.

"Between vision and fulfillment there is an arduous path to trod. If it seems to you that hades has broken loose, that nothing is going right, this may confirm your vision more than anything else!"
Anonymous

Sundried Tomato Pesto Pasta

1/3 cup sundried tomatoes (75 ml)
2 tbsp. fresh basil, chopped (30 ml)
2 tbsp. fresh parsley, chopped (30 ml)
1 tbsp. garlic, chopped (15 ml)
1/4 cup pine nuts, chopped (50 ml)
4 tbsp. onion, chopped (60 ml)
1/4 cup balsamic vinegar (50 ml)
1 tbsp. tomato paste (15 ml)
1/3 cup crushed tomatoes (75 ml)
1/4 cup red wine (50 ml)
1/2 cup olive oil (125 ml)
1/2 cup Parmesan cheese, grated (125 ml)
Salt and pepper to taste

Place sundried tomatoes in hot water until softened, about five minutes. Drain and chop. Add to food processor or blender. Add basil, parsley, garlic, pine nuts, onion, vinegar, tomato paste, crushed tomatoes, wine, olive oil, Parmesan cheese, and salt and pepper to taste. Blend well. Cook pasta of choice according to directions. Toss with pesto. Serves two.

Herb Butter Pasta

4 tbsp. butter, melted (60 ml)
1/4 tsp. basil (1 ml)
1/4 tsp. marjoram (1 ml)
1/4 tsp. dill (1 ml)
1/4 tsp. garlic salt (1 ml)
Dash of pepper
1/4 cup Parmesan cheese (50 ml)
8 ounces of pasta of choice (250 ml)

Cook pasta. Drain and keep hot in a serving dish. In a medium bowl, mix melted butter, basil, marjoram, dill, garlic salt, and pepper. Mix into warm pasta. Sprinkle with Parmesan cheese. Serves two.

"The term old friends! Seems a contradiction to me! For age cannot whither nor custom stale the infinite variety of friends who, for as long as you know them, remain as vibrant and stimulating as the first day you first met them!"
Anonymous

Penne with Tomato Eggplant Sauce

1/2 cup olive oil (125 ml)
4 cloves of garlic, peeled
1 1/2 lbs. eggplant, cut into cubes (672 g)
10 large white mushrooms, sliced
1/2 cup onion, chopped (125 ml)
Salt to taste
1/2 cup white wine (125 ml)
3 cups Italian plum tomatoes with juice (720 ml)
6 fresh basil leaves, chopped
Pinch of oregano
1 lb. penne pasta (500 g)
Fresh-grated Romano cheese to taste

Heat a large skillet over medium heat with olive oil. Add garlic and sauté for one minute. Remove and set aside. Add eggplant, mushrooms, and onions. Add salt to taste. Cook for ten minutes or until vegetables soften. Add wine and tomatoes, breaking tomatoes up gently with a fork. Bring to boil. Simmer for fifteen minutes. While sauce is simmering, cook penne. Drain. Stir half the sauce into the penne gently. Add chopped basil and oregano. Place in warm serving dish. Spoon remaining sauce on top. Sprinkle with cheese. Serves six.

Spaghettini with Vodka Tomato Sauce

1 tbsp. olive oil (15 ml)
1 onion, chopped finely
2 cloves of garlic, minced
1/4 cup vodka (50 ml)
1 twenty-eight-ounce can of tomatoes, with juice (795 ml)
1 tsp. salt (5 ml)
1/2 tsp. black pepper (2 ml)
Pinch of red chili flakes
1 lb. spaghettini pasta (500 g)
1/2 cup heavy cream (125 ml)
1/3 cup Parmesan cheese, grated (75 ml)

Add olive oil and onion to a medium-hot skillet. Sauté until onions are softened, around three to five minutes. In a small bowl, mix garlic and vodka. Add to onions. Add tomatoes with juice, salt, pepper, and chili flakes. Simmer for fifteen minutes. Meanwhile, cook spaghettini according to directions. Drain. Keep warm. Stir sauce into spaghettini. Mix gently. Add heavy cream. Stir just till blended. Sprinkle with Parmesan cheese. Serves four to six.

"A friend may well be reckoned
the masterpiece of God."
Anonymous

Italian Spaghetti
(with Meatballs)

1 lb. ground beef (448 g)
1/2 cup fresh breadcrumbs (125 ml)
1 tbsp. parsley (15 ml)
2 tbsp. Parmesan cheese, (30 ml)
1/2 tsp. pepper (2 ml)
1/4 tsp. garlic powder (1 ml)
1 egg, beaten
1 cup onion, chopped (250 ml)
4 cloves of garlic, minced
1/4 cup olive oil (50 ml)
2 cans whole tomatoes, 28 ounces each (796 ml) each
2 tsp. salt (10 ml)
1 tsp. sugar (5 ml)
1 bay leaf
6-oz. can of tomato paste (180 g)
1 tsp. basil (5 ml)
1 tsp. oregano (5 ml)
1/2 tsp. pepper (2 ml)
1 lb. spaghetti

In a large bowl, mix together ground beef, breadcrumbs, parsley, Parmesan cheese, pepper, garlic powder, and beaten egg. Form into balls. Refrigerate until needed. In a medium-hot skillet, sauté onion and garlic cloves in olive oil until onion is translucent. Stir in tomatoes, breaking up gently with a fork. Add salt, sugar, bay leaf. Cover. Simmer for 1 1/2 hours. Stir in tomato paste, basil, oregano, pepper, and meatballs. Simmer for thirty minutes. As sauce is simmering, cook spaghetti until desired doneness. Serve with sauce. Serves four.

"Since you alone are responsible for your thoughts, only you can change them. You will want to change them when you realize that each thought creates according to its own nature. Remember that the law works at all times and that you are always demonstrating according to the kind of thoughts you habitually entertain. Therefore, start now to think only those thoughts that will bring you health and happiness."
–Paramahansa Yogananda

Bronwyn's Favorite Tuna Casserole

My granddaughter Bronwyn and I have a standing joke about this recipe. Her daddy loves tuna casserole and often makes it, while Bronwyn declares she will never lift a fork to ever taste even a bite. Her favorite, tuna casserole? Not a chance! But I am hopeful. This recipe has potato chips in it. The door may very well open to new possibilities never dreamed of. That's always a good thing!

3 cups medium egg noodles (681 g)
1 cup celery, chopped (250 ml)
3/4 cup onion, chopped (175 ml)
4 tbsp. butter (30 ml)
1 can cream of mushroom soup (284 ml)
3/4 cup whole milk (175 ml)
3/4 cup grated cheddar cheese (175 ml)
2 six-ounce cans tuna fish, drained (375 ml)
1/4 cup chopped pimento (50 ml)
4 tbsp. Parmesan cheese (30 ml)
Pinch of thyme
Pinch of white pepper
1 cup crushed potato chips (250 ml)

Cook pasta according to package directions. Drain and set aside. In a medium-hot skillet, cook celery and onions in butter until softened, about four to five minutes. Stir in mushroom soup, milk, and cheese. Stir in tuna, pimento, thyme, and pepper. Add noodles. Transfer to a nine-by-thirteen-inch baking pan (22x33cm). Sprinkle with Parmesan cheese. Bake in preheated oven at 375°F (190°C) for twenty-five minutes or until heated through. Garnish with crushed chips. Bake five minutes more. Makes six servings.

"Health is an announcement of agreement between your body, mind and spirit. Honor your body, keep it in good shape. When you are not healthy, look to see which parts of you disagree. Your body will demonstrate the truth to you. Notice what it is showing you, listen to what it is saying."
—Neale Donald Walsch

Chili Eggplant Noodles

2 tbsp. sesame oil (30 ml)
2 tbsp. olive oil (30 ml)
4 tbsp. tamari sauce (60 ml)
2 tbsp. soy sauce (60 ml)
2 tbsp. cider vinegar (60 ml)
4 tbsp. honey (60 ml)
2 red Thai chilies, finely chopped or 2 jalapeño peppers, finely chopped
1 tbsp. fresh gingerroot, grated (15 ml)
2 cloves of garlic, minced
1 eggplant, cut into half-inch pieces (1 cm)
1/2 lb. soba noodles, cooked (225 g)
1 cup snow peas (250 ml)
1 cup edamame beans (250 ml)
1 cup bean sprouts (250 ml)
4 green onions, sliced

Preheat oven to 425°F (220°C). In a small bowl, whisk sesame oil, olive oil, Tamari sauce, soy sauce, vinegar, honey, chilies, and garlic. Taste. Adjust seasonings as desired. Toss eggplant with half the sauce and put in a single layer on a baking sheet. Put in hot oven and bake for twenty minutes. Meanwhile, cook and drain soba noodles. Transfer noodles to a large bowl and toss with additional sauce as desired. Add baked eggplant, snow peas, edamame beans, and green onions. Divide among two serving plates. Garnish with additional green onion if desired.

Greek Pasta with Shrimp

4 tbsp. olive oil (60 ml)
1 large garlic clove, chopped
2 cups canned tomatoes (500 ml)
1/2 cup white wine (125 ml)
Salt and pepper to taste
1/3 cup basil leaves, chopped (75 ml)
1 tsp. oregano (5 ml)
1 1/2 lbs. raw shrimp (672 g)
1 tbsp. butter (15 ml)
1/4 tsp. hot pepper flakes (1 ml)
1/2 lb. feta cheese, crumbled (224 g)
1/3 lb. spiral pasta (149 g)

Preheat oven to 400°F (200°C). Heat oil in medium-hot skillet. Add garlic and cook briefly until lightly browned. Add tomatoes, cutting up gently with a fork. Add wine. Add salt and pepper to taste. Add basil and oregano. Simmer for eight minutes. Remove from heat. Melt butter in separate medium-hot skillet and add shrimp. Cook for one minute. Sprinkle with red pepper flakes. Spoon into eight-by-eight-inch (20 x20 cm) baking dish. Spoon tomato mixture on top. Sprinkle with feta cheese. Bake for ten minutes. Meanwhile, cook pasta according to package directions. Drain. Put in warmed serving bowl. Gently stir in shrimp mixture. Serves two.

Rice Dishes

Sauterne Rice 274
Spanish Rice 275
Main Dish Mexican Rice 276
Indian Baked Rice 277
Risotto with Meat Sauce 278
Coconut Mango Rice 279
Wild Rice and Broccoli Pilaf 280
Persian Rice 281
Sweet Nanay's Champorato 282
Chinese Fried Rice 283

"If a man works hard, the land will not be lazy."
—Chinese proverb

Sauterne Rice

1/3 cup butter (75 ml)
2 cloves of garlic, sliced
1 1/2 cups white wine (375 ml)
3 cups water (175 ml)
2 cups white rice (500 ml)
1 tsp. salt (5 ml)
1/4 tsp. pepper (1 ml)
1/4 tsp. nutmeg (1 ml)
1/4 tsp. allspice (1 ml)
1/2 tsp. sugar (2 ml)
1/4 cup currants (50 ml)
1/4 cup chopped brazil nuts (50 ml)

Pour boiling water over currants and let sit for five minutes. Drain. Add butter to skillet over medium heat and melt. Add garlic. Sauté just until golden, about half a minute. Remove and discard. To skillet, add wine and water, rice, salt, pepper, nutmeg, allspice, and sugar. Bring to a boil. Cover tightly with a lid, and lower heat to simmer. Simmer for twenty minutes. Before serving, gently stir in currants and brazil nuts. Makes eight servings.

Spanish Rice

4 tbsp. butter (60 ml)
2 onions, chopped finely
2 green peppers, chopped finely
1 cup white rice (250 ml)
3 cups chicken or vegetable broth (750 ml)
1 cup vine-ripened tomatoes, diced (250 ml)
1 tbsp. chili powder (15 ml)
1/8 tsp. cumin (0.6 ml)
1/4 tsp. black pepper (1 ml)
1/4 tsp. salt (1 ml)
1/2 cup sharp cheddar cheese, grated (125 ml)

Melt butter in medium-hot skillet. Add onions and green pepper. Cook until very soft, about fifteen minutes. Add rice. Sauté until rice is toasted, for five to ten minutes. In a separate pot, boil chicken or vegetable broth. Add to onions, peppers, and rice. Add diced tomatoes, chili powder, cumin, black pepper, and salt. Stir well. Cover pan tightly. Bring to a boil. Lower heat and simmer for twenty-five to thirty minutes or until rice is tender. Stir lightly. Sprinkle with grated cheese. Serves four to six.

"The wind blows where it wills. You can't tell where it comes from, or where it is going. It is the same for everyone that is born through the Spirit."
—Jesus

Main Dish Mexican Rice

1 lb. lean ground beef (448 g)
1 onion, chopped
2 tbsp. chili powder (30 ml)
1/2 tsp. cumin (2 ml)
1/2 tsp. salt (2 ml)
1/4 tsp. black pepper (1 ml)
1 twenty-ounce can of black beans, drained (560 g)
2 cups tomato sauce (500 ml)
Dash of Tabasco sauce
2 cups corn niblets (500 ml)
1 1/2 cups uncooked rice (375 ml)
1/3 cup cilantro, chopped (75 ml)
1/3 cup grated cheese (75 ml)
1/3 cup black olives, sliced (75 ml)

Brown beef in medium-hot skillet until cooked through and no longer pink inside. Add onion, chili powder, cumin, salt, pepper, and beans. Stir in tomato sauce, Tabasco sauce, and corn. Taste. Adjust seasonings as desired. Add rice, and bring to boil. Lower heat and cover tightly with lid. Simmer until rice is tender, for twenty-five to thirty minutes, or until all visible liquid has disappeared. Place in a serving dish. Sprinkle with cilantro, cheese, and olives. Serves four.

"The best portion of a man's life is the nameless acts of kindness and love shown to him, and he, in turn, shows to others."
Anonymous

Indian Baked Rice

2 cups raw basmati rice (500 ml)
2 tbsp. olive oil (30 ml)
1 tbsp. butter (15 ml)
2 whole cardamom pods
1/2 cinnamon stick
4 cups chicken broth (1 L)
1/3 cup fresh dill, chopped (75 ml)

In a large cast-iron frying pan or oven- proof skillet, sauté raw rice in olive oil and butter on medium heat, until rice is toasted, five to ten minutes. Add cardamom pods and cinnamon stick. Add chicken broth. Add chopped dill. Stir well and remove from heat. Seal pan tightly with tinfoil or cover with lid. Place in oven and bake at 375°F (190°C) for forty to forty-five minutes. Place on a hot mat to serve right from the pan. (Pick out cardamom pods and cinnamon stick before serving.) Serves eight.

"Laughter is medicine to the heart. Come home each day with a sense of humor. See the opportunity it brings. When you see joy light another's face know God in His heaven is smiling on you."
—Le Rae

Risotto with Meat Sauce

4 cups rich beef stock (1 L)
1 1/2 cups meat stew, chopped finely (375 ml)
2 cups Arborio rice (500 g)
1/3 cup Parmigiano-Reggiano cheese, freshly grated (75 ml)
Salt to taste

Warm beef stock in saucepan over low heat. Keep warm. Put stew in a separate pot on medium heat. When simmering, add rice, stirring constantly for one minute. Still stirring, add warm beef stock half a cup at a time until rice absorbs enough liquid and is al dente (tender with a hint of firmness) and also has a rich, creamy consistency. Remove pan from heat. Stir in cheese. Serve immediately. Serves four to six.

"All tyranny needs to gain a foothold is for people of good conscience to remain silent."
—Thomas Jefferson

Coconut Mango Rice

2 cups white basmati rice (500 ml)
4 level tbsp. butter (60 ml)
1 regular onion, chopped
1 sweet orange pepper, chopped
1 clove of garlic, minced
2 level tbsp. fresh gingerroot, grated (30 ml)
2 tbsp. curry powder (30 ml)
1 fourteen-ounce can coconut milk (400 ml)
3 cups water (625 ml)
2 green onions, diced
1 ripe mango, peeled and chopped finely
1/2 cup fresh cilantro, chopped (125 ml)
1/3 cup filberts, toasted (50 ml)

Rinse rice well. Drain and set aside. In a large saucepan, melt butter on medium heat. Add onions and red pepper. Sauté for five to ten minutes. Add garlic and ginger. Stir briefly until fragrant. Add rice and curry powder, and stir gently to coat. Stir in coconut milk and water. Bring to a boil and then lower heat. Cover with lid and simmer for twenty minutes. Lightly stir in green onion, mango, cilantro, and almonds. Transfer to a serving dish. Serves four to six.

Wild Rice and Broccoli Pilaf

1 cup wild rice (250 ml)
2 cups chicken broth (500 ml)
1/4 cup sherry (50 ml)
2 tbsp. butter (30 ml)
3/4 cup mushrooms, sliced (175 ml)
3/4 cup celery, sliced (175 ml)
2 tbsp. green onion, sliced (30 ml)
2 tbsp. pimento (30 ml)
1/2 tsp. salt (2 ml)
1/4 tsp. thyme (1 ml)
Dash of pepper
1 ten-ounce package of frozen broccoli, chopped finely (283 g)

Rinse wild rice several times, straining the water through each rinse. Drain well. In a large skillet combine rice, chicken broth, and sherry. Bring to a boil. Cover and lower heat. Simmer for forty minutes. Heat up a separate skillet. Add butter and melt. Add mushrooms, celery, and green onion. Sauté for four to five minutes. Remove from heat. Stir in pimento, salt, thyme, and pepper. Stir mixture gently into cooked rice. Turn mixture into a lightly buttered two-quart casserole dish (2 L). Cover tightly with lid. Bake at 325°F (165°C) for twenty-five minutes. Stir once. Meanwhile, steam broccoli over simmering water until crisp and tender, three to four minutes. Drain and set aside. Remove rice from oven. Add broccoli and return to oven. Continue baking, covered, for ten to twelve minutes. Serves four.

Persian Rice

3 cups long-grain white rice, rinsed very well and strained (750 ml)
2 quarts water (2 L)
1/4 tsp. salt (1 ml)
1/3 cup melted butter (75 ml)
1/2 cup melted butter (125 ml)
1 cup water (250 ml) divided

Boil water with salt in a large pot. Add rice. Boil for ten minutes, uncovered, or until rice is half cooked. Remove from heat and strain the rice well in a colander. Pour 1/3 cup melted butter in a heavy pot, tilting to cover two inches (50.8 ml) up sides. Spoon the rice into the center of the pot, making a rice hill, avoiding the sides of the pot. With a chopstick or pointy object, make deep indentions in the rice hill, about six, evenly spaced. Pour 1/2 cup melted butter over rice. Drizzle 1/4 cup of divided water into holes. Cover pot with a tea towel to absorb steam. Place well-fitting lid on towel. Cook rice on very low heat. After fifteen minutes, add remaining water into holes. Replace lid. Steam rice for twenty-five to thirty minutes. Serves eight.

Sweet Nanay's Champorato
(Filipino Chocolate Rice)

My step-grandmother, a Philippine woman, made this dish, a staple of her country, when I was a young child. It has always been my favorite rice dish. I had to be very well behaved to get her to make champorato for me. Grandmother, a strict disciplinarian, taught me that love is not rude, so I was always very polite in order to get this tasty treat!

1 cup glutinous sweet sticky rice (250 ml)
2 1/2 cups water (625 ml)
1/2 cup packed unsweetened cocoa powder (125 ml)
1/2 cup white sugar (125 ml)
1/8 tsp. vanilla (0.6 ml)
1/2 cup sweetened condensed milk (125 ml)

In a medium-sized pot, boil rice with water uncovered, stirring constantly to prevent sticking. When rice is fluffy and soft, add cocoa powder, sugar, and vanilla. Spoon rice into serving bowls. Swirl sweetened condensed milk on top. Serves four. Note: if serving rice with a main course, use regular condensed milk instead of sweetened condensed milk.

```
"Music in the soul can be heard by the universe."
                    -Lao Tzu
```

Chinese Fried Rice

4 tbsp. oil, divided (60 ml)
2 cloves of garlic, crushed
2 green onions, chopped
1 cup cooked chicken, chilled and cubed (250 ml)
1 tsp. salt (5 ml)
Pepper to taste
3 tbsp. oil, divided (45 ml)
2 eggs, whisked lightly
4 cups cold cooked rice (1 L)
1 tbsp. soy sauce (15 ml)
Dash of fish sauce (optional)
1 tbsp. oyster sauce (15 ml)
1/2 cup cooked shrimp (125 ml) (optional)
1/2 cup blanched peas (125 ml)

In a large medium-hot wok, heat one tablespoon of oil. Add garlic and green onions. Stir fry for one to two minutes. Remove garlic and green onions. Set aside. Add cooked chicken to wok to reheat. Add salt and pepper to taste. Remove chicken and set aside. Wipe wok clean with a paper towel. Add one tablespoon of oil to wok. Add eggs and briefly scramble. Remove and set aside. Wipe wok clean with a paper towel. Add to wok two tablespoons of oil. Add rice, using a wooden spoon to break apart grains. When rice is hot, stir in soy, fish, and oyster sauces. Taste. Adjust seasonings as desired. Add garlic, green onions, eggs, and chicken. Add shrimp if desired. Add peas. Toss gently. Serves three to four.

```
"For a reward a man will hurry away on a
long journey.While for eternal life, many
   will hardly take the first step."
     -Thomas a` Kempis 1380-1471
```

Desserts

Fresh Peach Cobbler 287
Bacardi Rum Cake 288
Sonya's Pineapple Cheesecake. 289
Dahlynn Cheesecake 290
Banana Flambé 290
Norma's Easy Toffee 291
English Trifle 292
Bread Pudding 293
Quick Chocolate Cake 294
Flourless French Chocolate Cake 294
Chocolate Stout Brownies 295
Chai Chocolate Almond Biscotti 296
Caribbean Sweet Potato Rum Cake. 297
Rachel's Layered Dream Bars 298
McKowen's Wino Sauce 299
D. M.'s Double Chocolate Brownies 300
June's Chocolate Delight 301
Southern Comfort Apple Pie 302

Fresh Peach Cobbler

10 fresh ripe peaches, pitted, peeled, and sliced thin
1/3 cup white sugar (75 ml)
1/3 cup brown sugar (75 ml)
1/4 tsp. cinnamon (1 ml)
1/8 tsp. nutmeg (0.6ml)
1 1/4 tsp. lemon juice (6 ml)
2 tsp. cornstarch (10 ml)

Topping
1 heaping cup white flour (250 ml)
1/3 cup brown sugar (75 ml)
1/2 tsp. baking powder (2 ml)
1/2 tsp. salt (2 ml)
6 tbsp. cold butter cut small (90 ml)
1/3 cup boiling water (75 ml)

Topping Top
3–4 tbsp. brown sugar (45-60 ml)
1 tsp. cinnamon (5 ml)

Preheat oven to 425°F (220°C). In a large bowl, mix peaches, white and brown sugar, cinnamon, nutmeg, lemon juice, and cornstarch. Toss to coat. Place in two-quart baking dish (2 L). Place in oven and bake for ten minutes. In a separate large bowl, blend flour, sugar, baking powder, and salt. Blend in butter with a pastry blender until mixture resembles coarse crumbs. Add boiling water and stir until mixture is just combined. Take peaches out of oven and drop topping mix over them. Sprinkle with sugar and cinnamon. Return to oven. Bake for thirty minutes or until golden. Serves four.

"Unless Christians have the joy of
Christ in their hearts,
And manifest it, their words will carry
no conviction to their hearers."
—Steven Neill

Bacardi Rum Cake

1 package (18 1/2-oz.) plain yellow cake mix (515 g)
2 cups instant vanilla pudding mix (500 ml)
4 eggs
1/2 cup whole milk (125 ml)
1 cup pecans, toasted and chopped (250 ml)

Mix cake mix, pudding, eggs, and milk until thoroughly blended. Sprinkle pecans on bottom of greased and lightly floured angel food cake pan. Pour cake mix into pan. Bake in preheated oven at 325°F
(165°C) for sixty minutes or until toothpick inserted in center comes out clean. Cool on wire rack. Invert on serving platter. Prick top in several places with fork. Glaze with rum topping. Serves twelve.

Topping

1/2 cup butter, melted (125 ml)
1/4 cup water (50 ml)
1 cup brown sugar (250 ml)
1/2 cup dark rum (125 ml)

Combine butter, water, and sugar in a saucepan. Boil on high heat for five minutes. Remove. Stir in rum. Drizzle on cake.

Sonya's Pineapple Cheesecake

My friend Sonya appeared at my lonely door one night with this delectable cheesecake. With a good friend, you never walk in the dark alone. Or have to eat in the dark alone!

3 packages of cream cheese (250 g each)
1 cup sugar (250 ml)
1 eight-ounce can crushed pineapple, drained, juice reserved (250 ml)
1 envelope Knox gelatin (7 g)
1 cup whipped topping such as Cool Whip (250 ml) or whipped cream
1 commercially prepared graham cracker crumb crust
Sliced pineapple

Sprinkle gelatin in reserved pineapple juice in a small saucepan. Let stand for one minute. Cook on low heat for five minutes, stirring frequently until gelatin is dissolved. Remove from heat. In a large bowl, beat cream cheese and sugar until well blended. Slowly beat in gelatin mixture. Refrigerate for five to ten minutes until thickened. Stir whipped topping of choice into crushed pineapple. Pour into cream cheese mixture. Place in prepared piecrust. Refrigerate for several hours until well chilled. Serves eight.

"Friendship is always a sweet
responsibility, never an opportunity."
—Khalil Gibran

Dahlynn Cheesecake

1 commercially prepared graham cracker piecrust
1 package plain cream cheese, softened (250 g)
1/2 tsp. vanilla (2 ml)
1 fourteen-ounce can Eagle brand sweetened condensed milk (400 g)
1/3 cup lemon juice (75 ml)
1 small can of mandarin oranges, drained and chilled.

In a large bowl, whip cream cheese, vanilla, and sweetened condensed milk with an electric mixer until smooth. Slowly add lemon juice. Mix well. Pour into prepared piecrust of choice. Refrigerate for four hours. Before serving, arrange Mandarin oranges decoratively atop. Serves six.

Banana Flambé

4 large bananas, peeled and sliced lengthwise
4 tbsp. butter (60 ml)
1/3 cup dark brown sugar (75 ml)
Juice of 1 orange
Rind of 1 orange, grated
1/2 cup brandy (125 ml)
1/4 cup dark rum (50 ml)
Dash of cinnamon
Vanilla ice cream

Melt butter on medium heat in a large flameproof skillet. Add bananas. Sprinkle with brown sugar and cinnamon. Cook, stirring gently so as not to break up bananas, until the bananas are thoroughly caramelized, about five minutes. Add brandy. Swirl pan. Immediately add rum. Ignite carefully. Let flame subside before ladling into dessert dishes. Top vanilla ice cream. Serves eight.

"If Peace be in your heart, the wildest winter storm is full of solemn beauty, the midnight flash but shows your path of duty; Each living creature tells some new and joyous story; the very trees and stones catch a ray of glory; if peace be in your heart."
–Charles F. Richardson

Norma's Easy Toffee

1 cup broken pecan pieces (250 ml)
3/4 cup brown sugar, packed (175 ml)
1/2 cup butter (125 ml)
1/2 cup chocolate chip pieces (125 ml)

Butter a square eight-by-eight-inch dish. (20 x 20 cm). Spread pecans on the bottom of the dish. Set aside. In a medium saucepan, ove high heat, melt butter with sugar. Boil rapidly for seven minutes, stirring constantly. Remove from heat and immediately pour over pecans. Sprinkle with chocolate chips, smoothing with back of spoon as chocolate melts. Cover the dish with tinfoil until the chocolate chips melt completely. Put in fridge to chill. Cut into half-inch (1 cm) squares. Serves twelve.

English Trifle

1 prepared sponge cake, divided
2 eggs
1 egg yolk
2 cups heavy cream (500 ml)
1/4 cup sugar (50 ml)
1/2 cup sherry (125 ml)
1/2 cup currant jelly (125 ml)
2 canned peaches, drained and sliced, divided
1 cup fresh strawberries, sliced, divided (250 ml)
1 cup whipping cream, whipped (250 ml)
1/2 tsp. vanilla (2 ml)
Sprig of mint

Cut prepared sponge cake into cubes. Set aside. In a small saucepan, over medium-high heat, beat eggs with yolk, cream, and sugar. Cook until the custard coats a metal spoon, about three to five minutes. Remove from heat and set aside. Place half the cake cubes in a two-quart glass bowl (2 L). In a small bowl, mix the sherry with the currant jelly. Sprinkle the mixture over the cake cubes. Add half the peaches and half the strawberries. Spread with half the custard. Add the remaining cake, cubes, peaches, and strawberries. Spread with remaining custard. Mix whipping cream with vanilla. Swirl on top. Put in fridge for six hours or overnight. Before serving, sprinkle with additional fresh fruit and garnish with a sprig of mint. Serves twelve to fourteen.

"Your vision will become clear only when you can look into your own heart. Who looks outside, dreams; who looks inside, awakes."
—Carl Jung

Bread Pudding
(with Rum Sauce)

3 cups half and half cream (750 ml)
2 tbsp. butter (30 ml)
3 large organic eggs
1/2 cup dark brown sugar (125 ml)
1/4 tsp. salt (1 ml)
1/4 tsp. nutmeg (1 ml)
1/4 tsp. cinnamon (1 ml)
3 cups day-old bread, cubed (750 ml)
3/4 cup raisins (200 ml)

In a heavy-bottomed saucepan over high heat, scald cream with butter, stirring constantly. Set aside. Beat eggs with sugar, salt, nutmeg, and cinnamon. Gradually stir in scalded cream and butter. Mix in bread and raisins. Pour rum sauce over the top. Pour into an eight-by-eight-inch pan (20 by 20 cm). Place the pan in a larger pan filled halfway with warm water (so pudding can steam while in oven). Bake, covered, at 350°F (180°C) for thirty minutes. Serves six.

Rum Sauce

1/2 cup butter (125 ml)
1 cup packed brown sugar (250 ml)
1/2 cup cream (125 ml)
1/3 cup rum (75 ml)

Bring sauce to boil in a small saucepan. Pour over pudding.

"What we do is a symptom of our spiritual heart condition."
Anonymous

Quick Chocolate Cake

1 cup sour cream (250 ml)
1 cup sugar (250 ml)
1 tsp. vanilla (5 ml)
2 tbsp. melted butter (30 ml)
1 1/2 cups pastry flour (375 ml)
2/3 cup unsweetened cocoa powder (150 ml)
1 tsp. baking soda (5 ml)
1/2 tsp. salt (2 ml)
3 eggs, beaten

In a medium bowl, beat sour cream with sugar, vanilla, and butter. In a separate bowl, blend flour, cocoa, baking powder, and salt. Sprinkle into sour cream, sugar, vanilla, and butter mix. Stir well. Add beaten eggs one by one and mix until smooth. Spread batter in greased eight-by-eight-inch pan (20x20cm). Bake in a preheated 350°F (180°C) oven for twenty-five minutes or until toothpick inserted in center comes out clean. Serve warm with ice cream. Makes six servings.

Flourless French Chocolate Cake

7 oz. semisweet chocolate (200 g)
7 oz. butter, softened (200 g)
4 egg yolks
1/2 cup sugar (125 ml)
4 egg whites
1/2 cup sugar (125 ml)
1 cup frozen strawberries with juice, thawed (250 ml)
Whipped cream topping

Preheat oven to 350°F (180°C). Grease and flour a nine-inch round pan (22 cm). Break chocolate in small pieces and melt in double boiler over hot water. Add butter to melt. Mix well. Remove from heat. In a medium bowl, beat egg yolks with sugar. Fold in melted chocolate and butter. Set aside. Beat egg whites until frothy. Add sugar. Beat until stiff peaks form. Fold into batter. Bake for forty minutes or until knife inserted in center comes out clean. Cool. Cover with strawberries and whipped cream. Serves four to six.

"When we leave this earth for a better home someday,
The only thing we'll take is what we give away."
Anonymous

Chocolate Stout Brownies

6 oz. bittersweet chocolate (170 g)
2 tbsp. butter (30 ml)
1 tsp. vanilla (5 ml)
2 eggs
1 sweet potato, cooked and mashed (225 g)
1 cup stout beer (250 ml)
3/4 cup whole wheat flour (175 ml)
2/3 cup sugar (150 ml)
1/3 cup unsweetened cocoa powder (75 ml)
1 tsp. cinnamon (5 ml)
1/2 tsp. baking powder (2 ml)
1/4 tsp. salt (1 ml)
1/2 cup walnuts, chopped (125 ml)

Melt chocolate in double boiler over simmering water. Add butter and vanilla. Mix well. Remove from heat. Pour into large bowl. Mix in eggs, mashed sweet potato, and stout. In a separate bowl, mix flour with sugar, cocoa powder, cinnamon, baking powder, and salt. Add to first bowl. Stir in walnuts. Spoon batter into greased eight-by-eight-inch pan (20x20cm), spreading evenly. Place in 350°F (180°C) hot oven. Bake for twenty minutes or until a toothpick inserted in center comes out clean. Cool. Serves six to eight.

Chai Chocolate Almond Biscotti

1/2 cup butter, softened (125 ml)
3/4 cup white sugar (175 ml)
1/4 cup brown sugar, packed (50 ml)
2 large organic eggs
1 tbsp. vanilla extract (15 ml)
2 cups all-purpose flour (500 ml)
1/2 cup unsweetened cocoa powder (125 ml)
1 1/2 level tsp. baking powder (7 ml)
1 tsp. ginger (5 ml)
1/2 tsp. cardamom (2 ml)
1/2 tsp. cinnamon (2 ml)
1/2 tsp. salt (2 ml)
1 cup slivered almonds (250 ml)

Preheat oven to 350°F (180°C). In a large bowl, beat butter with white and brown sugar. Add eggs and vanilla. Blend well. In a separate bowl, combine flour, cocoa, baking powder, ginger, cardamom, cinnamon, and salt. Stir into butter, sugar, egg, and vanilla mix. Add almonds. Stir lightly. Shape dough into two logs. Place on an ungreased baking sheet. Press dough lightly to flatten. Place in an oven and bake for forty minutes. Take biscotti out of oven. Reduce temperature to 325°F (165°C). Cut biscotti on the diagonal with a serrated knife into half-inch slices (1 cm). Return to oven and bake for fifteen minutes more. Serves twelve to sixteen.

Caribbean Sweet Potato Rum Cake

1/2 cup raisins (125 ml)
1/4 cup dark rum (50 ml)
2 cups cooked mashed sweet potato (500 ml)
2 cups flour (500 ml)
1 1/2 cups brown sugar (375 ml)
1 tbsp. lemon or orange zest (15 ml)
2 level tsp. baking powder (10 ml)
1 level tsp. baking soda (5 ml)
1 tsp. cinnamon (5 ml)
1 tsp. nutmeg (5 ml)
1/2 tsp. ground cloves (2 ml)
1 tsp. ground ginger (5 ml)
1/2 tsp. salt (2 ml)
4 eggs
3/4 cup vegetable oil (175 ml)
1/4 cup fresh orange juice (50 ml)
1 cup unsweetened coconut (250 ml)

Put raisins in small bowl, and pour rum over raisins to soak. In a large bowl, stir sweet potatoes with flour, sugar, lemon, orange zest, baking powder, soda, cinnamon, nutmeg, cloves, ginger, and salt. Beat in eggs, vegetable oil, orange juice, and coconut. Add raisins with rum. Pour into nine-by-thirteen-inch lightly greased baking pan (22x33 cm) Bake at 350°F (180°C) for thirty minutes or until a toothpick inserted in center comes out clean. Cool on a wire rack. Wrap well and place in the fridge overnight. Frost. Serves fourteen to sixteen.

Frosting

1/2 cup melted butter (125 ml)
4 cups icing sugar (500 g)
3 tbsp. dark rum (45 ml)
1/2 cup unsweetened coconut (125 ml)
1 tsp. lemon or orange zest (5 ml)
Orange juice

Place melted butter into a medium bowl. Gradually mix in icing sugar. Sprinkle with rum and stir well. Add coconut, lemon, or orange zest. If necessary, thin with a bit of orange juice.

> "Trust God when dark doubts assail,
> Trust Him when faith is small,
> Trust Him when simply to trust Him
> Is the hardest thing of all."
> — Anonymous

Rachel's Layered Dream Bars

This recipe comes from my sister Rachel who, with love and faithfulness, has prepared many a delectable treat for her family over the years. These dream bars are aptly named. They are a dreamy smile inducer.

1 cup unbleached white flour (250 ml)
1/2 cup butter (125 ml)
2 large organic eggs
1 tsp. vanilla (5 ml)
2 tbsp. unbleached white flour (30 ml)
1/4 tsp. baking powder (1 ml)
1 1/2 cups dark brown sugar (375 ml)
1 cup semisweet coconut (250 ml)
1/4 tsp. sea salt (1 ml)
1 cup walnut pieces (250 ml)
1 tsp. fresh lemon juice (5 ml)
2 tbsp. melted butter (30 ml)
2 tbsp. icing sugar (30 ml)

Preheat oven to 350°F (180°C). For the first layer, mix 1 cup of flour with 1/2 cup of butter. Pat into a nine-by-nine-inch baking pan (22X22 cm). Bake for ten minutes. Remove from oven.

For the second layer, whisk eggs with vanilla and two tablespoons flour. Beat in baking powder. Spread over crust.

For the third layer, mix brown sugar, coconut, salt, and walnut pieces. Spread on second layer. Return bars to oven. Bake for thirty-five minutes. Remove and place on a wire rack. When bars are almost cool, blend lemon juice, melted butter, and icing sugar and drizzle over top. Cut into squares. Serves twelve.

McKowen's Wino Sauce

1 1/2 cups red wine, zinfandel or Syrah (375 ml)
1/2 cup sugar (125 ml)
1 whole vanilla bean, split lengthwise, pulp and seeds intact
2 whole star anise
1/2 tsp. pink peppercorns (2 ml)
Pinch of mint leaves or orange zest

In a medium-hot saucepan, combine wine, sugar, vanilla, anise, and mint or zest. If necessary, increase heat to bring to a rolling boil. Reduce heat. Cook for twenty minutes or until reduced by two-thirds, stirring frequently. Remove from heat. Set aside to cool. Strain the sauce in a colander to remove vanilla, peppercorns, star anise, and mint or zest. This sauce is delicious drizzled over ice cream, chocolate cake, or brownies. Makes about one cup. Store in an airtight container in fridge. Sauce keeps for three months.

```
"He is no fool who gives what he cannot
   keep to gain what he cannot lose."
            -Jim Elliot
```

D. M.'s Double Chocolate Brownies

1/2 cup white flour (125 ml)
1/8 tsp. baking powder (0.6 ml)
1/8 tsp. salt (0.6 ml)
1/2 cup softened butter (125 ml)
1/4 cup sugar (50 ml)
2 eggs
1/2 tsp. vanilla (2 ml)
12 tbsp. unsweetened cocoa powder (180 ml)
4 tbsp. vegetable oil (60 ml)
1/4 cup semisweet chocolate chips (50 ml)
1/4 cup chopped walnuts (50 ml)

Preheat oven to 325°F (165°C). Grease an eight-by-eight-inch glass dish (20x20cm). Set aside. In a medium bowl, combine flour, baking powder, and salt. In a separate bowl, beat butter, sugar, and eggs, mixing in eggs one at a time. Beat in vanilla. Gently mix in cocoa powder and oil. Add flour mixture. Beat until creamy. Fold in chocolate chips and walnuts. Pour into prepared baking pan. Bake for thirty minutes or until toothpick inserted in center comes out clean. Serve plain or with wino sauce and ice cream. Serves four to six.

June's Chocolate Delight

1 package of chocolate cake mix or (515 g)
Kahlua or dark rum
2 six-ounce packages instant chocolate pudding mix (180 g each)
4 cups whipped cream
6 dark chocolate bars or to equal 1 cup (250 ml)
2 cups canned cherries (500 ml)
1/2 cup toasted pecan pieces (125 ml)

Prepare cake according to directions on box. Let cool. With pastry brush, brush cake on top and all sides three or four times with Kahlua or rum. Cut into one-inch (2.54 cm) squares. Set aside. In a medium bowl, prepare instant pudding mix according to directions. In a separate bowl, beat whipping cream until stiff peaks form. Crush chocolate bars in food processor until very fine.

To assemble, in a large glass serving dish, layer cake cubes, pudding, whipped cream, and crushed chocolate bars. Repeat, finishing with whipped cream and crushed chocolate. Top with cherries. Sprinkle with toasted pecan pieces. Refrigerate until ready to serve. Makes sixteen servings.

"Love one another as I have loved you."
—Jesus Christ

Southern Comfort Apple Pie
(with Rum Sauce)

1 commercially prepared deep dish pie crust, unbaked
6 tart apples, peeled, cored, and sliced a quarter-inch thick (6.35 mm)
1/2 cup butter (125 ml)
3 tsp. cinnamon (15 ml)
1 cup white sugar (250 ml)
3/4 cup Southern Comfort (175 ml)
1/2 cup heavy cream (125 ml)

Preheat oven to 375°F (190°C). In a small bowl, mix cinnamon and sugar. Sprinkle on apples. Melt butter in a large medium-hot skillet. Add apples. Stir lightly and cook for one minute. Remove apples with slotted spoon, leaving sugar mixture in skillet. Lower heat. Transfer apples to a large platter, arranging in single layers. Pour Southern Comfort into skillet and simmer in sugar for five minutes. Add heavy cream. Continue simmering for ten minutes or until thickened. Return apples to skillet. Mix well and pour into piecrust. Set aside.

Topping

1/2 cup pecans, coarsely chopped and toasted (125 ml))
1/3 cup white sugar (75 ml)
4 tbsp. brown sugar (60 ml)
1/2 tsp. cinnamon (2 ml)
1/4 tsp. salt (1 ml)
1/3 cup white flour (75 ml)
1/3 cup butter (75 ml)

Combine pecans, sugar, cinnamon, salt, flour, and butter in food processor. Pulse until mixture is very crumbly. Sprinkle over pie. Put pie in oven and bake for fifty minutes. While baking, prepare rum sauce.

Rum Sauce
1 cup sugar (250 ml)
1/4 cup butter (50 ml)
1 cup liquid whipping cream (250 ml)
4 tbsp. dark rum (60 ml)
Vanilla ice cream (optional)

In a small medium-hot saucepan, heat sugar until amber in color. Lower heat. Add butter. Stir until melted. Add liquid whipping cream a bit at a time, stirring briskly to keep sauce from clumping. When thoroughly hot and smooth, remove from heat. Stir in rum. Serve the sauce warm over pie. If desired, add a dollop of vanilla ice cream on top of each serving. Makes eight servings.

A Selection of Four Complete Holiday Dinners

Holidays can be hectic. For your convenience, I have arranged a variety of complete dinners all the way from appetizers to dessert. In order to enjoy your holiday, do as much preparation as you can ahead of time. Some dishes, like sauces and dressings, can be made a day or two ahead. Casseroles can be made ahead too. (Just don't bake them.) Label your dishes clearly and put them in the fridge until time to assmble. Batters and doughs can also be assembled ahead of time. The same goes for sweet endings, the ever-important desserts! Preparing your happy holiday with a peaceful heart and eager anticipation ensures maximum enjoyment!

Holiday Dinner 1

Menu

Feta Artichoke Dip
Herb-Brined Organic Turkey (with Port Wine Gravy)
Southern Cornbread Dressing
Traditional Dressing
Green Bean Casserole
Citrus Brussels Sprouts (with Holiday Sauce)
Creamy Mashed Potatoes
Sassy Sweet Potato Bake
Spiced Cranberries
Country Biscuits
Plum Pudding
Pumpkin Pie
Turkey Tetrazzini (Leftovers)

Feta Artichoke Dip
(Appetizer)

Note: for a smaller crowd, cut the recipe in half.

2 fourteen-ounce cans of artichoke hearts, drained and chopped (800 g)
2 cups feta cheese, crumbled (1/2 L)
2 cups mayonnaise (1/2 L)
1 cup Parmesan cheese (1/4 L)
2 jars pimentos, drained (60 g)
2 cloves of garlic, minced
2 vine-ripened tomatoes, diced
4 green onions, minced
Pinch of oregano
Pinch of fennel seeds (optional)
1 package crackers of choice

Preheat oven to 350°F (180°C). Mix artichoke hearts, feta cheese, mayonnaise, Parmesan cheese, pimentos, garlic, oregano, and fennel in a large bowl. Divide into two equal portions and spread into two pie pans. Bake for twenty to twenty-five minutes or until lightly browned on top. Sprinkle with diced tomatoes and green onions. Serve with crackers. Makes eight to twelve servings.

"Let's all go forth to lead the land we love, asking God's blessing and help, knowing that here on earth, God's work must truly be our own."
–John F. Kennedy

Herb-Brined Organic Turkey
(with Port Wine Gravy)

1 fourteen-pound organic turkey (6 1/4 kg)
1 1/2 cups chicken broth (375 ml)

Brine

2 gallons cold water (8 L)
1 cup coarse sea salt (250 ml)
1/2 cup liquid honey (125 ml)
1 sweet onion, cut in chunks
2 stalks celery, coarsely chopped
1 carrot, coarsely chopped
1 whole head garlic, cut in half
4 bay leaves
4 branches each rosemary and thyme
2 branches fresh sage
1 tbsp. peppercorns (15 ml)

In a large pot or deep sink, mix the brine ingredients together. Place the turkey in the brine for several hours or overnight. (Keep water cold.) Discard the brine and pat the turkey dry with paper towel. Rub skin with a bit of olive oil if desired. Note: for a rich gravy, chop up a bit of celery, onion, garlic, and carrots and sprinkle on bottom of roasting pan. Toss in a sprig of rosemary and a sprig of thyme.

Fill the turkey cavity with your stuffing of choice. Place in a roasting pan. Pour chicken broth over the turkey and roast in a preheated oven 450°F (230°C) for forty minutes. Reduce heat to 350°F (180°C). Roast for 2 1/2 more hours or until juices run clear when pricked with a fork, and drumstick moves easily. Remove from oven and place on carving board. Rest for thirty minutes before carving. Serves fourteen to sixteen.

Port Wine Gravy

2/3 cup port wine (150 ml)
2 cups chicken broth (500 ml)
1 tbsp. arrowroot powder (15 ml)
1/3 cup cold water (75 ml)

Salt and pepper to taste

Pour pan juices from turkey into a bowl and skim off as much fat as possible. Set aside. Discard thyme and rosemary sprigs. Place roasting pan over two burners and heat to medium. Deglaze with port wine, scraping up any bits sticking to pan. Add chicken broth and mix well. Add pan juices. If you have roasted vegetables for gravy, remove with slotted spoon and puree in blender, then add back to pan. Mix arrowroot powder with cold water. Add to gravy. Continue cooking, stirring constantly, until thickened. Season with salt and pepper to taste. Pour into serving pitcher.

Non-Organic Turkey
Cooking Temperatures & Time
8–12-lb. turkey (3.5–5.5 kg) 4–5 hours
12–16-lb. turkey (5.5–7.25 kg) 5–6 hours
Cooking Temperature: 325–350°F (165–180°C)

Make sure you weigh the turkey and allow plenty of time to roast. Larger birds can take up to seven hours to roast. A turkey needs to sit for thirty minutes after roasting for easier carving. Always roast your turkey, tented with tinfoil, in preheated oven Remove the tinfoil the last thirty minutes of roasting to brown the top. If desired, pour a bottle of white wine over turkey before placing in the oven and baste periodically while roasting.

Note: If you plan on using stuffing, stuff turkey just before roasting to avoid the possibility of food poisoning.

Allow one to one and a half pounds of turkey per serving (450–675 g).

> "Neither natural love nor divine love
> will remain unless cultivated."
> —Oswald Chambers

Southern Cornbread Dressing

6 cups day-old cornbread, cubed (1360 g)
2 cups day-old wheat bread, cubed (510 g)
(Use less bread if using a smaller turkey.)
1 cup celery, chopped (250 ml)
1 onion, chopped
2 tart apples, chopped
1 cup pecan pieces (250 g)
1/4 cup fresh-chopped parsley (50 ml)
1 tsp. thyme (5 ml)
1/2 tsp. sage (2 ml)
1/2 tsp. salt (2 ml)
1/2 tsp. pepper (2 ml)
2 tbsp. butter (30 ml)
1-lb. pork sausage, cooked, chopped (448 g)

In a large skillet over medium heat, fry celery, onion, apples, pecans, parsley, thyme, sage, salt, and pepper in butter until golden or about five minutes. Remove to a large bowl. Add cooked sausage. (To save time, precook sausage the day before and keep in fridge.) Add cornbread and wheat bread and stir lightly. Stuff turkey. Put in preheated oven to roast. Keep warm wrapped in tinfoil until ready to serve.

Traditional Dressing

4 cups dry bread cubes (900 g)
(Use additional bread if using a larger turkey.)
1/2 cup minced onion (125 ml)
1/2 cup chopped celery (125 ml)
1/2 cup melted butter (125 ml)
1/2 tsp. salt (2 ml)
1/4 tsp. pepper (1 ml)
1/4 tsp. sage (1 ml)
1/4 tsp. poultry seasoning (1 ml)
1/2 tsp. parsley (2 ml)

In a medium-hot skillet, fry onion and celery in butter for four to five minutes or until golden. Add salt, pepper, sage, poultry seasoning, and parsley. Add bread cubes and stir lightly. Stuff turkey just before roasting.

"The most exquisite paradox … as soon as you give it all up you can have it all. As long as you want power you can't have it. The minute you don't want power, you'll have more than you ever dreamed possible."
—Ram Dash

Green Bean Casserole

2 cups French green beans, drained (500 ml)
3 cups chicken broth (750 ml)
1/4 cup butter (50 ml)
1/2 cup onion, chopped finely (125 ml)
1/2 cup mushroom pieces, chopped finely (125 ml)
1 ten-ounce can cream of mushroom soup (284 ml)
1 can French fried onion rings, divided
Pinch of salt and pepper
1 cup cheddar cheese, grated (250 ml)

Boil beans in broth for ten minutes. Drain and set aside. In a hot skillet, melt butter. Add onions and mushrooms. Fry for three to five minutes. Sprinkle with salt and pepper. Add mushroom soup and green beans and stir lightly. Add half the can of fried onion rings. Stir lightly. Turn casserole into greased eight-by-eight-inch pan (20x20 cm). Bake for twenty minutes at 350°F (180°C). Remove from oven and sprinkle with cheddar cheese. Top with remaining French-fried onion rings. Return to oven and bake for an additional ten minutes. Keep warm until serving. Makes six to eight servings.

Citrus Brussels Sprouts
(with Holiday Sauce)

1 lb. fresh Brussels sprouts(450 g)
Water to cover
Salt to taste

Soak Brussels sprouts in cold salted water for fifteen minutes after removing any wilted leaves. Drain. Put in saucepan and cook, covered, in boiling salted water for ten to twenty minutes or until just tender. Drain. Serve with Holiday sauce. Serves six.

Holiday Sauce

3 egg yolks
1/2 cup melted butter
1 tbsp. lemon juice (15 ml)
1 tbsp. frozen orange concentrate (15 ml)
1/4 tsp. salt (1 ml)

Blend egg yolks in a blender on low for several seconds. Slowly add melted butter. Add lemon and orange concentrate. Add salt. Taste. Adjust seasoning as desired. Keep warm until serving.

```
"If we ever forget we are one nation under
God, then we will be a nation gone under."
                                -Ronald Regan
```

Creamy Mashed Potatoes

3 1/2 lbs. potatoes (1 1/2 kg)
4 tbsp. butter (60 ml)
1/2 cup milk (125 ml)
1/2 tsp. salt (2 ml)
Butter
Sweet paprika

Note: use as many potatoes as you think you need for your holiday dinner. The general rule is two potatoes per man, one potato per woman. Do not use new potatoes, as firm older potatoes make the best mashed potatoes. If using a larger amount of potatoes than called for in this recipe, adjust butter, milk, and salt accordingly in order to get a creamy consistency. Peel potatoes, wash, and cut into quarters. Put in pot of cold salted water to cover. Bring to rolling boil. Lower heat and gently boil until a fork pierces through potatoes easily, about fifteen to twenty minutes. Drain. Put potatoes back in pot. Add butter, milk and salt. Whip until thoroughly smooth. Transfer potatoes to a serving dish. Add a dollop of butter atop and sprinkle with paprika.

Sassy Sweet Potato Bake

4 cups sweet potatoes, cooked and mashed (896 g)
1/2 cup sugar (125 ml)
2 eggs, beaten
Pinch of cayenne
1/2 cup canned milk (125 ml)
4 tbsp. softened butter (60 ml)
1 tsp. lemon juice (5 ml)

Topping
1 cup brown sugar (250 ml)
1/2 cup butter (125 ml)
1/3 cup flour (75 ml)
Salt to taste
1 cup pecan pieces (250 ml)

In a medium bowl, combine cooked sweet potatoes with sugar, eggs, cayenne, milk, butter, and lemon juice. Turn into an eight-by-eight-inch buttered baking dish (20x20 cm). In a another bowl, mix brown sugar, butter, and flour. Sprinkle with salt to taste. Add pecan pieces. Sprinkle over sweet potatoes. Bake in preheated 350°F (180°C) oven for thirty to forty minutes. Serve hot. Makes eight servings.

"He that answers a matter before he hears it, is folly and shame to him. A wise man hears. And increases learning."
–King Solomon

Spiced Cranberries

3/4 lb. frozen cranberries (340 g)
1/2 cup honey (125 ml)
3 tbsp. brown sugar
3/4 cup water (175 ml)
1/4 tsp. nutmeg (1 ml)
6 whole cloves
1 six-inch cinnamon stick (15 cm)
orange zest

In a medium saucepan, combine cranberries, honey, brown sugar, water, nutmeg, cloves, and cinnamon stick. Bring to a gentle boil. Lower heat. Simmer until berries are cooked through and are starting to burst, about ten minutes. Remove from heat. Pick out cinnamon stick and cloves. Transfer to a serving dish. Sprinkle with orange zest. Chill in fridge until ready to use.

> "Three things in human life are important. The first is to be kind. The second is to be kind. The third is to be kind."
> —Mother Theresa

Country Biscuits

3 cups unbleached white flour (750 ml)
1 tbsp. baking powder (15 ml)
3 tbsp. sugar (45 ml)
1 tsp. salt (5 ml)
3/4 tsp. cream of tartar (4 ml)
3/4 cup softened butter (175 ml)
1 cup whole milk (250 ml)

In a medium bowl, mix flour and baking powder, sugar, salt, and cream of tartar. Add softened butter. Mix well, using a pastry blender or two forks. Add milk slowly. Turn biscuits onto a lightly floured board. Knead eight to ten times with the heels of your hands. Roll biscuit dough with floured rolling pin until half an inch (1 cm) thick. Cut out with biscuit cutter. Bake at 450°F (230°C) for ten minutes. Wrap biscuits in a clean tea towel. Makes twelve.

```
"Each friend represents a world in us, a world
possibly not born until they arrive, and it is
only by this meeting that a new world is born."
-Anais Nin
```

Plum Pudding

(This is an English Christmas pudding recipe you can do the day before. This plum pudding recipe dates back to the 1800s.)

1 cup hot whole milk (250 ml)
1 cup dry breadcrumbs (250 ml)
1/2 cup white sugar (125 ml)
4 egg yolks
4 egg whites
1 cup raisins, lightly floured (250 ml)
1/2 cup figs, chopped (125 ml)
4 tbsp. lemon peel, grated (60 ml)
1/2 lb. suet, chopped (225 g)
1/4 cup wine (50 ml)
1 tsp. nutmeg (5 ml)
3/4 tsp. cinnamon (4 ml)
1/4 tsp. ground cloves (1 ml)
1/4 tsp. mace (1 ml)
1 1/2 tsp. salt (7 ml)

In a large bowl, mix together hot milk and breadcrumbs. Let stand until cool. Add sugar. Lightly beat egg yolks and stir in. In a separate bowl, beat egg whites until stiff peaks form. Add to first bowl. Add lightly floured raisins, figs, and lemon peel. Work in chopped suet. When well mixed, add wine, nutmeg, cinnamon, cloves, mace, and salt. Pour pudding into two small or one large empty coffee can. Place on a rack in a large pot. Add boiling water to pot until it comes halfway way up coffee cans. Cover pot tightly. Steam the pudding for six hours, keeping water gently boiling throughout, adding more water as it boils away. To Unmold: Set cans in cold water for several seconds and then uncover. Turn out onto a platter. Cut pudding with a sharp knife and serve with sterling sauce and lemon sauce. Serves fourteen to eighteen.

Sterling Sauce

1/3 cup butter, softened (75 ml)
2/3 cup brown sugar (150 ml)
2 tbsp. heavy cream (30 ml)
1 1/2 tbsp. sherry (22 ml)
2 tsp. brandy (10 ml)

Put butter in small bowl. Beat brown sugar into butter gradually. Add heavy cream, sherry, and brandy, drop by drop, until well blended. Serve with plum pudding. Makes about 1 1/2 cups (375 ml).

```
"I never knew how to worship until
      I knew how to love."
        -Henry Ward Beecher
```

Lemon Sauce

1 cup sugar (250 ml)
1 tbsp. cornstarch (15 ml)
1 cup boiling water (250 ml)
2 tbsp. melted butter (30 ml)
1 1/2 tbsp. lemon juice (22 ml)
Dash of nutmeg
Dash of salt

In a small saucepan, mix sugar and cornstarch together. Add boiling water. Boil for five minutes, stirring all the while. Remove from heat. Stir in melted butter, lemon juice, nutmeg, and salt. Serve with plum pudding. Makes about one cup (250 ml).

```
"Every time you speak your faith, it
   creates a stronger image inside you."
              -Charles Capps
```

Pumpkin Pie
(This recipe is for two pies.)

2 cups pure pumpkin (500 ml)
4 eggs
2 cups brown sugar, packed (500 ml)
2 tsp. cinnamon (10 ml)
1 tsp. nutmeg (5 ml)
1/2 tsp. ginger (2 ml)
1/2 tsp. salt (2 ml)
1 1/2 cups canned milk (375 ml)
2 deep-dish pie shells, unbaked
Whipped cream

In a large bowl, mix pumpkin, eggs, sugar, cinnamon, nutmeg, ginger, salt, and milk. Pour into unbaked pie shells. Bake in preheated oven at 425°F (220°C) for fifteen minutes. Reduce heat to 350°F (180°C). Bake for an additional thirty to thirty-five minutes or until knife inserted in center of pies comes out clean. Serve with whipped cream. Serves twelve to fourteen.

"The grace of God does not come forth to bring rest and renewal to our soul until we completely reach the point of stillness before Him."
Anonymous

Turkey Tetrazzini
(Leftovers)

4 cups leftover turkey, chopped (560 g)
1 sixteen-ounce package linguine, cooked and drained (455 g)
3/4 cup butter (175 ml)
1 1/2 cups mushrooms, sliced (375 ml)
1 cup celery, diced (250 ml)
2 medium onions, diced
2 bell peppers, diced
1/2 cup sherry (125 ml)
2 cans cream of mushroom soup (368 ml)
2 cups chicken broth (500 ml)
2 cups sharp cheddar or Swiss cheese, grated (500 ml)
3/4 cup Parmesan cheese, grated (175 ml)

Melt butter in a large skillet, medium-hot. Add mushrooms and fry until golden, about two to three minutes. Remove mushrooms from skillet and set aside. Add celery, onions, and peppers to skillet. Cook until tender, about four to five minutes. Return mushrooms. Add sherry. Stir in linguine and turkey. Combine soup with chicken broth and add to skillet. Stir in cheddar or Swiss cheese. Place in a large casserole dish, lightly buttered, or two small casserole dishes. Bake in preheated oven 350°F (180°C) for forty-five minutes. Remove from oven. Sprinkle with Parmesan cheese. Place under broiler and broil two minutes or until cheese melts. Serves twelve.

"Never forget that you are one of a kind.
Never forget that if there weren't any need for
you in all your uniqueness to be on this earth,
you wouldn't be here in the first place.
And never forget, no matter how overwhelming
life's challenges and problems seem to be, that
one person can make a difference in the world.
In fact, it is always because of one person that all
the changes that matter in the world come about.
So be that one person."
—Richard Buckminster Fuller

Holiday Dinner 2

Menu

Jenny's Faux Pâté
Creamy Mediterranean Salad
Herb-Roasted Leg of Lamb
Lemon Garlic Roasted Potatoes
Baked Eggplant with Tomatoes
Farmers' Bread
Lemon Meringue Pie

Jenny's Faux Pâté
(Appetizer)

My twin sister, Jenny, got this recipe after working in the Greek Village in Vancouver, BC. This faux pâté is creamy and savory, with melt-in-your-mouth flavor, like a kind word, gently spoken.

>1 lb. organic chicken livers (448 g)
>1/2 cup white flour (125 ml)
>1/2 tsp. lemon pepper (2 ml)
>1/2 tsp. Greek oregano (2 ml)
>1/4 tsp. garlic salt (1 ml)
>1/2 tsp. dried mint (2 ml)
>1/4 tsp. thyme (1 ml)
>1/4 tsp. basil (1 ml)
>1/2 tsp. marjoram (2 ml)
>1/2 tsp. dried minced onion (2 ml)
>1/8 cup olive oil (30 ml)
>1/8 cup butter (30 ml)
>Juice of 1 lemon

Put flour in a plastic bag. Add lemon pepper, oregano, garlic salt, mint, thyme, basil, marjoram, and dried minced onion. Add organic chicken livers. Shake bag several times to coat well, and then put in a sieve and shake off excess flour. Add olive oil and butter to a smoking hot skillet. When butter melts, add chicken livers and fast fry, shaking skillet often and turning frequently until liver is cooked and crisp, about two minutes per side. Do not overcook, as overcooking makes liver tough. Transfer to a warm serving platter. Sprinkle with lemon. Serves six.

Creamy Mediterranean Salad

1 package vine-ripened small tomatoes, cut in half
2 cucumbers, diced
1 large red onion, cut into rings
1 green pepper, chopped
1/2 block feta cheese, crumbled
2/3 cup Kalamata olives, pitted (150 ml)
4 sundried tomatoes in oil, drained and chopped
1/2 tsp. oregano (2 ml)
1/4 tsp. pepper (1 ml)
2 tbsp. mayonnaise (30 ml)
2 tbsp. olive oil (30 ml)
2 tbsp. lemon juice (30 ml)
Pinch of dry mustard

In a medium bowl, combine tomatoes, cucumber, onion, feta cheese, olives, and sundried tomatoes. For dressing, in a separate bowl, combine oregano, pepper, mayonnaise, olive oil, lemon juice, and pinch of dry mustard. Taste. Adjust seasonings as desired. Drizzle over salad. Toss lightly. Chill salad thoroughly until serving. Makes six to eight servings

Herb-Roasted Leg of Lamb

5–6 lbs. boneless leg of lamb (2 3/4 kg)
4–5 garlic cloves, sliced thin
1 sprig rosemary, crumbled
1 tsp. oregano (5 ml)
1 tsp. salt (5 ml)
1/2 tsp. pepper (2 ml)
4 tbsp. lemon juice (60 ml)
2 tbsp. olive oil (30 ml)
splash white wine
mint jelly –opt–

Make slits in roast with a sharp knife and insert garlic cloves. In a small dish, combine oregano, salt, pepper, lemon juice, olive oil, and wine. Rub over roast. Put roast on a rack in shallow roasting pan without a cover. Roast at 325°F (165°C) for thirty to thirty-five minutes per pound (448 g) or until a meat thermometer registers 170°F for medium rare, 175°F for medium, or 180°F for well done. Remove roast from oven and put on a carving board. Let sit several minutes before carving. Serve with mint jelly and gravy if desired. Serves six to eight.

Gravy

Place roasting pan on stove top on medium-hot heat. With a fork, vigorously scrape up dripping bits. Whisk in three tablespoons of flour (45 ml). Add half a cup of wine and two cups of chicken broth (500 ml). Bring to boil to thicken, stirring constantly, adding more broth as needed. Add salt and pepper to taste if desired. Keep warm until serving.

"Be careful what you water your dreams with. Water them with worry and fear and you will produce weeds that choke the life from your dream. Water them with optimism and solutions and you will cultivate success. Always be on the lookout for ways to turn a problem into an opportunity for success. Always be on the lookout for ways to nurture your dream."
–Lao Tzu

Lemon Garlic Roasted Potatoes

6–8 russet potatoes
3/4 cup olive oil (175 ml)
2 1/2 cups chicken broth (625 ml)
Juice of 1 large lemon
3 cloves of garlic, crushed
3/4 tsp. Greek oregano (3 ml)
1 tsp. sea salt (5 ml)
Fresh-cracked pepper
Juice of half an orange

Preheat oven to 375°F (180°C). Peel and wash potatoes. Pat the potatoes dry with a paper towel and cut into quarters. Put in large bowl. In another bowl, mix sea salt, oregano, pepper, garlic, and oil. Add to potatoes, coating well. Pour into large baking pan. Sprinkle liberally with lemon. Add chicken broth all around, careful not to pour broth onto potatoes. Put on lowest rack in oven, and roast until broth comes to a rolling boil. Once boiling, turn oven down to 350°F (180°C). Roast potatoes for sixty minutes. Sprinkle with orange juice. Roast sixty more minutes or until potatoes pierce through easily with a fork. Before serving, toss thoroughly with broth and juices. Serves eight.

"Courage is contagious. When a brave man takes a stand, the spines of others are stiffened."
—Billy Graham

Baked Eggplant with Tomatoes

8 slim, elongated eggplants
3/4 cup olive oil, divided (175 ml)
1/2 tsp. coarse salt (2 ml)
1/2 tsp. fresh cracked pepper (2 ml)
3 cups onions, diced (3/4 L)
6 garlic cloves, peeled and sliced
3 1/2 cups vine ripened tomatoes, diced (829 ml)
1 cup water (250 ml)
1 tsp. Greek oregano (5 ml)
1 tsp. Greek seasoning (2 ml)
1 tsp. sugar (5 ml)

Slit eggplants lengthwise, careful not to slice all through. Set aside. Put four tablespoons of olive oil (60 ml) in a large skillet. Turn to medium-hot. When oil is sizzling, add eggplant. Cook for two minutes. Remove from heat. Arrange side by side in a large baking dish so as not to crowd. Season with salt and pepper. Set aside. Add remaining olive oil to skillet and heat. Add onions and garlic. Fry until golden, four to five minutes. Add tomatoes and water, oregano, Greek seasoning, and sugar. Reduce heat and simmer for fifteen minutes. Generously fill eggplants with mixture. Put in 350°F (180°C) oven and bake for forty-five minutes, basting occasionally. Serves eight.

Farmers' Bread

Pointers for kneading bread: Flour your hands. Use the heels of your hands to compress and push the dough away from you, and then fold it back over itself. Give the dough a small turn and repeat the motion. Put the weight of your body into the motion, and get into a flow. Kneading one loaf of bread should take about ten minutes.

2 cups unbleached white flour (500 ml)
4 tsp. instant yeast (20 ml)
2 tsp. sugar (10 ml)
1 1/4 cups warm water (300 ml)
1 tbsp. oil (15 ml)
2 tsp. salt (10 ml)

Put flour in large mixing bowl. Make a well in center. Sprinkle yeast and sugar into well. Pour warm water into well. Mix lightly with a wooden spoon until thoroughly blended. Cover bowl with a clean tea towel and keep in warm area free of drafts for fifteen minutes. Turn dough out on lightly floured surface, and knead until smooth and elastic, sprinkling with salt and oil. Cover with tea towel. Keep in a warm place for fifteen minutes. Take the dough out and knead once again. Shape dough into an oblong shape. Place on a greased baking sheet. Cover. Keep warm for fifteen minutes. Place in cold oven and turn oven to 375°F (190°C). Bake for forty to forty-five minutes until bread is golden and makes a hollow sound when rapped. Let cool for twenty minutes before slicing.

"A word well chosen can open a heart."
Anonymous

Lemon Meringue Pie

1 commercially prepared piecrust baked and set aside
4 tbsp. cornstarch (60 ml)
4 tbsp. flour (60 ml)
1/2 tsp. salt (2 ml)
1 1/2 cups sugar (375 ml)
1 1/2 cups boiling water (375 ml)
1 tbsp. butter (15 ml)
dash lemon zest
1/3 cup lemon juice (75 ml)
4 egg yolks (Reserve whites)

Thoroughly mix in top of a double boiler cornstarch, flour, salt, and sugar. Add boiling water. Stir until well blended. Bring to a boil. Lower heat and simmer covered for twenty minutes. Add butter, zest, lemon juice, and egg yolks. Cook and stir till thickened. Remove from heat. Let cool. Pour into prepared piecrust. Top with meringue.

Meringue

4 egg whites
¼–1/2 cup sugar (50-125 ml)
2 tsp. lemon juice. (10 ml)
Few grains of salt

Beat egg whites with electric beaters until soft peaks form. Gradually beat in desired amount of sugar, lemon juice, and salt. Spread meringue on the cooled lemon pie, spreading generously to the edges so meringue does not shrink into center of pie as it bakes. Place in 425°F (220°C) oven until meringue is delicately browned on top, about five minutes. Remove from oven. Let cool. To cut pie easily, dip knife in hot water. Serves six.

"Generosity is a requirement of the spirit. When we are generous with others it refreshes not only them. But us."
Anonymous

Holiday Dinner 3

Menu

King Crab Cocktail
Orange-Roasted Salmon Steaks
Saffron Rice Pilaf
Green Beans with Citrus Tahini
Moroccan Carrot Salad (with Curry Vinaigrette)
Corn Fritters
Raspberry Granité

King Crab Cocktail
(Appetizer)

2 bunches fresh spinach or lettuce leaves, torn
1 1/2 lb. King crab meat (672 g)
1 1/2 cups green pepper, diced fine (375 ml)
1 1/2 cups celery, diced fine (375 ml)

In a medium bowl, mix together crab, green pepper, and celery, careful not to break lumps of crabmeat. Cover and chill. Make cocktail sauce.

Cocktail Sauce

1 cup ketchup (250 ml)
1 tbsp. horseradish (15 ml)
Dash of Tabasco sauce
2 tsp. Worcestershire sauce (10 ml)
1 tsp. white pepper(5 ml)
1 tsp. black pepper (5 ml)
1 tsp. salt (5 ml)
1/2 tsp. garlic powder (2 ml)
1 tsp. onion powder (5 ml)

Mix ingredients well in small bowl. Taste and adjust seasonings as desired. Cover and put in fridge to chill at least one hour or until ready to use. Arrange lettuce or spinach leaves on a large platter. Sprinkle evenly with crab mixture. Spoon cocktail sauce atop. Makes six servings.

Orange-Roasted Salmon
(Double this recipe for a crowd.)

2 tbsp. extra virgin olive oil (30 ml)
6 salmon steaks
1 tbsp. orange zest (15 ml)
1 tsp. sea salt (5 ml)
1/2 tsp. cracked pepper (2 ml)
1/2 cup thick plain yogurt (125 ml)
1/2 cup mayonnaise (125 ml)
4 tbsp. fresh chopped parsley (60 ml)
3 tbsp. chopped capers (45 ml)
3 tbsp. orange juice (45 ml)
3 tbsp. frozen orange juice concentrate (45 ml)

Put salmon steaks on a lightly oiled baking sheet. Drizzle steaks with olive oil. Sprinkle with zest, salt, and pepper. For sauce: in medium bowl, mix together yogurt, mayonnaise, parsley, capers, orange juice, and orange concentrate. Set aside. Place salmon in 400°F (200°C) preheated oven. Bake for ten minutes or until just a trace of pink remains in center. Remove. Drizzle with sauce. Serves six.

Saffron Rice Pilaf

1 tsp. crumbled saffron threads (5 ml)
2 tbsp. very hot water (30 ml)
1/3 cup olive oil (75 ml)
1 large onion, chopped
3 cups basmati rice (675 g)
4 1/2 cups water (1 1/8 L)
1/2 tsp. salt (2 ml)
1 cup almonds, slivered (250 ml)
1/2 cup dried currants (125 ml)

Put saffron threads in hot water to soften and set aside. Rinse basmati rice several times until water runs clear, and then strain and put in large bowl. Cover with fresh cold water and let soak for two hours. Drain well and set aside. Add olive oil to a large skillet and heat to medium-hot. Add almonds and fry until fragrant, about one minute. Remove with slotted spoon and drain on paper towel. Set aside. Add onion to remaining oil in skillet; reduce heat to medium, and fry until golden and soft, about ten minutes. Add rice to skillet. Sauté until fragrant and golden, two to three minutes. Add water. Add softened saffron threads. Cover and simmer for twenty minutes. Remove from heat. Let rice stand, covered, for five minutes. Remove to serving dish. Gently stir in almonds and currants. Serves eight to ten.

Green Beans with Citrus Tahini

2 lbs. organic green beans (1 K)
2 cloves of garlic
6 tbsp. Tahini paste (90 ml)
6 tbsp. lemon juice (90 ml)
1/4 tsp. cumin (1 ml)
salt to taste
2 tbsp. roasted sesame seeds (30 ml)

Steam beans until crisp and tender, about three to five minutes. In a medium bowl, mash garlic, tahini, lemon juice, cumin, salt, and sesame seeds. Thin with a few drops of water if too thick. Taste. Adjust seasonings as desired. Drizzle over steamed beans. Serves ten to twelve.

```
      Truth is just truth. It never has
         to worry about its image."
                ANONYMOUS
```

Moroccan Carrot Salad
(with Curry Vinaigrette)

1/3 cup raisins (75 ml)
1/2 cup orange juice (125 ml)
2 cups carrots, shredded (500 ml)
2 cups green apple, shredded (500 ml)
Salt and pepper to taste

Soak rains in orange juice for several minutes or until raisins are plump. In a medium bowl, combine carrots and apples. Add raisins and orange juice. Mix lightly. Drizzle with curry vinaigrette. Serves eight.

Curry Vinaigrette

1/4 cup white wine vinegar (50 ml)
2 tbsp. olive oil (30 ml)
2 tbsp. lemon juice (30 ml)
1 tsp. curry powder (5 ml)
1/2 tsp. salt (2 ml)
1/8 tsp. pepper (0.6 ml)
1/2 tsp. sugar (2 ml)
1/4 tsp. minced garlic (1 ml)
1/4 tsp. dill weed (1 ml)
Dash of hot pepper sauce.

Shake ingredients in covered jar until well blended. Taste and adjust seasonings to personal preference.

Corn Fritters

1 cup white flour (250 ml)
1/2 cup cornmeal (125 ml)
2 tsp. baking powder (10 ml)
1/2 tsp. salt (2 ml)
1/2 tsp. sugar (2 ml)
1/8 tsp. cayenne (0.6 ml)
1 cup milk (250 ml)
1 egg
2 tbsp. melted butter (30 ml)
1 1/2 cups frozen corn, thawed (375 ml)
4 cloves of garlic, thinly sliced
Oil for frying

In a large bowl, mix flour, cornmeal, baking powder, salt, sugar, and cayenne. Stir in milk, egg, and melted butter until just combined. Fold in corn and garlic. Pour oil in heavy-bottomed skillet and heat on medium-high. When oil is sizzling, drop batter by tablespoons into hot oil. Fry until golden, about two minutes per side. Drain on paper towels. Serves six to eight.

Raspberry Granité

1 cup white berry sugar (250 ml)
2 cups raspberries, pureed (500 ml)
1 1/2 tsp. lemon juice (7 ml)
2 cups water (500 ml)
1/2 cup fresh whole raspberries (125 ml)
Champagne

In a medium bowl, mix sugar, raspberries, lemon juice, and water. Cover with saran wrap and put in freezer for thirty minutes or until very cold. When ready to serve, spoon raspberry granité into four large champagne flutes. Top with fresh raspberries. Float with Champagne.

Holiday Dinner 4

Menu

Beef Wellington
Pistachio Cheese Log
Radicchio Apple Walnut Salad
Orange-Glazed Carrots
Roasted Potatoes
Baked Alaska

Beef Wellington
(Tenderloin wrapped in pastry.)

2 lbs. beef tenderloin (900 g)
1 1/2 cups mushrooms, chopped (375 ml)
1/2 cup onion, chopped (125 ml)
2 tbsp. butter (30 ml)
2 three-ounce cans liver pâté (85 g) each
3 tbsp. panko breadcrumbs (45 ml)
2 tbsp. burgundy wine (30 ml)
Commercial pastry dough (enough for two double pie crusts)
1 tbsp. butter, softened (15 ml)
1 egg, beaten
2 well-rounded tbsp. flour (30 ml)
1 cup beef stock (250 ml)
1/4 cup burgundy wine (50 ml)
1/4 tsp. basil (1 ml)
Salt and pepper to taste
Chopped parsley

In a skillet on medium-hot heat, cook mushrooms and onions in butter for five to ten minutes or until onions are tenderized. Stir in pâté, breadcrumbs, and two tablespoons burgundy wine. Cover and remove from heat. Let cool. Insert meat thermometer in beef and place on rack in shallow roasting pan. Roast at 425°F (220°C) for thirty-five to forty-five minutes or until thermometer registers 130°F. Remove beef from pan. Place in fridge and cool for two hours. Reserve pan drippings.

For Pastry

On a floured surface, roll out pastry dough into a rectangle large enough to completely enfold tenderloin. Spread pate mixture over pastry to within half an inch (1 cm) of the edges. Take the tenderloin out of the fridge and centrally place atop pastry. Wrap dough completely around the tenderloin. Spread butter on top. Seal edges with beaten egg, trimming excess dough from ends. (Save excess dough.) Brush ends with additional beaten egg to seal. Place wrapped tenderloin seam side down on greased baking sheet. Make cut outs of flowers, hearts, or diamonds with excess dough and place atop tenderloin. Brush with remaining egg. Bake in preheated oven at 425°F (220°C) for thirty-five minutes, or until pastry is golden brown. Make gravy. Serves six.

Gravy

Heat reserved meat drippings. Stir in flour. Whisk in beef stock, burgundy wine, and basil. Bring to a boil, stirring constantly. Lower heat and cook until thickened. Season with salt and pepper. Taste and adjust seasonings as desired. Garnish with parsley.

```
"Nearly all of God's jewels are crystallized tears."
Anonymous
```

Pistachio Cheese Log
(Appetizer)

1 cup cream cheese, room temperature (250 ml)
1 cup sharp white cheddar cheese, grated (250 ml)
1 tbsp. Dijon mustard (15 ml)
1 dash of liquid smoke
1 dash of Worcestershire sauce
Salt and pepper to taste
8 oz. shelled unsalted pistachios, coarsely chopped (250 ml)
Crackers for serving

In a medium bowl, beat cream cheese, cheddar cheese, Dijon mustard, liquid smoke, and Worcestershire sauce until well blended. Taste. Adjust seasonings as desired. Cover and put in fridge for one hour or until slightly firm. In a skillet over medium heat, toast pistachios, stirring until fragrant, for about five minutes. Remove from heat. Let cool. Take cheese mixture from fridge and center on a piece of wax paper. Using the wax paper as a tool, shape cheese mixture into a six-inch log (15 cm). Cover with cooled pistachios, pressing lightly to stick. Wrap cheese log in a fresh sheet of wax paper. Place in fridge and chill until firm, one hour. Serve with crackers. Serves eight.

Radicchio Apple Walnut Salad

6 cups Radicchio lettuce (1.5 L)
1 1/2 tbsp. white wine vinegar (22 ml)
4 tbsp. shallots, minced (60 ml)
1 1/2 tsp. Dijon mustard (7 ml)
1/2 tsp. coarse salt (2 ml)
fresh ground pepper to taste
4 1/2 tbsp. olive oil (67 ml)
1 1/2 cups walnut halves, toasted (375 ml)
2 granny smith apples, sliced thin
extra olive oil for drizzling

In a small bowl, whisk vinegar, shallot, mustard, salt, and pepper. Add olive oil in a slow, steady stream, whisking until well blended. Taste and adjust seasonings as desired. In a large serving bowl, toss lettuce with toasted walnuts and apples. Drizzle with dressing. Makes six servings.

"The ways of right living people glow with light.
The longer they live, the brighter they shine."
—Proverbs 4:18

Orange-Glazed Carrots

3 cups baby carrots (750 ml)
1/3 cup orange juice with pulp (75 ml)
1/3 cup dark brown sugar (75 ml)
3 tbsp. salted butter (45 ml)
Pinch of salt
Pinch of ground ginger

Place carrots in a saucepan in moderate amount of water and boil gently until crisp and tender, five to eight minutes. Drain. Pour orange juice over carrots. Cover and lower heat. Simmer for five minutes. Stir in brown sugar, butter, salt, and pinch of ginger. Keep warm until serving. Makes six servings.

```
"God writes the gospel not in the Bible alone but in
the trees. In the flowers. In the clouds. In the stars."
                                          —Billy Graham
```

Roasted Potatoes

3 1/2 lbs. potatoes, peeled and quartered (1 1/2 k)
6 1/2 oz. lard (195 g)
1/2 tsp. coarse salt (2 ml)
1/2 tsp. fresh-cracked black pepper (2 ml)

Preheat oven to 425°F (220°C). Boil potatoes for ten minutes exactly in a large pot of water. Remove from heat and drain thoroughly. Drag tines of a fork over edges of potatoes to rough up a bit. Place lard in a roasting pan and put in preheated oven. When lard is smoking hot, take pan from oven and add potatoes, shaking pan vigorously to coat potatoes with the melted fat. Sprinkle liberally with salt and pepper. Put back in oven. Bake for forty-five minutes, turning and stirring the potatoes frequently until browned and crispy. Serves six to eight.

"The people who influence us the most are not those who detain us with their continual talk, but those who live their lives like the stars in the sky, and the lilies of the field, simply and unaffectedly."
—O. Chambers

Baked Alaska

1 sponge cake, baked, cooled, and set aside
1 quart vanilla ice cream, softened (1 L)
4 egg whites
1 tsp. vanilla (5 ml)
1/2 tsp. cream of tartar (2 ml)
2/3 cup sugar (150 ml)
1/4 cup walnuts, chopped (50 ml)

Place softened ice cream in a 1 1/2 quart–size bowl (1419 ml). With a spatula, press and level ice cream evenly all around, making top very flat. Cover bowl and place ice cream in freezer until it becomes very frozen. Place prepared sponge cake on serving platter. Remove ice cream from the freezer. Run a spatula gently around the edges of the bowl to loosen the ice cream. Invert the bowl onto the center of the sponge cake to dispense ice cream. Cover and freeze. Beat egg whites, vanilla, cream of tartar, and sugar in a medium bowl until soft peaks form. Gently fold in walnuts. Preheat oven to 500°F (260°C). Generously spread mixture over frozen cake and ice cream, to look like an igloo. Place in oven. Bake for three minutes. Cut into wedges. Serve immediately. Makes eight servings.

"There is a looker-on who sits behind my eyes. It seems he has seen things in ages and worlds beyond memory's shore, and those forgotten sights glisten on the grass and shiver on the leaves. He has seen under new veils the face of the one beloved, in twilight hours of many a nameless star. Therefore his sky seems to ache with the pain of countless meetings and partings, and a longing pervades this spring breeze, -the longing that is full of the whisper of ages without beginning."
–from *Lover's Gifts,* Rabindranath Tagore, Nobel Prize winner, 1913

Desiderata

Go placidly amid the noise and haste, and remember what peace there may be in silence. As far as possible, without surrender, be on good terms with all persons. Speak your truth quietly and clearly; and listen to others, even to the dull and ignorant; they too have their story.

Avoid loud and aggressive persons, they are vexations to the spirit. If you compare yourself with others, you may become vain and bitter, for always there will be greater and lesser persons than yourself. Enjoy your achievements as well as your plans.

Keep interested in your own career, however humble; it is a real possession in the changing fortunes of time. Exercise caution in your business affairs, for the world is full of trickery. But let this not blind you to what virtue there is; many persons strive for high ideals, and everywhere life is full of heroism.

Be yourself. Especially do not feign affection. Neither be cynical about love; for in the face of all aridity and disenchantment it is as perennial as the grass. Take kindly the counsel of the years, gracefully surrendering the things of youth. Nurture strength of spirit to shield you in sudden misfortune. But do not distress yourself with dark imaginings. Many fears are born of fatigue and loneliness.

Beyond a wholesome discipline, be gentle with yourself. You are a child of the universe no less than the trees and the stars; you have a right to be here. And whether or not it is clear to you, no doubt the universe is unfolding as it should.

Therefore be at peace with God, whatever you conceive Him to be. And whatever your labors and aspirations, in the noisy confusion of life, keep peace with your soul. With all its sham, drudgery and broken dreams, it is still a beautiful world. Be cheerful. Strive to be happy.

—Max Ehrman

Conclusion

Cooking with Spirits for the Spirit has been a joy to prepare. It is my fondest hope that your culinary repertoire has expanded delightfully and enjoyably as much as did mine in the preparing of this book. It is my fondest hope you are not only well fed of body but also well fed of spirit! Truly yours,

—Janet Hall Svisdahl

CPSIA information can be obtained at www.ICGtesting.com
Printed in the USA
LVOW021848210113

316613LV00001B/1/P